Pattern Recognition and Classification in Time Series Data

Eva Volna
University of Ostrava, Czech Republic

Martin Kotyrba
University of Ostrava, Czech Republic

Michal Janosek
University of Ostrava, Czech Republic

A volume in the Advances in Computational Intelligence and Robotics (ACIR) Book Series

www.igi-global.com

Published in the United States of America by
>   IGI Global
>   Information Science Reference (an imprint of IGI Global)
>   701 E. Chocolate Avenue
>   Hershey PA 17033
>   Tel: 717-533-8845
>   Fax: 717-533-8661
>   E-mail: cust@igi-global.com
>   Web site: http://www.igi-global.com

Library of Congress Cataloging-in-Publication Data

Names: Volna, Eva, 1961- editor. | Kotyrba, Martin, 1984- editor. | Janosek,
    Michal, 1981- editor.
Title: Pattern recognition and classification in time series data / Eva
    Volna, Martin Kotyrba, and Michal Janosek, editor.
Description: Hershey PA : Information Science Reference, 2016. | Includes
    bibliographical references and index.
Identifiers: LCCN 2016018118| ISBN 9781522505655 (hardcover) | ISBN
    9781522505662 (ebook)
Subjects: LCSH: Pattern perception. | Artificial intelligence. | Algorithms.
    | Time-series analysis.
Classification: LCC Q327 .P375 2016 | DDC 519.5/5--dc23 LC record available at https://lccn.loc.
gov/2016018118

This book is published in the IGI Global book series Advances in Computational Intelligence and Robotics (ACIR) (ISSN: 2327-0411; eISSN: 2327-042X)

British Cataloguing in Publication Data
A Cataloguing in Publication record for this book is available from the British Library.

All work contributed to this book is new, previously-unpublished material. The views expressed in this book are those of the authors, but not necessarily of the publisher.

Advances in Computational Intelligence and Robotics (ACIR) Book Series

ISSN: 2327-0411
EISSN: 2327-042X

MISSION

While intelligence is traditionally a term applied to humans and human cognition, technology has progressed in such a way to allow for the development of intelligent systems able to simulate many human traits. With this new era of simulated and artificial intelligence, much research is needed in order to continue to advance the field and also to evaluate the ethical and societal concerns of the existence of artificial life and machine learning.

The **Advances in Computational Intelligence and Robotics (ACIR) Book Series** encourages scholarly discourse on all topics pertaining to evolutionary computing, artificial life, computational intelligence, machine learning, and robotics. ACIR presents the latest research being conducted on diverse topics in intelligence technologies with the goal of advancing knowledge and applications in this rapidly evolving field.

COVERAGE

- Automated Reasoning
- Agent technologies
- Cyborgs
- Evolutionary Computing
- Fuzzy Systems
- Intelligent control
- Cognitive Informatics
- Synthetic Emotions
- Brain Simulation
- Computational Intelligence

IGI Global is currently accepting manuscripts for publication within this series. To submit a proposal for a volume in this series, please contact our Acquisition Editors at Acquisitions@igi-global.com or visit: http://www.igi-global.com/publish/.

Titles in this Series

Integrating Cognitive Architectures into Virtual Character Design
Jeremy Owen Turner (Simon Fraser University, Canada) Michael Nixon (Simon Fraser University, Canada) Ulysses Bernardet (Simon Fraser University, Canada) and Steve DiPaola (Simon Fraser University, Canada)
Information Science Reference • copyright 2016 • 346pp • H/C (ISBN: 9781522504542) • US $185.00 (our price)

Handbook of Research on Natural Computing for Optimization Problems
Jyotsna Kumar Mandal (University of Kalyani, India) Somnath Mukhopadhyay (Calcutta Business School, India) and Tandra Pal (National Institute of Technology Durgapur, India)
Information Science Reference • copyright 2016 • 1015pp • H/C (ISBN: 9781522500582) • US $465.00 (our price)

Applied Artificial Higher Order Neural Networks for Control and Recognition
Ming Zhang (Christopher Newport University, USA)
Information Science Reference • copyright 2016 • 511pp • H/C (ISBN: 9781522500636) • US $215.00 (our price)

Handbook of Research on Generalized and Hybrid Set Structures and Applications for Soft Computing
Sunil Jacob John (National Institute of Technology Calicut, India)
Information Science Reference • copyright 2016 • 607pp • H/C (ISBN: 9781466697980) • US $375.00 (our price)

Handbook of Research on Modern Optimization Algorithms and Applications in Engineering and Economics
Pandian Vasant (Universiti Teknologi Petronas, Malaysia) Gerhard-Wilhelm Weber (Middle East Technical University, Turkey) and Vo Ngoc Dieu (Ho Chi Minh City University of Technology, Vietnam)
Engineering Science Reference • copyright 2016 • 960pp • H/C (ISBN: 9781466696440) • US $325.00 (our price)

Problem Solving and Uncertainty Modeling through Optimization and Soft Computing Applications
Pratiksha Saxena (Gautam Buddha University, India) Dipti Singh (Gautam Buddha University, India) and Millie Pant (Indian Institute of Technology - Roorkee, India)
Information Science Reference • copyright 2016 • 403pp • H/C (ISBN: 9781466698857) • US $225.00 (our price)

www.igi-global.com

701 E. Chocolate Ave., Hershey, PA 17033
Order online at www.igi-global.com or call 717-533-8845 x100
To place a standing order for titles released in this series,
contact: cust@igi-global.com
Mon-Fri 8:00 am - 5:00 pm (est) or fax 24 hours a day 717-533-8661

Table of Contents

Detailed Table of Contents

Chapter 1
Eva Volna, University of Ostrava, Czech Republic
Martin Kotyrba, University of Ostrava, Czech Republic

The chapter is focused on an analysis and pattern recognition in time series, which are fractal in nature. Our goal is to find and recognize important Elliott wave patterns which repeatedly appear in the market history for the purpose of prediction of subsequent trader's action. The pattern recognition approach is based on neural networks. Artificial neural networks are suitable for pattern recognition in time series mainly because of learning only from examples. This chapter introduces a methodology that allows analysis of Elliot wave's patterns in time series for the purpose of a trend prediction. The functionality of the proposed methodology was validated in experimental simulations, for whose implementation was designed and created an application environment. In conclusion, all results were evaluated and compared with each other. This chapter is composed only from our published works that present our proposed methodology. We see the main contribution of this chapter in its range, which allows us to present all our published works concerning our proposed methodology together.

Chapter 2
Martin Žáček, University of Ostrava, Czech Republic

The goal of this chapter is a description of the time series. This chapter will review techniques that are useful for analyzing time series data, that is, sequences of measurements that follow non-random orders. Unlike the analyses of random samples of observations that are discussed in the context of most other statistics, the analysis of time series is based on the assumption that successive values in the data file represent consecutive measurements taken at equally spaced time intervals. There are two main goals of time series analysis: (a) identifying the nature of the phenomenon represented by the sequence of observations, and (b) forecasting (predicting future values of the time series variable). Both of these goals require that the pattern of observed time series data is identified and more or less formally described. Once the pattern is established, we can interpret and integrate it with other data.

Classification tasks can be solved using so-called classifiers. A classifier is a computer based agent which can perform a classification task. There are many computational algorithms that can be utilized for classification purposes. Classifiers can be broadly divided into two categories: rule-based classifiers and computational intelligence based classifiers usually called soft computing. Rule-based classifiers are generally constructed by the designer, where the designer defines rules for the interpretation of detected inputs. This is in contrast to soft-computing based classifiers, where the designer only creates a basic framework for the interpretation of data. The learning or training algorithms within such systems are responsible for the generation of rules for the correct interpretation of data.

Chapter 4

Patterns are mentioned usually in the extraction context. Little stress is posed in their representation and management. This chapter is focused on the representation of the patterns, manipulation with patterns and query patterns. Crucial issue can be seen in systematic approach to pattern management and specific pattern query language which takes into consideration semantics of patterns. In the background we discuss two different approaches to the pattern store and manipulation (based on inductive database and PANDA project). General pattern model is illustrated using abstract data type implemented in Oracle. In the following chapters the introduction to querying patterns and simple scheme of the architecture PBMS is shown.

Chapter 5

The chapter puts into the business of financial markets area in greater detail at FOREX currency market. It describes the main methods used for in currencies trade. The main goal of this paper is to explain the principle of creating an Automated Trading System (ATS) with the MQL4 language. The chapter shows concrete architectural elements of the program on the demonstration examples and it is a guide for the development of an ATS. The main benefit is creation of the original trading system, which optimizes an ATS usage on the base of historical data in practice. Optimization of the trading parameters is based on the equity performance in the historical periods.

    Dora Lapkova, Tomas Bata University in Zlin, Czech Republic
    Zuzana Kominkova Oplatkova, Tomas Bata University in Zlin, Czech
       Republic
    Michal Pluhacek, Tomas Bata University in Zlin, Czech Republic
    Roman Senkerik, Tomas Bata University in Zlin, Czech Republic
    Milan Adamek, Tomas Bata University in Zlin, Czech Republic

This chapter deals with the pattern recognition in the time series. The data was obtained from the measurement of the force profiles via strain gauge sensor. This pattern recognition should help to classify different techniques of the professional defence (direct punch, direct and round kicks) and gender of the attacker. The aim is to find a suitable feature sets from the measured raw data which has to be transferred in appropriate way; in the case of this research spectral analysis or discrete cosine transformation were used. Based on the previous experience of authors, artificial neural networks with Levenberg-Marquardt training algorithm were selected as a classifier. In these experimentations, students from the Faculty of Applied Informatics, Tomas Bata University in Zlin participated. The results were successful and higher level than expected accuracy of 85% was achieved. The future plans include involving more participants and repeating the simulations to confirm the proposed technique.

    Jaromir Svejda, Tomas Bata University in Zlin, Czech Republic
    Roman Zak, Tomas Bata University in Zlin, Czech Republic
    Roman Senkerik, Tomas Bata University in Zlin, Czech Republic
    Roman Jasek, Tomas Bata University in Zlin, Czech Republic

The basic idea of BCI (Brain Computer Interface) is to connect brain waves with an output device through some interface. Human brain activity can be measured by many technologies. In our research, we use EEG (Electroencephalography) technology. This chapter will deal with processing of EEG signal and its utilization in practical applications using BCI technology mentioned above. This chapter is organized as follows. Firstly, the basic knowledge about EEG technology, brain and biometry is briefly summarized. Secondly, research of authors is presented. Finally, the future research direction is mentioned.

Chapter 8
Ivo Lazar, Tomas Bata University in Zlin, Czech Republic
Said Krayem, Tomas Bata University in Zlin, Czech Republic
Denisa Hrušecká, Tomas Bata University in Zlin, Czech Republic

What we have solved: the possibility to receive DVB-T (Digital Video Broadcasting Terrestrial) with respect to local conditions for signal. We have deduced: variables that represent a set of so-called useful signal, i.e. the signal suitable for further processing – amplification and distribution. As a case study we have choosed few examples using Event B Method to show possibilty of solving komplex projects by this method. The resulting program can be proven to be correct as for its theoretical backgrounds. It is based on Zermelo-Fraenkel set theory with axion of choice, the concept of generalized substitution and structuring mechanismus (machine, refinement, implementation). B methods are accompanied by mathematical proofs that justify them. Abstract machine in this example connected with mathematical modelling solves an ability to receive DVB-T signal from the plurality of signals, both useful and useless for further processing.

Preface

What is a pattern? In common sense it is something that occurs repeatedly so some part of a thing or action repeats many times. There can be a patterns in the textile, leather, river flow, trees etc. We can find some pattern in the behaviour of animals, like birds periodically migrating to warm countries during winter and back. There are many patterns in human activities. For example, traffic. In the morning there is a traffic peak, second one occurs when people return from work back home. Patterns can be found in many techniques and skills like design patterns in software engineering.

Generally, we can say that patterns can be static or dynamic. I can be something that we can perceive regardless on duration or it is be something that will emerge only after some period of time, or both.

In our book we concentrate on dynamic patterns mainly. That means that the pattern would be acquired by observing the original action through time. Of course, any such pattern written down on a paper is static. Or better, the recorded information about that action is static. But this is more about storing patterns than recognizing them. Patterns and their recognition is just a beginning. There are many things we have to do prior pattern recognition and there are many things which can be done when we have had successfully recognized a pattern. Let's go through most related tasks momentarily.

Firstly, we have to observe an event or thing where we suspect there can be a pattern, so we should have all necessary means of reception to successfully perceive that pattern. That includes any signal or noise filtering. Next, it is necessary to store this observation, our pattern candidate. Working with computers, any digital form can be suitable which will encode acquired data. Then we can hand over this observation to a pattern recognition algorithm which should have been trained before to be able to do such thing. This is the main part of pattern recognition. By this we gain some classes where all observations are categorized. But what to do then? This leads us to a reflection what to do with patterns? Having patterns, we can do many things. It can help us with decisions, control, adaptations, or just description what is happening with our observed system.

The book's main topic is Patter Recognition and Classification in Time Series Data. The reader can proceed from introduction to time series, pattern management, pattern recognition and system adaptation based on recognized pattern to more application level articles.

Maybe we still haven't had answered a question, what is pattern recognition? Shortly, pattern recognition focuses on finding similarities in data, to classify or cluster them into bunch of similar occurrences – patterns. More you can find in our book.

Eva Volna
University of Ostrava, Czech Republic

Michal Janosek
University of Ostrava, Czech Republic

Martin Kotyrba
University of Ostrava, Czech Republic

Chapter 1
Recognition of Patterns with Fractal Structure in Time Series

Eva Volna
University of Ostrava, Czech Republic

Martin Kotyrba
University of Ostrava, Czech Republic

ABSTRACT

The chapter is focused on an analysis and pattern recognition in time series, which are fractal in nature. Our goal is to find and recognize important Elliott wave patterns which repeatedly appear in the market history for the purpose of prediction of subsequent trader's action. The pattern recognition approach is based on neural networks. Artificial neural networks are suitable for pattern recognition in time series mainly because of learning only from examples. This chapter introduces a methodology that allows analysis of Elliot wave's patterns in time series for the purpose of a trend prediction. The functionality of the proposed methodology was validated in experimental simulations, for whose implementation was designed and created an application environment. In conclusion, all results were evaluated and compared with each other. This chapter is composed only from our published works that present our proposed methodology. We see the main contribution of this chapter in its range, which allows us to present all our published works concerning our proposed methodology together.

DOI: 10.4018/978-1-5225-0565-5.ch001

INTRODUCTION

This chapter is composed only from our published works (Kotyrba et al. 2012; Kotyrba, Volná, & Jarušek, 2012; Kotyrba et al. 2013; Volna, Kotyrba, & Jarusek, 2013; Volná, Kotyrba, & Kominkova Oplatkova, 2013), that present our proposed methodology including experimental verification. We see the main contribution of this chapter in its range, which allows us to present all our published works concerning our proposed methodology together.

The main topic of the chapter is to develop and optimize the pattern recognition algorithm in order to recognize Elliott wave patterns in time series for the purpose of prediction. Elliott wave theory is a form of market analysis based on the theory that market patterns repeat and unfold in cycles. Ralph Nelson Elliott developed this theory in the 1930s. Elliott argued that upward and downward market price action was based on mass psychology and always showed up in the same repetitive patterns. These patterns were divided into what Elliott called "waves." According to Elliott, crowd psychology moves from optimism to pessimism and back again and this is seen in the price movements of market trend which are identified in waves. The Elliott Wave Principle is a detailed description of how groups of people behave (Poser 2003). It reveals that mass psychology swings from pessimism to optimism and back in a natural sequence, creating specific and measurable patterns. One of the easiest places to see the Elliott Wave Principle at work are the financial markets, where changing investor psychology is recorded in the form of price movements. When people are optimistic about the future of a given issue, they bid the price up. Two observations will help to grasp this: First, investors have noticed for hundreds of years that events external to the stock markets seem to have no consistent effect on the progress. The same news that today it seems to drive the markets up is as likely to drive them down tomorrow. The only reasonable conclusion is that the markets simply do not react consistently to outside events. Second, when historical charts are studied, it can be seen that the markets continuously unfold in waves. Using the Elliott Wave Principle is an exercise in probability. Elliott wave patterns are not exact, they are slightly different every time they appear. They can have different amplitude and different duration, albeit visually the same pattern can look differently despite being the same. Moreover, these patterns do not cover every time point in the series, but are optimized so that the developed classifier would be able to learn their key characteristics and accurately recognize them. Such optimized inputs also reduce calculation costs. One of important challenges is to recognize the input pattern reliably.

The aim of this experimental study is focused on recognition Elliott models in the chart. The proposed classifiers have been tested in this paper for Elliott wave's pattern recognition. We use an interdisciplinary approach (see Figure 1), which consists from artificial neural networks, Elliott wave theory and knowledge modelling (Kotyrba, Volná, and Jarušek, 2012). We used an artificial neural network that is adapted by backpropagation (Atsalakis, Dimitrakakis, & Zopounidis, 2011). Neural network uses Elliot wave's patterns in order to extract them and recognize. Artificial neural networks are suitable for pattern recognition in time series mainly because of learning only from examples. There is no need to add additional information that could bring more confusion than recognition effect. Neural networks are able to generalize and are resistant to noise. On the other hand, it is generally not possible to determine exactly what a neural network learned and it is also hard to estimate possible recognition error. They are ideal especially when we do not have any other description of the observed series.

The chapter proposes the Elliott waves pattern recognition approach based on a backpropagation neural network. We focus on prediction by means of Elliott wave's recognition. Our experimental studies show that the patterns of Elliott wave theory can be also observed on the Volume waveforms. Volume (often abbreviated VOL), or the volume of trading is simply an indicator expressing the total number of contracts traded within a specific time period (e.g., hour, day, week, month ...).

THE ELLIOTT WAVE-PRINCIPLE

The Elliott Wave Principle is based on the fact that prices usually move in fives waves in the direction of the larger trend and in three waves contrary to it. In an uptrend a five wave advance will be followed by a three wave decline; in a down trend a five wave decline will be followed by a three wave advance. Five-wave patterns are called impulse waves, three-wave patterns are called corrective waves (Figure 2). The Elliott Wave Principles is defined as follows (Frost and Prechter 2001).

Figure 1. Interdisciplinary approach

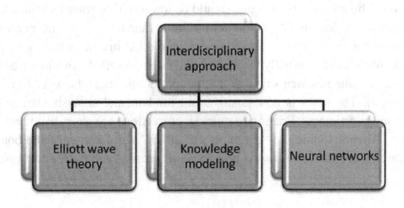

Figure 2. The basic pattern of Elliott wave

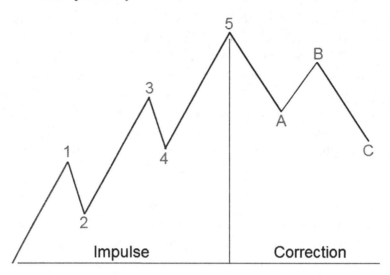

Five Wave Pattern: Dominant Trend

Wave 1: Wave one is rarely obvious at its inception. When the first wave of a new bull market begins, the fundamental news is almost universally negative. The previous trend is considered still strongly in force. Fundamental analyses continue to revise their earnings estimates lower; the economy probably does not look strong. Sentiment surveys are decidedly bearish, put options are in vogue, and implied volatility in the options market is high. Volume might increase a bit as prices rise, but not by enough to alert many technical analysts.

Wave 2: Wave two corrects wave one, but can never extend beyond the starting point of wave one. Typically, the news is still bad. As prices retest the prior low, bearish sentiment quickly builds, and "the crowd" haughtily reminds all that the bear market is still deeply ensconced. Still, some positive signs appear for those who are looking: volume should be lower during wave two than during wave one, prices usually do not retrace more than 61.8% (Fibonacci relationship) of the wave one gains, and prices should fall in a three wave pattern.

Wave 3: Wave three is usually the largest and most powerful wave in a trend (although some research suggests that in commodity markets, wave five is the largest). The news is now positive and fundamental analysts start to raise earnings estimates. Prices rise quickly, corrections are short-lived and shallow. Anyone looking to "get in on a pullback" will likely miss the boat. As wave three starts, the news is probably still bearish, and most market players remain negative; but by wave three's midpoint, "the crowd" will often join the new bullish trend. Wave three often extends wave one by a ratio of 1.618:1.

Wave 4: Wave four is typically clearly corrective. Prices may meander sideways for an extended period, and wave four typically retraces less than 38.2% of wave three (see Fibonacci relationships). Volume is well below than that of wave three. This is a good place to buy a pull back if you understand the potential ahead for wave 5. Still, fourth waves are often frustrating because of their lack of progress in the larger trend.

Wave 5: Wave five is the final leg in the direction of the dominant trend. The news is almost universally positive and everyone is bullish. Unfortunately, this is when many average investors finally buy in, right before the top. Volume is often lower in wave five than in wave three, and many momentum indicators start to show divergences (prices reach a new high but the indicators do not reach a new peak). At the end of a major bull market, bears may very well be ridiculed (recall how forecasts for a top in the stock market during 2000 were received).

Three Wave Pattern: Corrective Trend

Wave A: Corrections are typically harder to identify than impulse moves. In wave A of a bear market, the fundamental news is usually still positive. Most analysts see the drop as a correction in a still-active bull market. Some technical indicators that accompany wave A include increased volume, rising implied volatility in the options markets and possibly a turn higher in open interest in related futures markets.

Wave B: Prices reverse higher, which many see as a resumption of the now long-gone bull market. Those familiar with classical technical analysis may see the peak as the right shoulder of a head and shoulders reversal pattern. The volume during wave B should be lower than in wave A. By this point, fundamentals are probably no longer improving, but they most likely have not yet turned negative.

Wave C: Prices move impulsively lower in five waves. Volume picks up, and by the third leg of wave C, almost everyone realizes that a bear market is firmly entrenched. Wave C is typically at least as large as wave A and often extends to 1.618 times wave a or beyond (Frost and Prechter 2001).

Elliott wave is another technical tool that may be used to try to identify market trends and determine whether trends are about to change. Elliott wave can be used to generate short-term trading opportunities and analyze whether current market trends will continue. To apply Elliott wave to some analysis we need to identify which wave is being formed. The major waves determine the major trend of the market. The minor waves determine the minor trends in the market. Once we identify the main wave look to buy the market in the 1, 3 and 5 waves, and sell the market in waves to 2 and 4. In the corrective phase look to buy wave A and C and look to sell wave B. The most difficult part of Elliott wave analysis to correctly label the waves. Waves are usually identified by looking back at historic price action. The hard part in applying Elliott wave is try to anticipate drawing of the waves before the market action takes place. The usefulness of the Elliott wave analysis for the trader is also highlighted by the fact that the major waves on the currency markets usually develop in close correspondence with the interest rate cycles specific for the currency pairs that somebody is trading. Potentially profitable Elliott wave setups occur 50% of the time on the currency markets which makes it important for the traders to be at least aware of the basic principles of recognizing them, (Frost & Prechter 2001).

Elliot Wave Patterns Detection

Many studies show that there are mainly two kinds of pattern recognition algorithms: an algorithm based on rule-matching (Anand, Chin & Khoo, 2001) and an algorithm based on template-matching (Leigh, Modani & Hightower, 2004). Nonetheless, both of these two categories have to design a specific rule or template for each pattern. However, both types of algorithms require participation of domain experts and lack the ability to learn.

Elliott waves are characterized by wide and numerous descriptions of their distinctive phases, thus they are difficult to detect in time series.

- **Detection According to the Rules:** The first eventuality is the classification which gradually runs from smallest to largest parts of Elliott waves. This method is described in (Dostál & Sojka 2008). The process starts with finding a scale and separate mono-waves marking. There are completed patterns according to particular ratios. These patterns are a base for other patterns. This approach is often used for manual evaluation with their subsequent processing. The method uses seven rules, which classify waves into groups depending on a ratio of heights of neighbouring waves. The rules use Fibonacci ratios with a deviation of 5%. The only possibility of searching is to check each mono-wave through the conditions and some experience of a researcher is expected as well. Here, the aim is not to deal with the evaluated segment, but to respect single figures as complex units. This method is accurate, but it is computationally very time consuming and it is limited to the detection of mono-waves according to the predetermined number of specific rules.

- **Detection Units and Their Progressive Separation:** The second eventuality is classification of big parts of Elliott waves and their subsequent decomposition into smaller parts. Patterns of impulsive character can be detected clearly thanks to more accurate conditions than patterns of correction phase. Therefore it is possible to detect patterns proposed in input data. Here, the aim is to find a figure and then to classify its smaller units. A disadvantage is that impulse phases are only detected directly, while correction phases must be derived. Another disadvantage during detection of large parts is that their internal structure is unknown as long as other pulses are not found in these parts.

- **Detection According to Characteristic Figures:** The third eventuality is to restrict detection to some significant figures, which are significant with respect to parts of patterns according to the Elliott theory. Therefore, the method does not restrict to detecting mono-waves. Found figures can be processed further, while found figures generate additional parameters for further processing. A disadvantage is that we are able to find a lot of characteristic patters in input data, which is time consuming. Here, we have to choose patterns correctly for detection and to have sufficient amount of test data to disposal. However, this approach is very effective and, therefore, it was chosen as a detection method in the chapter.

THE BASIC PATTERN OF IMPULSE PHASE

Impulse waves are five wave patterns. Impulse waves always unfold in the same direction as the larger trend - the next higher degree impulse or corrective wave. Waves 1, 3 and 5 within an impulse are themselves impulse waves of lower degree which should also subdivide into a five-wave pattern (Figure 3). One of the impulse waves within an impulse wave will usually be extended or much longer than the other two. Most extensions in the currency markets occur in wave three. When one of the impulse waves extends the other two will frequently be of an equal size. Waves 2 and 4 within impulse waves are corrective waves. Once an impulse wave is completed it will be followed by a corrective wave. An impulse wave is always followed by a corrective wave of the same degree unless the impulse wave completes a higher degree wave, (Poser 2003).

There are three rules which should hold true for an impulse wave (Figure 4) to be valid:

- Wave two cannot move past the start of wave one;
- Wave three cannot be the shortest wave of the three impulse waves (1,3,5);
- Wave four cannot move past the end of wave one.

Figure 3. The basic pattern of impulse phase

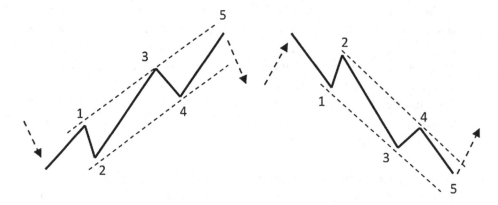

Figure 4. Valid impulse wave

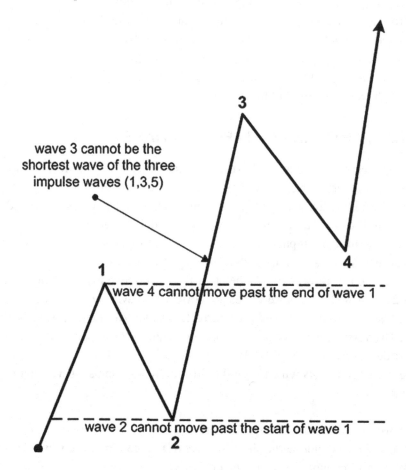

If any of these rules are violated, you should try a different wave count. In some cases, the wave count can still be considered valid if the currency prices violate any of the above rules but not on a closing basis, (Poser 2003).

THE BASIC PATTERN OF CORRECTIVE PHASE

Corrective waves are three wave patterns. Corrective waves always unfold in the opposite direction to the larger trend - the next higher degree impulse or corrective wave. There are two different groups of corrective waves: simple corrective waves (zigzags, flats and irregulars) and complex corrective waves (triangles, double and triple threes). Corrective waves have much more variations than the impulse waves which makes it less easy to identify them while they are still being formed. These corrective waves are broadly called ABC corrections. They differ by the distance their subwaves move in relation to each other and by the way they subdivide. A zigzag consists of a 5-3-5 sequence in which wave B doesn't move past the start of wave A and wave C moves far beyond the end of wave A. A flat is formed by a 3-3-5 sequence in which all the three subwaves are of the same length. An irregular is made up of a 3-3-5 sequence in which wave B exceeds the start of wave A and waves C moves close to or beyond the end of wave A. In Figure 5 you can see the basic pattern of correction phase, i.e. zigzag. (Frost & Prechter 2001).

Fibonacci Analysis and Elliott Wave Theory

Fibonacci numbers provide the mathematical foundation for the Elliott Wave Theory. While the Fibonacci ratios have been adapted to various technical indicators, their utmost use in technical analysis remains the measurement of correction waves (Frost and Prechter 2001). The Fibonacci number sequence 1, 1, 2, 3, 5, 8, 13, 21, 34, 55,

Figure 5. Ideal Zizgaz

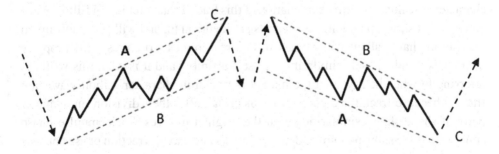

89,...is made by simply starting at 1 and adding the previous number to arrive at the new number. This series has very numerous interesting properties:

- The ratio of any number to the next number in the series approaches 0.618 or 61.8% (the golden ratio) after the first 4 numbers. For example: 34/55 = 0.618.
- The ratio of any number to the number that is found two places to the right approaches 0.382 or 38.2%. For example: 34/89 = 0.382.
- The ratio of any number to the number that is found three places to the right approaches 0.236 or 23.6%. For example: 21/89 = 0.236.

These relationships between every number in the series are the foundation of the common ratios used to determine price retracements and price extensions during a trend (Figure 6). A retracement is a move in price that "retraces" a portion of the previous move. Usually a stock will retrace at one of three common Fibonacci levels-38.2%, 50%, and 61.8%. Fibonacci price retracements are determined from a prior low-to high swing to identify possible support levels as the market pulls back from a high. Retracements are also run from a prior high-to-low swing using the same ratios, looking for possible resistance levels as the market bounces from a low (Frost & Prechter 2001). Fibonacci price extensions are used by traders to determine areas where they will wish to take profits in the next leg of an up-or downtrend. Percentage extension levels are plotted as horizontal lines above/below the previous trend move. The most popular extension levels are 61.8%, 100.0%, 138.2% and 161.8%. In reality it is not always so easy to spot the correct Elliott wave pattern, nor do prices always behave exactly according to this pattern. Therefore, it is advisable for a trader not to rely solely on Fibonacci ratios, but rather to use them in conjunction with other technical tools.

Fractal Structure of Elliott Waves

One of the basic tenets of Elliott Wave theory is that market structure is fractal in character. The non-scientific explanation of this fractal character is that Elliott Wave patterns that show up on long term charts are identical to, and will also show up on short term charts, albeit with sometimes more complex structures. This property of fractals is called "self-similarity" or "self-affinity" and it is what this writer is referring to when he says that the market is fractal in character. Elliott waves are fractals because fractal is a geometric object that after their division into smaller parts of shape shows similarities with the original motives. Each impulse phase consists of three subwaves upward of five breaks and each correction phase consists

Figure 6. Fibonacci price retracements and price extensions
Adapted from http://www.markets.com/education/technical-analysis/fibonacci-elliot-wave.html.

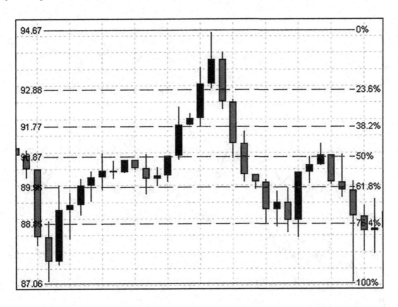

of two subwaves downward of three breaks. For a detailed view of the Elliott wave, we can find more and more fractures in each subwave. Just such repeating pattern is a fundamental property of fractals (Figure 7).

BACKPROPAGATION NEURAL NETWORKS

Artificial Neural Networks (ANN) are inspired in the biological neural nets and are used for complex and difficult tasks (Fausett, 1994). The most often usage is classification of objects as also in this case. ANNs are capable of generalization and hence the classification is natural for them. Some other possibilities are in pattern recognition, control, filtering of signals and also data approximation and others. There are several kinds of ANN. In our experimental study, simulations were based on backpropagation neural networks. The ANN needs a training set of known solutions to be trained on them. Supervised ANN has to have inputs and also required output(s). The neural network works so that properties or attributes of items in the training sets are transferred into suitable input values. These inputs are multiplied by weights which are adjusted and optimized during the training to produce an inner potential inside the neuron. In the node the sum of inputs multiplied by weights is transferred through mathematical function like sigmoid, linear function or hyperbolic tangent etc. Therefore, ANN can be used also for data approximation – when

Figure 7. Fractal structure of Elliott wave
Adapted from (Poser 2003).

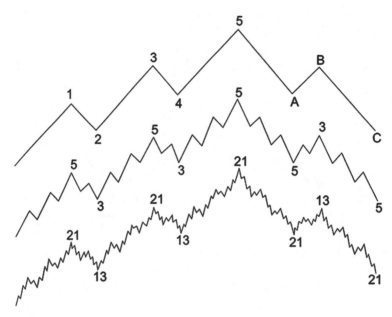

a regression model on measured data, i.e. the relation between input and required (measured data) output is synthesizes.

The neuron (Figure 8), as the main computational unit, performs only a very simple operation: it sums its weighted inputs and applies a certain activation function on the sum. Such a value then represents the output of the neuron. However great such a simplification is (according to the biological neuron), it has been found as plausible enough and is successfully used in many types of ANN, (Fausett 1994).

A neuron X_i obtains input signals x_i and relevant weights of connections w_i, optionally a value called bias b_i is added in order to shift the sum relative to the origin. The weighted sum of inputs is computed and the bias is added so that we obtain a value called stimulus or inner potential of the neuron s_i. After that it is transformed by an activation function f into output value o_i that is computed as it is shown in equations (Figure 8) and may be propagated to other neurons as their input or be considered as an output of the network. Here, the activation function is a sigmoid. The purpose of the activation function is to perform a threshold operation on the potential of the neuron.

Backpropagation network is one of the most complex neural networks for supervised learning. This ANN is a multilayer feedforward neural network, Figure 9. Usually a fully connected variant is used, so that each neuron from the *n-th* layer is connected to all neurons in the *(n+1)-th* layer, but it is not necessary and in general

Figure 8. Model of neuron

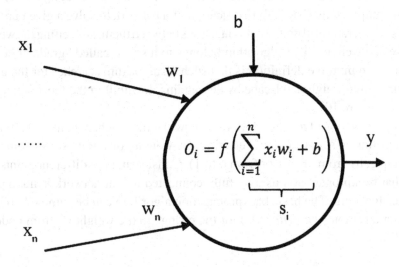

some connections may be missing – see dashed lines, however, there are no connections between neurons of the same layer. A subset of input units has no input connections from other units; their states are fixed by the problem. Another subset of units is designated as output units; their states are considered the result of the computation. Units that are neither input nor output are known as hidden units.

Figure 9. A general three-layer neural network

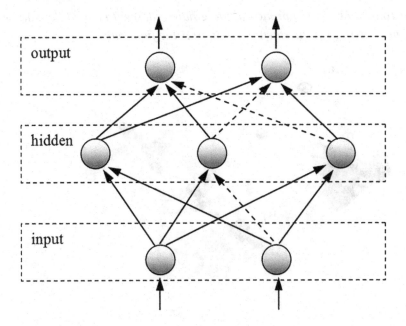

Each problem specifies a training set of associated pairs of vectors for the input units and output units. The full specification of a network to solve a given problem involves enumerating all units, the connections between them, and setting the weights on those connections. This algorithm belongs to a group called "gradient descent methods". An intuitive definition is that such an algorithm searches for the global minimum of the weight landscape by descending downhill in the most precipitous direction (Figure 10).

Backpropagation algorithm works as follow (Hertz, Kogh, & Palmer, 1991). The initial position is set at random selecting the weights of the network from some range (typically from -1 to 1 or from 0 to 1). Considering the different points, it is clear, that backpropagation using a fully connected neural network is not a deterministic algorithm. The basic backpropagation algorithm can be summed up in the following equation (the *delta rule*) for the change to the weight w_{ji} from node i to node j (1):

$$\Delta w_{ji} = \eta \times \delta_j \times y_i \tag{1}$$

where Δw_{ij} is the weight change, η is the learning rate, y_i is the input signal to node j, and the local gradient δ_j is defined as follows:

1. If node j is an output node, then δ_j is the product of $\varphi'(v_j)$ and the error signal e_j, where $\varphi(\_)$ is the logistic function and v_j is the total input to node j (i.e.

Figure 10. An intuitive approach to the gradient descent method, looking for the global minimum: a) is the starting point, b) is the final one.

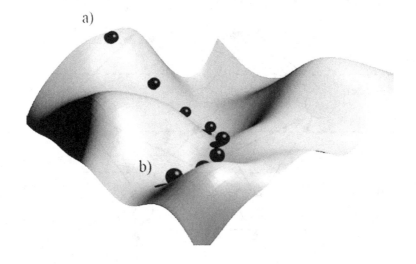

$\Sigma_i\, w_{ji} y_i$), and e_j is the error signal for node j (i.e. the difference between the desired output and the actual output);

2. If node j is a hidden node, then δ_j is the product of $\varphi'(v_j)$ and the weighted sum of the δ's computed for the nodes in the next hidden or output layer that are connected to node j.

Note: The actual formula is $\delta_j = \varphi'(v_j) = \Sigma_k\, \delta_k w_{kj}$ where k ranges over those nodes for which w_{kj} is non-zero (i.e. nodes k that actually have connections from node j. The δ_k values have already been computed as they are in the output layer (or a layer closer to the output layer than node j).

MULTI-CLASSIFIER

The core of the multi-classifier consists of the detection system for the pattern recognition of structures with fractal dynamics. The multi-classifier (Figure 11) is based on neural networks which are adapted by backpropagation. (Volna, Kotyrba & Jarusek 2013)

Figure 11. The multi-classifier proposal for the purpose of pattern recognition with consecutive prediction

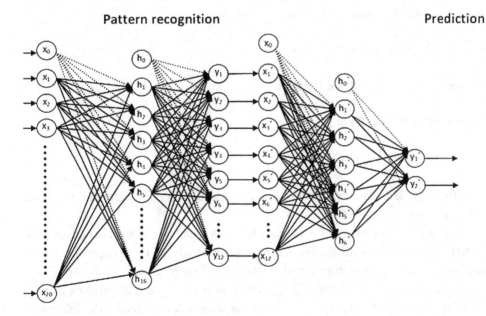

- The first neural network is designed to recognize selected Elliott wave's patterns. Emphasis is placed on the ability of a network to evaluate the found patterns with a degree of consensus of similarity with the defined pattern from training set. It is also necessary to network guarantee information about a quality of the found pattern.
- The second neural network evaluated prediction of trend component on the basis of the recognized pattern. The whole prediction is based on the IF-THEN rules from which the training set is composed for the second neural network. In essence, the neural network represents a rule-based of knowledge system that is able to decide whether a time series respects corrective or impulse direction.

Pattern Recognition Classifier

For the purpose of adaptation of the pattern recognition classifier, it is necessary to remark that determination of training patterns is one of the key tasks. Improperly chosen patterns can lead to confusion of neural networks. The search for the training set patterns is a complicated process which is usually performed manually by the user. All patterns of training set were defined in order to represent the characteristics of Elliott wave to be identified in dependently of the time scale or the nature of the monitored data. When creating patterns, we used the properties of the Fibonacci sequence, which we used as a time filter so we could estimate when the impulse or correction would terminate. Time incorrections:

A wave $= X$ units of time

B wave $= 1.681 \times X$ or $B =< 0.618 \times X$

C wave $= 0.618 \times A$ (B) or

$C => 1.618 \times A$ (B) or $C = A+B$

In the impulsive waves were taken into consideration waves where the first, third and fifth wave extended (Figure 12).

For example, when wave 3 is extended, waves 1 and 5 tend towards equality or a 0.618 relationship, as illustrated in Figure 12. Actually, all three impulsive waves tend to be related by Fibonacci mathematics, whether by equality, 1.618 or 2.618 (whose inverses are 0.618 and 0.382). These impulse wave relationships usually occur in percentage terms. Wave 5's length is sometimes related by the Fibonacci ratio to the length of wave 1 through wave 3, as illustrated in Figure 12. In those

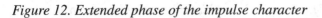

Figure 12. Extended phase of the impulse character

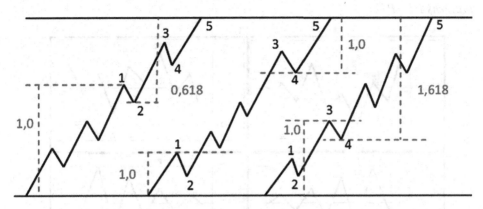

rare cases when wave 1 is extended, it is wave 2 that often subdivides the entire impulse wave into the wave. In such cases, the latter portion is 0.382 of the total distance when wave 5 is not extended. This guideline explains why a retracement following the fifth wave often has double resistance at the same level: the end of the preceding fourth wave and the 0.382 retracement point (Frost & Prechter 2001).

The training set consisted of 12 patterns representing the basic structure of the various phases of Elliott waves that include patterns containing impulse phase (P2, P5, P6, P8 and P10), the correction phase (P1, P7, P9 and P11), special triangle pattern (P3 and P4) and the basic structure oh whole Elliott wave (P12), see Figure 13. Input data is sequences always including n consecutive numbers, which are transformed into interval $\langle 0, 1 \rangle$. The proposed pattern recognition classifiers are able to recognize Elliot wave structures in given time series.

Input vector contains 20 components. We used 20 input neurons so that each component of the input vector was accepted with the same weight, therefore the used training set contains together with each component its complement to value "1", i.e. $(x_1, x_2, x_3, x_4, x_5, x_6, x_7, x_8, x_9, x_{10}, 1-x_1, 1-x_2, 1-x_3, 1-x_4, 1-x_5, 1-x_6, 1-x_7, 1-x_8, 1-x_9, 1-x_{10})$. Such a proposed input vectors representing patterns is a guarantee that equal emphasis is placed on each value, because backpropagation algorithm usually has a tendency to put less emphasis on inputs near zero. Output vector has got 12 components and each output unit represents one of 12 different types of Elliott wave samples. A neural network architecture is *20 - 16 - 12* (e.g. 20 units in the input layer, 16 units in the hidden layer, and 12 units in the output layer). The net is fully connected. Adaptation of the neural network starts with randomly generated weight values.

We used the backpropagation method for the adaptation with the following parameters: first 5000 iterations have the learning rate value 0.5, and for the next 2000 iterations the learning rate value is 0.1, momentum is 0. The conducted experimental

Figure 13. Different types of Elliott wave's samples represented in the training set , patterns P1 - P12

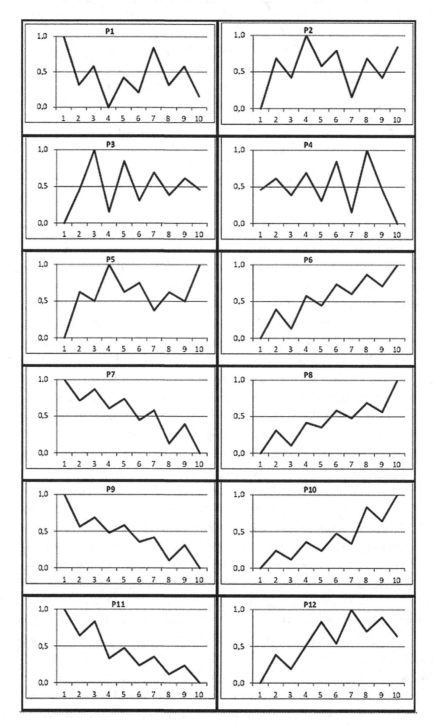

studies also showed that in each cycle of adaptation is to present an adequate network of training patterns mixed randomly to ensure their greater diversity, but also acts as a measure of system stability. Uniform system in a crisis usually collapses entirely, while in the diversion system through a crisis of its individual parts, but the whole remains functional. The condition of end of the adaptation algorithm specified the limit value of the overall network error, E < 0.07. It concerns the perfect the training set adaptation from Figure 13. The final network configuration is shown in Figure 14.

The Test Phase

In order to test the efficiency of the method, we applied a database from the area of financial forecasting (www.forexrate.co.uk) that is a set of data that reflects the situation on the market. We used time series which shows the development of market values of EUR/USD, which reflect the exchange rate between EUR and USD.

We used four different kind of financial time series, e.g. daily, hourly, 10-minutes and minutes. Our classifier (Volná, Kotyrba, and Jarušek, 2013) was able to recognize all given types of Elliott wave's samples represented in the training set (Figure 13). Comparison of the pattern P4 looks, how is learned via neural network versus its present in test set is represented in Figure 15. Pattern P4, which is recognized in test time series is shown in Figure 16. There is shown number of pattern P1-P12 that was recognized from financial time series with consensus of similarity greater than 90% in Table 1.

Our experimental studies show that the patterns of Elliott waves theory can be also observed on the Volume waveforms. Volume of trading is simply an indicator expressing the total number of contracts traded within a specific time period (e.g., hour, day, week, month ...). Our test set is made from the time series (www.google.com/finance) and includes 259 values (Figure 17). We used forex EUR/USD from 11 April 2013. The foreign exchange market (forex) is a global, worldwide-decen-

Figure 14. The final network configuration - pattern recognition classifier

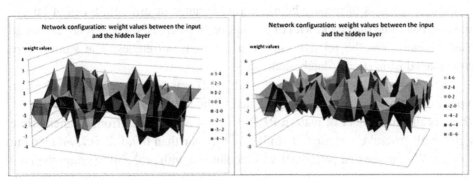

Figure 15. Training pattern P4 and its representation in used test sets

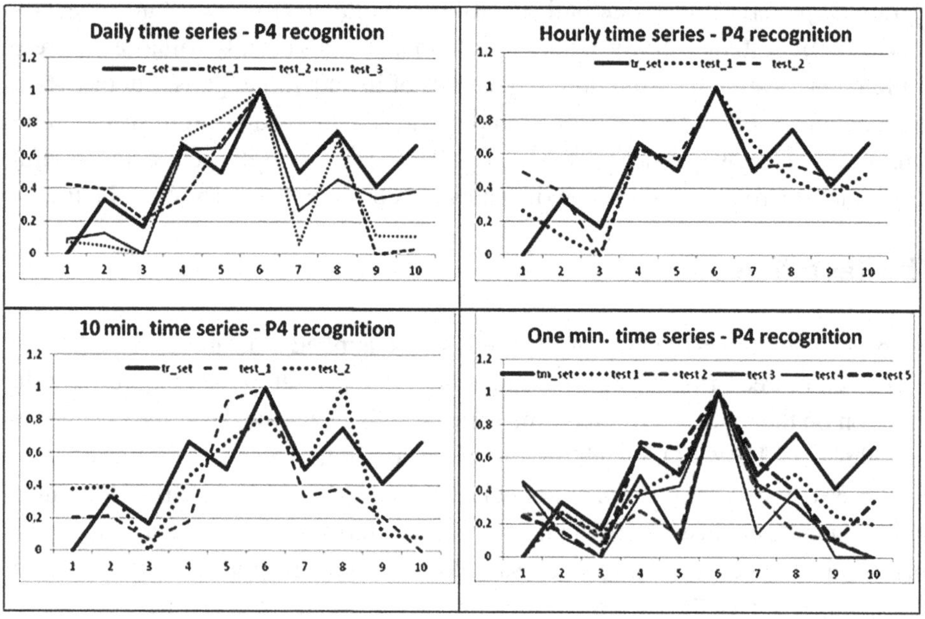

Table 1. Pattern recognition with consensus of similarity greater than 90%

Time Series	Patterns											
	P1	**P2**	**P3**	**P4**	**P5**	**P6**	**P7**	**P8**	**P9**	**P10**	**P11**	**P12**
Daily	0	19	8	24	13	0	28	5	21	25	35	11
Hourly	3	3	5	39	5	0	13	9	38	72	78	23
10 min.	6	25	4	44	1	1	14	10	33	59	95	4
One min.	5	31	1	39	0	0	4	21	35	62	87	2

tralized financial market for trading currencies. Financial centers around the world function as anchors of trading between a wide range of different types of buyers and sellers around the clock, with the exception of weekends. The foreign exchange market determines the relative values of different currencies. The values were downloaded from (Forex databases).

The proposed classifier (Kotyrba at al.2012) was able to recognize all given types of Elliott wave's samples represented in the training set (Figure 13, Table 2). There is shown number of pattern P1-P11 that was recognize from financial time series with several consensus of similarity (greater than 0.9, 0.8, 0.7, and 0.6) in Table 2. We can see that pattern P1 was recognized with probability grater then 0.9

Figure 16. P4 recognized patterns that occur in financial time series

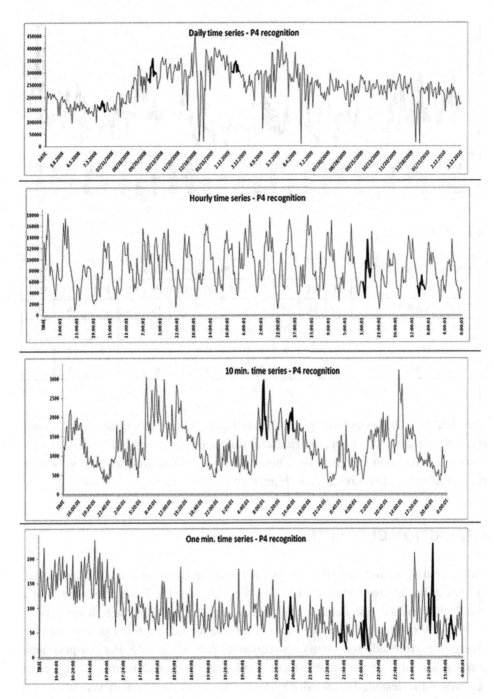

Figure 17. Financial time series

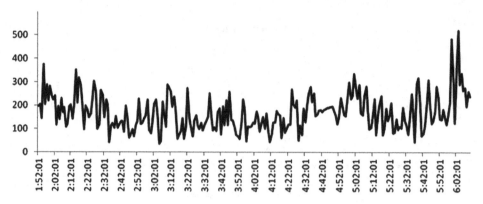

Table 2. Test results

Consensus of Similarity	Number of Patterns											
	P1	P2	P3	P4	P5	P6	P7	P8	P9	P10	P11	P12
> 0.9	6	18	19	12	5	3	5	15	22	8	6	6
> 0.8	2	6	0	2	2	0	6	9	5	1	4	2
> 0.7	4	2	0	0	1	0	3	5	5	1	3	4
> 0.6	4	1	1	0	0	0	4	0	1	1	1	4

quite 6 times, with probability grater then 0.9 quite 2 times etc. Illustration of some recognized patterns that occur in financial time series is shown in Figure 18. Comparison of the sixth pattern looks, how is learned via neural network versus its present in test set is represented in Figure 19.

PREDICTION CLASSIFIER

The second neural network of the proposed multi classifier simulates the knowledge system. A knowledge base is designed in the form of rules. Each rule consists of a conditional and a consequential part. All rules are expressed in the following form: *IF a THEN b*. The left side of each rule represents a conditional part of the rule whereas its right side represents consequential part of the rule. For our purposes, it was essential to create suitable form of rules which should include all important features of the designed knowledge system. The rules in our system were presented in the following form:

Figure 18. Some recognized patterns that occur in financial time series

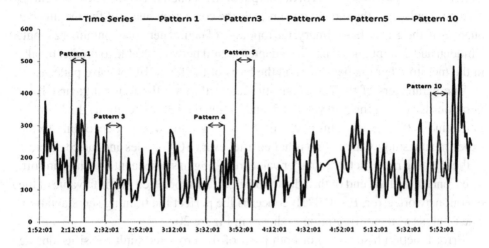

Figure 19. Training patterns P2 and P1 and their representation in the test set

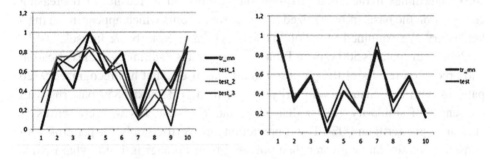

IF *found pattern & fulfilment of consensus of similarity* THEN *trend direction*

There are two basic variables in the antecedent. It means fulfilment of consensus of similarity and found patterns which we gained as results (outputs) from the first part of classifier. After prediction of trend direction the consequent is composed like this: UT-upward trend, DT-downward trend. Outputs from the first classifier produce sets of values that are assigned to each recognized training pattern in the given test time series. It is important to appreciate what can be considered as an effective criterion related to consensus of similarity. The proposed threshold resulting from our experimental study was determined at least 90%. We consider 12 basic rules, where each represents one pattern in the used training set. It means one rule for one pattern of used Elliott wave from Figure 13. It is sufficient because the neural network is able to generalize relationships from the training set into the weight values. Two neurons form the output of the second network. The first neuron predicts a pulse and the second one predicts the correction phase of the monitoring quantity in the graph. In summary, the topology of neural network contains 12 input, 6 hidden and 2 output neurons. The adapted neural network is able to predict breaks in the monitored graph behaviors on the basis of the found Elliot wave patterns.

The parameters of the backropagation algorithm are the following: first 1000 iterations have learning rate value 0.5, and for the next 3000 iterations the learning rate value is 0.1, momentum is 0. These learning rates were set according to the experimental study. Calculation is halted after every 1000 cycles and the coefficient of the learning rate is set to a smaller value, resulting in subsequent weight gain soft. The Condition of the end of the adaptation algorithm specified the limit value of the overall network error, $E < 0.07$. It concerns the perfect the training set adaptation. The final network configuration is shown in Figure 20.

Error function history (E) of both parts of the proposed multiclassifier during adaptation is shown in Figure 21 (Kotyrba et al. 2013).

Outputs from the second classifier carry a predictive character. The neural network determines if the trend direction should have an increasing or decreasing character on the basis of recognized Elliott wave patterns which appear in the market history. We examined a total of 25 data sets (Volna, Kotyrba, & Jarusek, 2013). Each of them contains 500 values. Table 3 demonstrates a summary of classification and prediction results of the proposed multi-classifier. That has recognized 9326 patterns with consensus of similarity greater than 70%, next 6859 patterns with consensus of similarity greater than 80%, and 2361 patterns with consensus of similarity greater than 90%. Trend prediction was verified only for patterns with consensus of similarity greater than 90% and their number is 1440, what is 61% successful prediction in total. In this case, the proposed multi-classifier is justifiable because the prediction percentage greater than 50% means success in the case of predictive exchange software.

Figure 20. The final network configuration - prediction classifier

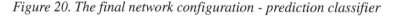
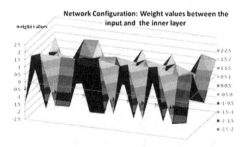
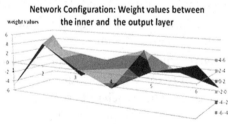

Figure 21. Error function history

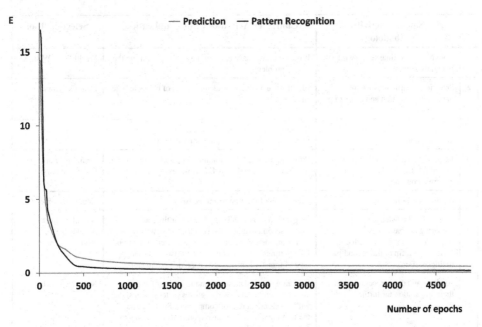

Table 3. A summary of classification and prediction results

The number of recognized patterns with consensus of similarity greater than 70%	9326
The number of recognized patterns with consensus of similarity greater than 80%	6859
The number of recognized patterns with consensus of similarity greater than 90%	2361
The number of successful trend predictions based on found patterns with consensus of similarity greater than 90%	1440
Successful prediction in total	61%

METHODOLOGY OF RECOGNITION OF STRUCTURES WITH FRACTAL DYNAMICS

Aim of the proposed methodology (Kotyrba et al. 2013) is to propose a procedure for automatic pattern recognition in the systems with fractal dynamics in order to predict the trend. Using the proposed methodology, in the context of this chapter is limited to the stock market, but the area of application is much wider character, such as the prediction of sunspots or volume wave forms etc. The proposed methodology represents a sequence of actions whose implementation will help in the recommended sequence recognition of individual parts of structures Elliott waves, which can be used to predict the trend of the analyzed time series. The sequence of these activities is shown in Table 4.

Table 4. Steps of the proposed methodology

	Name of Activity Methodology	**Character Activities within Publications**	**Selection Tool**
1	Obtaining data- time series with fractal dynamics.	It is essential to have appropriate data representing the solved problem.	World Wide Web.
2	Selection of structures for the purpose of detection and analyzing their characteristics.	Elliott wave analysis for identification of characteristic structures.	Elliott's theory.
3	Choice of classification methods and setting its parameters.	Settings of the first neural network topology, type of transfer function and adaptation parameters.	Neural network.
4	Preparing data for the first part of multiclassifier which realizes pattern recognition.	Preparation of standard training set patterns which represent individual parts Elliott waves.	Neural network, Elliott´s theory.
5	Application of methods.	Adaptation of the first neural network.	Neural network.
6	Proposal of knowledge system, preparing the base rules. Implementation of knowledge system in a form of the second part multiclassifier.	Preparation of normalized patterns for the training set for the second neural network that represents a rules-based knowledge system, designed to predict the trend line. Settings of the second neural network topology, type of transfer functionand adaptation parameters.	Neural network, Knowledge modeling.
7	Analysis and data processing and their preparation for further use.	Selection of test data series and its standardization. Adapted neural network recognizes patterns in test data with different degrees of compliance. Real outputs of the first neural network, also represents the inputs to the second neural network.	Neural network.
8	Evaluation of the solution results.	Validation of the results and their comparison with existing methods for overall evaluation.	Analytic Programming, Box-Jenkins methodology, Refined Elliott Trader, etc. Fuzzy logic toolbox etc.

COMPARATIVE STUDY

Our comparative study was aimed at comparing outputs from the proposed multi-classifier with other approaches (Volna, Kotyrba, & Jarusek, 2013). We focused on the classification of Elliott figures in the chart with a follow-up prediction of trend in the graph of the monitored system. Software NCSS with implemented Box-Jenkins methodology comprised an alternative approach for prediction. Box-Jenkins forecasting method introduces a self-projecting time series forecasting method. The underlying goal is to find an appropriate formula so that the residuals are as small as possible and exhibit no pattern. The model-building process involves four steps. Repeated as necessary, to end up with a specific formula that replicates the patterns in the series as closely as possible and also produces accurate forecasts (Box, Jenkins, and Reinsel, 1994). This methodology is implemented in many different models and is very well known for its success and variability of use.

The graph in Figure 22 shows the trend prediction of a minute time series that shows the course of EUR/USD forex from 11 March 2010 containing 500 minute values. The first proposed classifier detected pattern P6 with consensus of similarity 98%. On the basis of P6 pattern recognition (green line), the second proposed classifier predicted that the trend direction should have decreasing character (green rectangle). For comparison, the Box-Jenkins methodology also predicted a downward trend of the minute time series (red line).

The graph in Figure 23 shows the trend prediction of a hourly time series that shows the volume behavior of Coca Cola corp. from 1 January 2012 containing 500 hourly values. The first proposed classifier detected pattern P9 with consensus of similarity 93%. On the basis of P9 pattern recognition (green line), the second proposed classifier predicted that the trend direction should have increasing character (green rectangle). For comparison, the Box-Jenkins methodology also predicted an upward trend of the minute time series (red line).

The graph in Figure 24 shows the trend prediction of a daily time series that shows the stock price development of Boeing corp. 1 January – 6 May 2012. The first proposed classifier detected pattern P6 with consensus of similarity 89%. On the basis of P6 pattern recognition (green line), the second proposed classifier predicted that the trend direction should have decreasing character (green rectangle). In comparison with it, the Box-Jenkins methodology incorrect predicted a downward trend of the daily time series (red line).

Other experimental simulations provided similar numerical results.

The proposed multiclassifier has also tested in (Volná, Kotyrba, M. & Kominkova Oplatkova, 2013), where sets of experiments have been performed. The artificial neural network classifiers were performed in two approaches - one classical with

Figure 22. Trend prediction of a minute time series; green rectangle represents an area, where the trend direction is located according to the proposal multi-classifier after pattern P6 detection.

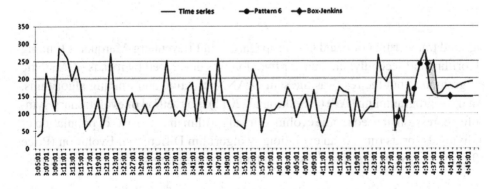

Figure 23. Trend prediction of a hour time series. Green rectangle represents an area, where the trend direction is located according to the proposal multi-classifier after pattern P9 detection.

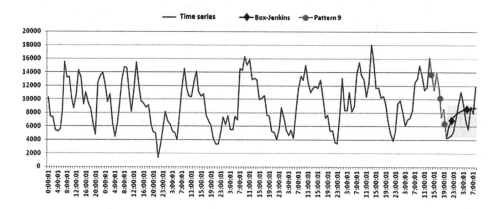

Figure 24. Trend prediction of a daily time series; green rectangle represents an area, where the trend direction is located according to the proposal multi-classifier after pattern P6 detection.

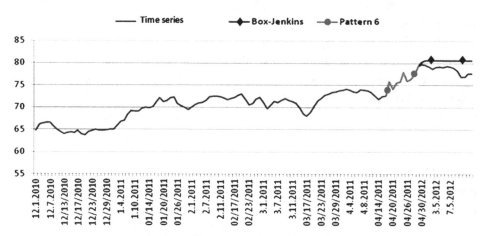

sigmoid transfer function and backpropagation and Levenberg-Marquardt training algorithm and secondly, the transfer function was developed by means of Analytic Programming but the rest was the same - ANN structure and training algorithms. Analytic programming (AP) (Zelinka at al. 2011) is a method of evolutionary symbolic regression. It needs some evolutionary algorithm that consists of population of individuals for its run. As an evolutionary algorithm Differential Evolution (Price 1999) was used in this study case. Analytic programming serves as an optimization tool for finding suitable form of transfer functions of neurons. It means that AP represents a tool which maps symbols from the basic set to the set of possible programs that can be constructed from these symbolic objects. AP has been used for optimizing parameters of used neural networks. In conclusion, the overall classification success of all these mentioned methods is compared. A consensus of similarity in charts with course of Volume is considered to be results of evaluation of classification.

CONCLUSION

In this chapter, a short introduction into the field of time series pattern recognition using artificial intelligence methods has been given. We used method based on backpropagation neural network. According to the results of experimental studies, it can be stated that Elliot wave's patterns were successfully extract in given time series and recognize using suggested method, how as can be seen from figures in experimental section. Elliott waves recognition allows time series trend prediction, as follows. If we recognize impulse phase of Elliott wave, trend prediction is downwards. If we recognize correction phase of Elliott wave or triangle patterns, trend prediction is upwards. The proposed methodology of recognition of structures with fractal dynamics is based on an interdisciplinary approach that combines various methods of artificial intelligence. Experimental results show that the methodology can also be used on a wider class of problems than just detection of Elliott waves in the price charts and achieving successful prediction. The future work will be focused on development of some method, which could be able to recognize a fractal structure in Elliot wave's patterns. It means, that the method should recognize Elliot wave's patterns in a varied time scale. . It might result in better mapping of the time series behavior for better prediction.

ACKNOWLEDGMENT

The research described here has been financially supported by the University of Ostrava grant SGS14/PrF/2016. Any opinions, findings and conclusions or recommendations expressed in this material are those of the authors and do not necessarily reflect the views of the sponsors.

REFERENCES

Anand, S., Chin, W. N., & Khoo, S. C. (2001). Chart Patterns on Price History.*Proc. of ACM SIGPLAN Int. Conf. on Functional Programming.*

Atsalakis, G. S., Dimitrakakis, E. M., & Zopounidis, C. D. (2011). Elliott Wave Theory and neuro-fuzzy systems, in stock market prediction: The WASP system. *Expert Systems with Applications, 38*(8), 9196–9206. doi:10.1016/j.eswa.2011.01.068

Box, G. E. P., Jenkins, G. M., & Reinsel, G. C. (1994). Time Series Analysis: Forecasting and Control (3rd ed.). Prentice-Hall.

Dostál, P., & Sojka, Z. (2008). Elliottovy vlny (in Czech). Tribuns.r.o.

Fausett, L. V. (1994). *Fundamentals of Neural Networks.* Englewood Cliffs, NJ: Prentice-Hall, Inc.

Frost, A. J., & Prechter, R. (2001). *Elliott Wave Principle: Key to Market Behavior.* John Wiley & Sons.

Hertz, J., Kogh, A., & Palmer, R. G. (1991). *Introduction to the Theory of Neural Computation.* Redwood City, CA: Addison – Wesley publishing Company.

Kotyrba, M., Volná, E., Bražina, D., & Jarušek, R. (2012). Elliott waves recognition via neural networks. In *Proceedings 26th European Conference on Modellingand Simulation, ECMS 2012.*

Kotyrba, M., Volná, E., Janošek, M., Habiballa, H., & Bražina, D. (2013). Methodology for Elliott waves pattern recognition. In *Proceedings 27th European Conference on Modelling and Simulation, ECMS 2013.*

Kotyrba, M., Volná, E., & Jarušek, R. (2012). Artificial intelligence methods for pattern recognition with fractal structure. In *Proceedings of the 18th International Conference on Soft Computing, Mendel 2012.*

Leigh, W., Modani, N., & Hightower, R. (2004). A Computational Implementation of Stock Charting: Abrupt Volume Increase As Signal for Movement in New York Stock Exchange Composite Index. *Decision Support Systems, 37*(4), 515–530. doi:10.1016/S0167-9236(03)00084-8

Poser, S. (2003). *Applying Elliott Wave Theory Profitably.* John Wiley & Sons.

Price, K. (1999). An Introduction to Differential Evolution. In *New Ideas in Optimization* (pp. 79–108). London: McGraw-Hill.

Volna, E., Kotyrba, M., & Jarusek, R. (2013). Multiclassifier based on Elliott wave's recognition. *Computers & Mathematics with Applications (Oxford, England), 66*(2), 213–225. doi:10.1016/j.camwa.2013.01.012

Volná, E., Kotyrba, M., & Jarušek, R. (2013). Prediction by means of Elliott waves recognition. In Nostradamus: Modern Methods of Prediction, Modeling and Analysis of Nonlinear Systems, AISC 192. Springer-Verlag Berlin Heidelberg. doi:10.1007/978-3-642-33227-2_25

Volná, E., Kotyrba, M., & Kominkova Oplatkova, Z. (2013). Elliott waves classification via softcomputing. In *Proceedings of the 19th International Conference on Soft Computing, Mendel 2013*.

Zelinka, I., Davendra, D., Jasek, R., Senkerik, R., & Oplatkova, Z. (2011). *Analytical programming-a novel approach for evolutionary synthesis of symbolic structures.* INTECH Open Access Publisher. doi:10.5772/16166

KEY TERMS AND DEFINITIONS

Artificial Neural Network: An Artificial Neural Network (ANN) is the information-processing paradigm that is inspired by the way biological nervous systems. Its key element is the structure of the information processing system. It is composed of a large number of highly interconnected processing elements (neurons) working in unison to solve specific problems.

Classification: A classification problem occurs when an object needs to be assigned into predefined group or class based on a number of observed attributes related to that object. A classifier is a computer based agent which can perform a classification task.

Elliott Wave: The Elliott Wave Principle is a form of technical analysis that traders use to analyze financial market cycles and forecast market trends by identifying extremes in investor psychology, highs and lows in prices, and other collective factors.

Pattern Recognition: Pattern recognition is a branch of machine learning that focuses on the recognition of patterns and regularities in data.

Time Series: A time series is a sequence of data points that consists of successive measurements made over a time interval, where the time interval is continuous and the distance in this time interval between any two consecutive data point is the same. Each time unit in the time interval has at most one data point.

Chapter 2
Introduction to Time Series

Martin Žáček
University of Ostrava, Czech Republic

ABSTRACT

The goal of this chapter is a description of the time series. This chapter will review techniques that are useful for analyzing time series data, that is, sequences of measurements that follow non-random orders. Unlike the analyses of random samples of observations that are discussed in the context of most other statistics, the analysis of time series is based on the assumption that successive values in the data file represent consecutive measurements taken at equally spaced time intervals. There are two main goals of time series analysis: (a) identifying the nature of the phenomenon represented by the sequence of observations, and (b) forecasting (predicting future values of the time series variable). Both of these goals require that the pattern of observed time series data is identified and more or less formally described. Once the pattern is established, we can interpret and integrate it with other data.

INTRODUCTION

Many statistical methods relate to data which are independent, or at least uncorrelated. There are many practical situations where data might be correlated. This is particularly so where repeated observations on a given system are made sequentially in time. (Reiner, 2010)

Data gathered sequentially in time are called a *time series*.

DOI: 10.4018/978-1-5225-0565-5.ch002

The analysis of these experimental data that have been observed at different points in time leads to new and unique problems in statistical modeling and inference. The obvious correlation introduced by the sampling of adjacent points in time can severely restrict the applicability of the many conventional statistical methods traditionally dependent on the assumption that these adjacent observations are independent and identically distributed. The systematic approach by which one goes about answering the mathematical and statistical questions posed by these time correlations is commonly referred to as time series analysis.

Historically, time series methods were applied to problems in the physical and environmental sciences. This fact accounts for the basic engineering flavor permeating the language of time series analysis. The first step in any time series investigation always involves careful scrutiny of the recorded data plotted over time.

Before looking more closely at the particular statistical methods, it is appropriate to mention that two separate, but not necessarily mutually exclusive, approaches to time series analysis exist, commonly identified as the time domain approach and the frequency domain approach. ()

A time series is a set of statistics, usually collected at regular intervals. Time series data occur naturally in many application areas:

- **Economics and Finance:** E.g., monthly data for unemployment, hospital admissions, daily exchange rate, a share price, etc. (Barro, 1987).
- **Environmental Modelling:** E.g., daily rainfall, air quality readings.
- **Meteorology and Hydrology:** E.g., weather forecast.
- **Demographics:** E.g., population development.
- **Medicine:** E.g., ECG brain wave activity every 2–8 secs.
- Engineering and Quality Control.

Example 1: New York Stock Exchange (Brockwell, 2002; Shumway, 2015)

Figure 1 shows the daily returns (or percent change) of the New York Stock Exchange (NYSE) from February 2, 1984 to December 31, 1991. It is easy to spot the crash of October 19, 1987 in Figure 1. The data shown in Figure 1 are typical of return data. The mean of the series appears to be stable with an average return of approximately zero, however, the volatility (or variability) of data changes over time. In fact, the data show volatility clustering; that is, highly volatile periods tend to be clustered together. A problem in the analysis of these type of financial data is to forecast the volatility of future returns. For example, GARCH models have been developed to handle these problems.

Figure 1. Daily weighted market returns from February 2, 1984 to December 31, 1991; the crash of October 19, 1987 occurs at t = 938.
Shumway, 2015.

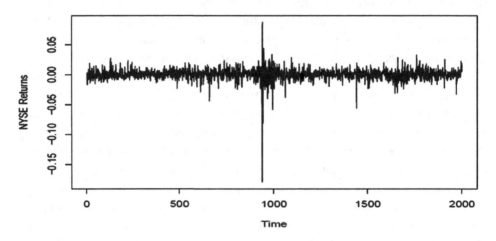

Example 2: Johnson & Johnson Quarterly Earnings (Brockwell, 2002; Shumway, 2015)

Figure 2 and Figure 3 show quarterly earnings per share for the U.S. company Johnson & Johnson. There are 84 quarters (21 years) measured from the first quarter of 1960 to the last quarter of 1980. Modeling such series begins by observing the primary patterns in the time history. In this case, note the increasing underlying trend and variability, and a somewhat regular oscillation superimposed on the trend that seems to repeat over quarters. (Shumway, 2015; Chan, 2002)

Figure 2. Johnson & Johnson quarterly earnings per share, 1960-I to 1980-IV
Shumway, 2015.

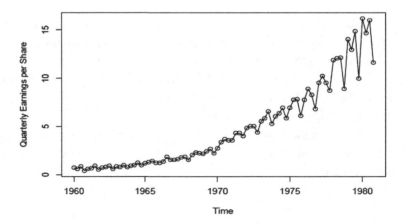

Figure 3. Left: quarterly value of initial deposits of $75, $100, $125, and $150 over 15 years, with a quarterly growth rate of 5%; $x_t = (1 + 0.05) x_{t-1}$; right: logs of the quarterly values; $log(x_t) = log (1 + 0.05) + log(x_{t-1})$. When marked in terms of quarters, Figure 3 looks like Figure 2.
Shumway, 2015.

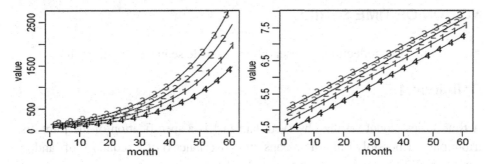

The simplest form of data is a longish series of continuous measurements at equally spaced time points.

That is: (Reiner, 2010)

- Observations are made at distinct points in time, these time points being equally spaced, and
- The observations may take values from a continuous distribution.

The above setup could be easily generalized: for example, the times of observation need not be equally spaced in time, the observations may only take values from a discrete distribution, ...

If we repeatedly observe a given system at regular time intervals, it is very likely that the observations we make will be correlated. So we cannot assume that the data constitute a random sample. The time-order in which the observations are made is vital.

Objectives of time series analysis: (Reiner, 2010)

- **Description:** Summary statistics, graphs;
- **Analysis and Interpretation:** Find a model to describe the time dependence in the data, can we interpret the model?
- **Forecasting or Prediction:** Given a sample from the series, forecast the next value, or the next few values;
- **Control:** Adjust various control parameters to make the series fit closer to a target;

- **Adjustment:** In a linear model the errors could form a time series of correlated observations, and we might want to adjust estimated variances to allow for this.

NOTION OF TIME SERIES

A *time series* is a collection of observations x_t made sequentially through time.

Definition 1

A time series model for the observed data $\{x_t\}$ is a specification of the joint distributions (or possibly only the means and covariances) of a sequence of random variables $\{X_t\}$ of which $\{x_t\}$ is postulated to be a realization.

In reality it is possible to observe only the time series at a finite number of times, and in that case the underlying sequence of random variables $(X_1, X_2, ..., X_n)$ is just a an n-dimensional random variable (or random vector). Often, however, it is convenient to allow the number of observations to be infinite. In that case $\{X_t, t = 1, 2,...\}$ is called a *stochastic process* (or a *random function*). This model is called as a *stochastic model*. In order to specify its statistical properties we then need to consider all n-dimensional distributions

$$P\left[X_1 \leq x_1, \cdots, X_n \leq x_n\right] \text{ for all } n = 1, 2, \cdots$$

The theory of stochastic processes is the theoretical mathematical foundation for studying stochastic time series models. (Anderson, 1971)

A *deterministic model* is a model that is not based on probability theory. There are two main types of deterministic models:

1. **Deterministic Functions of Time:** $X_t = f(t)$,
2. **Recurrence Equations:** $X_t = f(t, X_{t-1}, X_{t-2}, ...)$.

Provided $f(\cdot)$ and (if required) past values of X_t are known, a deterministic model for X_t allows one to predict perfectly the future of X_t (Box, 1976) (Novák, 2015)

Example 3: A Binary Process (Brillinger, 1975)

A very simple example of a stochastic process is the binary process $\{X_t, t = 1, 2,...\}$ of independent random variables with

$$P\left(X_t = 1\right) = p; P\left(X_t = -1\right) = 1 - p,$$

$$P\left(X_t = 1\right) = P\left(X_t = -1\right) = \frac{1}{2}.$$

In this case

$$P\left(X_1 = i_1, X_2 = i_2, \cdots, X_n = i_n\right) = 2^{-n}$$

where $i_k = 1$ or -1.

The time series obtained by tossing a penny repeatedly and scoring $+1$ for each head and -1 for each tail is usually modeled as a realization of this process. (Hillmer, 1983)

Example 4: Random Walk (Brillinger, 2001)

The random walk $\{S_t, t = 0, 1, 2, \ldots\}$ (starting at zero) is obtained by cumulatively summing (or "integrating") IID random variables. Thus a random walk with zero mean is obtained by defining $S_0 = 0$ and

$$S_t = X_1 + X_2 + \cdots X_n \ for \ t = 1, 2, \cdots$$

where $\{Xt\}$ is IID noise. If $\{Xt\}$ is the binary process of Example 3, then $\{S_t, t = 0, 1, 2, \ldots\}$ is called a *simple symmetric random walk*. This walk can be viewed as the location of a pedestrian who starts at position zero at time zero and at each integer time tosses a fair coin, stepping one unit to the right each time a head appears and one unit to the left for each tail. A realization of length 200 of a simple symmetric random walk is shown in Figure 4. Notice that the outcomes of the coin tosses can be recovered from $\{S_t, t = 0, 1, 2, \ldots\}$ by differencing. Thus the result of the tth toss can be found from $S_t - S_{t-1} = X_t$.

Definition 2: IID Noise (Brillinger, 2001)

Perhaps the simplest model for a time series is one in which there is no trend or seasonal component and in which the observations are simply independent and identically distributed (IID) random variables with zero mean.

Figure 4. One realization of a simple random walk {S_t, t = 0, 1, 2, ..., 200}
Shumway, 2015.

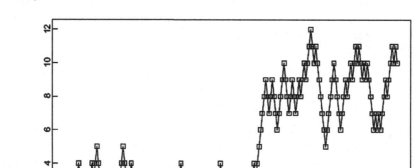

A process {X_t, $t \in \mathbf{Z}$} is said to be an IID noise with mean 0 and variance σ^2, written

$$\left\{ X_t \right\} \sim IID\left(0, o^2\right),$$

if the random variables X_t are independent and identically distributed $EX_t = 0$ with and $Var(X_t) = \sigma^2$.

The binary process is obviously an IID(0, 1)-noise.

In most situations to be considered in this course, we will not need the "full" specification of the underlying stochastic process. The methods will generally rely only on its means and covariances and – sometimes – on some more or less general assumptions. (Zeller, 1983)

Consider a stochastic process {X_t, $t \in T$}, where T is called the *index* or parameter set. Important examples of index sets are

$$\mathbf{Z} = \left\{0, \pm 1, \pm 2, \cdots\right\}, \left\{0, 1, 2, \cdots\right\}, \left(-\infty, \infty\right) \text{ and } \left[0, \infty\right)$$

A stochastic process with $T \subset \mathbf{Z}$ is often called a time series.

Definition 3

Let $\{X_t, t \in T\}$ be a *stochastic process* with $Var(X_t) < \infty$. The mean function of $\{X_t\}$ is

$$\mu_X(t) \overset{def}{=} E(X_t), t \in T.$$

The covariance function of $\{X_t\}$ is

$$\gamma_X(r,s) = Cov(X_r, X_s), r, s \in T.$$

STATIONARITY TIMES SERIES

Loosely speaking, a stochastic process is stationary, if its statistical properties do not change with time. Since, as mentioned, we will generally rely only on properties defined by the means and covariances, we are led to the following definition. (Grandell, 2012)

Definition 3 (Gouriéroux, 1997)

The time series $\{X_t, t \in Z\}$ s said to be (weakly) stationary if

1. $Var(X_t) < \infty$ for all $t \in Z$,
2. $\mu_X(t) = \mu$ for all $t \in Z$,
3. $\gamma_X(r, s) = \gamma_X(r + t, s + t)$ for all $r, s, t \in Z$.
4. Implies that for all $\gamma_X(r, s)$ is a function of $r - s$, and it is convenient to define

$$\gamma_X(h) \overset{def}{=} \gamma_X(h, 0).$$

The value "h" is referred to as the "*lag*".

Definition 4

Let $\{X_t, t \in Z\}$ be a stationary time series. The autocovariance function (ACVF) of $\{X_t\}$ is

$$\gamma_X\left(h\right) = Cov\left(X_{t+h}, X_t\right)$$

The autocorrelation function (ACF) is

$$\rho_X\left(h\right) \stackrel{def}{=} \frac{\gamma_X\left(h\right)}{\gamma_X\left(0\right)}.$$

A simple example of a stationary process is the white noise, which may be looked a upon as the correspondence to the IID noise when only the means and the covariances are taken into account. (Novák, 2014) (Chan, 2002)

Definition 5: White Noise (Shumway, 2015)

A process $\{X_t, t \in Z\}$ is said to be a white noise with mean μ and variance σ^2, written

$$\left\{X_t\right\} \sim WN\left(\mu, \sigma^2\right),$$

if $EX_t = \mu$ and $\gamma\left(h\right) = \begin{cases} \sigma^2 & if\ h = 0 \\ 0 & if\ h \neq 0 \end{cases}$

The time series generated from uncorrelated variables is used as a model for noise in engineering applications where it is called white noise.

In some literature white noise means IID.

Figure 5 shows in the upper panel a collection of 500 such random variables, with $\sigma^2 = 1$, plotted in the order in which they were drawn.

Figure 5. Gaussian white noise series
Shumway, 2015.

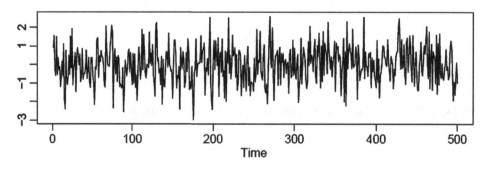

IMPORTANT TYPES OF DETERMINISTIC TRENDS

Different types of deterministic trends can be obtained by varying the functional form of $f(t)$. Especially important ones the following.

1.   Trigonometric Trend:

$$f(t) = A_0 + \sum_{j=1}^{q} \left[A_j \cos(\omega_j t) + B_j \sin(\omega_j t) \right]$$

This function is periodic (or quasi-periodic). From the very start of time series analysis, such models were considered in order to represent series whose behavior appeared to exhibit periodicities. An important issue in such analyses consists in determining the important frequencies ω_j (*harmonic analysis* of *spectral analysis*).

2.   Linear Trend:

$$f(t) = \beta_0 + \beta_1 t.$$

3.   Polynomial Trend:

$$f(t) = \beta_0 + \beta_1 t + \cdots + \beta_k t^k.$$

4.   Exponential Curve:

$$f(t) = \beta_0 + \beta_k r^t.$$

5.   Logistic Curve:

$$f(t) = \frac{1}{\beta_0 + \beta_k r^t}, \ where \ r > 0.$$

6.   Gompertz Curve:

$$f(t) = \exp\left\{ \beta_0 + \beta_k r^t \right\}, \ where \ r > 0$$

IMPORTANT CATEGORIES OF STOCHASTIC MODELS

Adjustment Model

$$X_t = f(t, u_t),$$

where t represents time and u_t is a random disturbance.

Usually, it is assumed that the u_t are mutually independent or uncorrelated. Important types of adjustment models:

1. Additive Trend:

$$X_t = f(t) + u_t.$$

2. Multiplicative Trend:

$$X_t = f(t) u_t$$

where $f(t)$ is independent of (or uncorrelated with) u_t. Usually, it is assumed that $f(t)$ is a deterministic (nonrandom) function of time as considered above. In certain cases, $f(t)$ can be viewed as random (*unobserved components models*).

3. **Trend Estimation and Elimination:** Methods for estimating or eliminating trends belong to two basic types:
    a. **Global Adjustment Methods:** Where all the observations play equivalent roles,
    b. **Local Adjustment Methods:** Where nearby observations (in time) play more important roles: moving averages and exponential smoothing.
4. **Persons Decomposition:** In economics, this following standard decomposition has often been used:

$$X_t = Z_t + C_t + S_t + u_t$$

where

T_t is a secular (long-run) trend,

C_t is a relatively smooth deviation from the secular trend (business cycle),
S_t is a seasonal component,
u_t is a random perturbation (unpredictable).

Filtering Models (Generalized Moving Averages)

$$X_t = f\left(\cdots, u_{t-1}, u_t, u_{t+1}, \cdots\right)$$

where the u_t are random disturbances (independent or mutually uncorrelated random variables).

Important case – Moving average of order q:

$$X_t = \bar{u} + u_t - \sum_{j=1}^{q} \theta_j u_{t-j}$$

Autopredictive Models

$$X_t = f\left(X_{t-1}, X_{t-2}, \cdots, u_t\right)$$

where the u_t are random disturbances.

Important case – Autoregressive process of order p:

$$X_t = \bar{u} + \sum_{j=1}^{p} \varphi_j X_{t-j} + u_t.$$

Explanatory Models

$$X_t = f\left(Z_t^*, u_t\right)$$

where Z_t^* contains various explanatory variables (exogenous variables) and (possibly) lagged values of X_t.

BASIC OF FORECASTING

Time series are any univariate or multivariate quantitative data collected over time either by private or government agencies. Common uses of time series data include:

1. Modeling the relationships between various time series;
2. Forecasting the underlying behavior of the data; and
3. Forecasting what effect changes in one variable may have on the future behavior of another variable.

There are two major categories of forecasting approaches: Qualitative and Quantitative (Awokuse, 2004).

- **Qualitative Techniques:** Qualitative techniques refer to a number of forecasting approaches based on subjective estimates from informed experts. Usually, no statistical data analysis is involved. Rather, estimates are based on a deliberative process of a group of experts, based on their past knowledge and experience. Examples are the Delphi technique and scenario writing, where a panel of experts are asked a series of questions on future trends, the answers are recorded and shared back to the panel, and the process is repeated so that the panel builds a shared scenario. The key to these approaches is a recognition that forecasting is subjective, but if we involve knowledgeable people in a process we may get good insights into future scenarios. This approach is useful when good data are not available, or we wish to gain general insights through the opinions of experts.
- **Quantitative Techniques:** Refers to forecasting based on the analysis of historical data using statistical principles and concepts. The quantitative forecasting approach is further sub-divided into two parts: causal techniques and time series techniques. Causal techniques are based on regression analysis that examines the relationship between the variable to be forecasted and other explanatory variables. In contrast, Time Series techniques usually use historical data for only the variable of interest to forecast its future values.
- **Forecast Horizon:** The forecast horizon is defined as the number of time periods between the current period and the date of a future forecast. For example, for the case of monthly data, if the current period is month T, then a forecast of sales for month T+3 has a forecast horizon of three steps. For quarterly data, a step is one quarter (three months), but for annual data, one step is one year (twelve months). The forecast changes with the forecast horizon. The choice of the best and most appropriate forecasting models and strategy usually depends on the forecasting horizon. (Awokuse, 2004)

Three Types of Time Series Forecasts

1. **Point Forecast:** A single number or a "best guess." It does not provide information on the level of uncertainty around the point estimate/forecast. For example, an economist may forecast a 10.5% growth in unemployment over the next six months.
2. **Interval Forecast:** Relative to a point forecast, this is a range of forecasted values which is expected to include the actual observed value with some probability. For example, an economist may forecast growth in unemployment rate to be in the interval, 8.5% to 12.5%. An interval forecast is related to the concept of confidence intervals.
3. **Density Forecast:** This type of forecast provides information on the overall probability distribution of the future values of the time series of interest. For example, the density forecast of future unemployment rate growth might be normally distributed with a mean of 8.3% and a standard deviation of 1.5%. Relative to the point forecast, both the density and the interval forecasts provide more information since we provide more than a single estimate, and we provide a probability context for the estimate. However, despite the importance and more comprehensive information contained in density and interval forecasts, they are rarely used by businesses. Rather, the point forecast is the most commonly used type of forecast by businesses managers and policymakers. (Awokuse, 2004)

Steps to Modeling and Forecasting Time Series

Step 1: Determine Characteristics/Components of Series.

Some time series techniques require the elimination of all components (trend, seasonal, cyclical) except the random fluctuation in the data. Such techniques require modeling and forecasting with stationary time series. In contrast, other methods are only applicable to a time series with the trend component in addition to a random component. Hence, it is important to first identify the form of the time series in order to ascertain which components are present. All business data have a random component. Since the random component cannot be predicted, we need to remove it via averaging or data smoothing. The cyclical component usually requires the availability of long data sets with minimum of two repetitions of the cycle. For example, a 10-year cycle requires, at least 20 years of data. This data requirement often makes it unfeasible to account for the cyclical component in most business and industry forecasting analysis. Thus, business data is usually inspected for both trend and seasonal components. (Awokuse, 2004)

How can we detect trend component?

- Inspect time series data plot.
- Regression analysis to fit trend line to data and check p-value for time trend coefficient.

How can we detect seasonal component?

- Requires at least two years' worth of data at higher frequencies (monthly, quarterly).
- Inspect a folded annual time series data plot – each year superimposed on others.
- Check Durbin-Watson regression analysis diagnostic for serial correlation.

Step 2: Select Potential Forecasting Techniques.

For business and financial time series, only trend and random components need to be considered. Figure 6 summarizes the potential choices of forecasting techniques for alternative forms of time series. For example, for stationary time series (only random component exist), the appropriate approach are stationary forecasting methods such as moving averages, weighted moving average, and exponential smoothing. These methods usually produce less accurate forecasts if the time series is non-stationary. Time series methods that account for trend or seasonal techniques are best for non-stationary business and financial data. These methods include: seasonal multiple regression, trend and seasonal autoregression, and time series decomposition. (Awokuse, 2004)

Figure 6. Seasonally adjust housing starts
Awokuse, 2004.

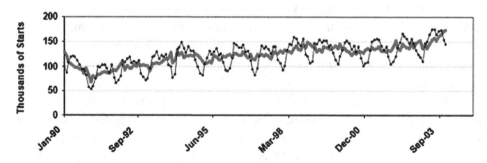

Step 3: Evaluate Forecasts from Potential Techniques (Figure 7).

After deciding on which alternative methods are suitable for available data, the next step is to evaluate how well each method performs in forecasting the time series. Measures such as R^2 and the sign and magnitude of the regression coefficients will help provide a general assessment of our models. However, for forecasting, an examination of the error terms from the model is usually the best strategy for assessing performance.

First, each method is used to forecast the data series. Second, the forecast from each method is evaluated to see how well it fits relative to the actual historical data. Forecast fit is based on taking the difference between individual forecast and the actual value. This exercise produces the forecast errors. Instead of examining

Figure 7. Potential choices of forecasting techniques
Awokuse, 2004.

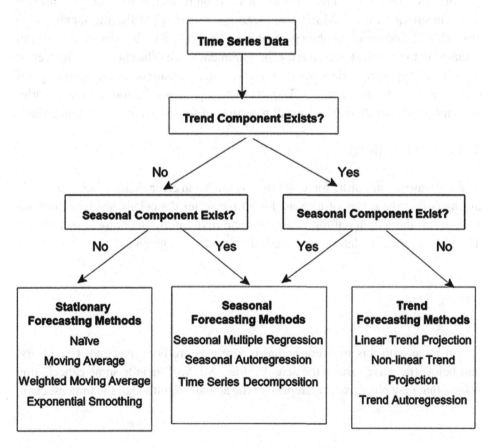

individual forecast errors, it is preferable and much easier to evaluate a single measurement of overall forecast error for the entire data under analysis. Error (et) on individual forecast, the difference between the actual value and the forecast of that value, is given as:

$$e_t = Y_t - F_t,$$

where:

e_t = the error of the forecast,
Y_t = the actual value,
F_t = the forecast value.

There are several alternative methods for computing overall forecast error. Examples of forecast error measures include: mean absolute deviation (MAD), mean error (ME), mean square error (MSE), root mean square error (RMSE), mean percentage error (MPE), and mean absolute percentage error (MAPE). The best forecast model is that with the smallest overall error measurement value. The choice of which error criteria are appropriate depends on the forecaster's business goals, knowledge of data, and personal preferences. The next section presents the formulas and a brief description of five alternative overall measures of forecast errors (Awokuse, 2004)

1. Mean Error (ME)

A quick way of computing forecast errors is the mean error (ME) which is a simple average of all the errors of forecast for a time series data. This involves the summing of all the individual forecast errors and dividing by the number of forecast. The formula for calculating mean absolute deviation is given as:

$$ME = \frac{\sum_{i=1}^{N} e_i}{N}$$

An issue with this measure is that if forecasts are both over (positive errors) and below (negative errors) the actual values, ME will include some cancellation effects that may potentially misrepresent the actual magnitude of the forecast error.

2. Mean Absolute Deviation (MAD)

The mean absolute deviation (MAD) is the mean or average of the absolute values of the errors. The formula for calculating mean absolute deviation is given as:

$$MAD = \frac{\sum_{i=1}^{N} |e_i|}{N}$$

Relative to the mean error (ME), the mean absolute deviation (MAD) is commonly used because by taking the absolute values of the errors, it avoids the issues with the canceling effects of the positive and negative values. N denotes the number of forecasts.

3. Mean Square Error (MSE)

Another popular way of computing forecast errors is the mean square error (MSE) which is computed by squaring each error and then taking a simple average of all the squared errors of forecast. This involves the summing of all the individual squared forecast errors and dividing by the number of forecast. The formula for calculating mean square error is given as:

$$MSE = \frac{\sum_{i=1}^{N} e_i^2}{N}$$

The MSE is preferred by some because it also avoids the problem of the canceling effects of positive and negative values of forecast errors.

4. Mean Percentage Error (MPE)

Instead of evaluating errors in terms of absolute values, we sometimes compute forecast errors as a percentage of the actual values. The mean percent error (MPE) is the ratio of the error to the actual value being forecast multiplied by 100. The formula for calculating mean percent error is given as:

$$MPE = \frac{\sum\limits_{i=1}^{N} \frac{e_i}{Y_i} \cdot 100}{N}$$

5. Mean Absolute Percentage Error (MAPE)

Similar to the mean percent error (MPE), the mean absolute percent error (MAPE) is the average of the absolute values of the percentage of the forecast errors. The formula for calculating mean absolute percent error is given as:

$$MAPE = \frac{\sum\limits_{i=1}^{N} \left|\frac{e_i}{Y_i}\right| \cdot 100}{N}$$

The MAPE is another measure that also circumvents the problem of the canceling effects of positive and negative values of forecast errors.

CONCLUSION

In this chapter has been introduced some basic ideas of time series analysis and stochastic or deterministic processes. Of particular importance are the concepts of stationarity and the autocovariance and sample autocovariance functions. Some standard techniques are described for the estimation and removal of trend and seasonality (of known period) from an observed time series.

In last part of this chapter was introduced some basic skills for analyzing and forecasting data over time. Next, it discussed several forecasting techniques and how they are used in generating forecasts. Furthermore, it was also examines important issues on how to evaluate and judge the accuracy of forecasts and discuss some of the common challenges to developing good forecasts.

REFERENCES

Anderson, T. W. (1971). *The Statistical Analysis of Time Series*. New York: John Wiley & Sons.

Awokuse, T., & Ilvento, T. (2004). *Module 6: Introduction to Time Series Forecasting*. Retrieved December 31, 2015, from http://www.udel.edu/FREC/ilvento/BUAD820/MOD604.pdf

Barro, R. J. (1987). *Macroeconomics* (2nd ed.). New York: John Wiley & Sons.

Box, G. E. P., & Jenkins, G. M. (1976). *Time Series Analysis: Forecasting and Control* (2nd ed.). San Francisco: Holden-Day.

Brillinger, D. R. (1975). *Time Series: Data Analysis and Theory*. New York: Holt, Rinehart & Winston Inc.

Brillinger, D. R. (1981, 2001). Time Series: Data Analysis and Theory (2nd ed.). San Francisco: Holden-Day.

Brockwell, P. J., & Davis, R. A. (2002). *Introduction to Times Series and Forecasting*. Springer-Verlag New York, Inc. doi:10.1007/b97391

Chan, N. H. (2002). *Time Series: Applications to Finance*. New York: Wiley.

Gouriéroux, C., & Monfort, A. (1997). *Time Series and Dynamic Models*. Cambridge, UK: Cambridge University Press.

Grandell, J. (2012). *Time series analysis*. Retrieved December 31, 2015, from https://www.math.kth.se/matstat/gru/sf2943/ts.pdf

Hillmer, C., Bell, R., & Tiao, C. (1983). Modeling Considerations Considerations in Seasonal Adjustment of Economic Time Series. Academic Press.

Novák, V. (2015). Linguistic Characterization of Time Series. *Fuzzy Sets and Systems*.

Novák, V., Pavliska, V., Štěpnička, M., & Štěpničková, L. (2014). *Time Series Trend Extraction and Its Linguistic Evaluation Using F-Transform and Fuzzy Natural Logic. In Recent Developments and New Directions in Soft Computing (Studies in Fuzziness and Soft Computing 317)*. Switzerland: Springer.

Reiner, G. (2010). *Time Series. Hilary Term*. Retrieved December 31, 2015, from http://www.stats.ox.ac.uk/~reinert

Shumway, R. H., & Stoffer, D. S. (2015). *Times Series Analysis and Its Applications*. Springer-Verlag New York Inc.

Zellner, A. (Ed.). (1983). *Applied Time Series Analysis of Economics Data*. Bureau of the Census.

KEY TERMS AND DEFINITIONS

Density Forecast: This type of forecast provides information on the overall probability distribution of the future values of the time series of interest.

IID Noise: The simplest model for a time series is one in which there is no trend or seasonal component and in which the observations are simply independent and identically distributed (iid) random variables with zero mean.

Interval Forecast: Relative to a point forecast, this is a range of forecasted values which is expected to include the actual observed value with some probability.

Point Forecast: A single number or a "best guess." It does not provide information on the level of uncertainty around the point estimate/forecast.

Random Walk: The random walk is obtained by cumulatively summing (or "integrating") IID random variables.

Times Series: Time series analysis refers to problems in which observations are collected at regular time intervals and there are correlations among successive observations. Applications cover virtually all areas of Statistics but some of the most important include economic and financial time series, and many areas of environmental or ecological data.

Trend Analysis: There are no proven "automatic" techniques to identify trend components in the time series data; however, as long as the trend is monotonous (consistently increasing or decreasing) that part of data analysis is typically not very difficult. If the time series data contain considerable error, then the first step in the process of trend identification is smoothing.

Chapter 3
Artificial Intelligence Algorithms for Classification and Pattern Recognition

Robert Jarušek
University of Ostrava, Czech Republic

Vaclav Kocian
University of Ostrava, Czech Republic

ABSTRACT

Classification tasks can be solved using so-called classifiers. A classifier is a computer based agent which can perform a classification task. There are many computational algorithms that can be utilized for classification purposes. Classifiers can be broadly divided into two categories: rule-based classifiers and computational intelligence based classifiers usually called soft computing. Rule-based classifiers are generally constructed by the designer, where the designer defines rules for the interpretation of detected inputs. This is in contrast to soft-computing based classifiers, where the designer only creates a basic framework for the interpretation of data. The learning or training algorithms within such systems are responsible for the generation of rules for the correct interpretation of data.

DOI: 10.4018/978-1-5225-0565-5.ch003

INTRODUCTION

Research and development in the field of artificial intelligence have been carried out over several decades, from the 50's of the 20th century, when the term of artificial intelligence began to form (Turing, 1950). As John Searle indicated in the Chinese Room argument (Cole, 2014), it not necessary some intelligence to achieve intelligent behaviour if there are sufficient amount of information available. In the 50's, Alan Turing considered that an artificial intelligence system corresponding to its own definition of intelligent behaviour will be available in 2000 (Turing, 1950). At present, it can be noted that despite the disappointment that followed the euphoria of the 50s, there are successful applications of artificial intelligence systems, although not at such level that Alan Turing imagined. In the field of pattern recognition, which will be the aim of the chapter, it is for example a face or smile detection in a picture, which is commonly used in compact digital cameras. On the other hand, for example, we can say that there is much to discover in areas such as speech recognition or text. Lots of old manuscripts are waiting in archives to be digitized. Systems for hand-writing recognition, which could replace a computer keyboard, operate only partially and their massive use has not occurred yet.

OVERVIEW OF CLASSIFICATION AND PATTERN RECOGNITION TECHNIQUES

Classification is one of the most frequently encountered decision making tasks of human activity. A classification problem occurs when an object needs to be assigned into a predefined group or class based on a number of observed attributes related to that object. In general, we can say that each task, the output of which is a value from a finite set, can be considered as a classification task.

The whole issue of classification and pattern recognition lies on the border between computer science, mathematics, and artificial intelligence. Pattern recognition is not just limited to work with 2D images which are scanned optically. The issue is the class of procedures that are used for 1D, 2D and 3D signal processing coming from any sensor. For input values, we can consider all data, regardless of their origin, i.e. text, audio, image, etc. Due to the fact that we work on computer input data, all objects can be presented in a binary form without loss of generality. If we assume that a vector can be formed in a different way than the measurement of values, then image recognition receives much wider significance for practical applications. In the last ten years, there has been an expansion of industrial applications that use both optical sensors and special diagnostic procedures to provide the most appropriate solutions of technical or medical problems. More of this issue has been discussed in (Bishop, 2005), (Bishop, 2006) etc.

Classification tasks can be solved using so-called classifiers. A classifier is a computer based agent which can perform a classification task. There are many computational algorithms that can be utilized for classification purposes. Classifiers can be broadly divided into two categories (Ranawana & Palade, 2006): *rule-based classifiers* and *computational intelligence based classifiers*, usually called soft computing (Zadeh, 1994).

Rule-based classifiers are generally constructed by the designer, where the designer defines rules for the interpretation of detected inputs. In other words, the programmer has to cover all possible combinations of ranges of values of the input vector using decision tables in cooperation with a domain expert.

This is in contrast to soft-computing based classifiers, where the designer only creates a basic framework for the interpretation of data. The learning or training algorithms within such systems are responsible for the generation of rules for the correct interpretation of data. Then the system tries to optimally apply these rules or to deduce rules by which their decision-making will be controlled.

In practice, there are often used soft-computing classifiers that use one or more rule-based method for preprocessing inputs before their own classification. Such classifiers are a combination of both approaches and their activities can be divided into two steps.

- **Selection of Key Features:** At first, input data is preprocessed by an algorithm which extracts the key features from the input objects. This is to eliminate the effect of noise, move, rotation, or damage to enter the classification. For feature extraction, there is no general rule. Their choice is related to a given application and it depends on the type of data, but experience and intuition of the expert play a great role here.
- **Own Classification:** Features extracted from objects are presented to classifier for classification.

Therefore, the classifier does not work directly with objects, but with their images obtained during preprocessing. A typical classification scheme is shown in Figure 1. It is quite clear that the better the preprocessing is the easier classification algorithm can be used. In doing so, two extreme situations may occur.

Ideal preprocessing means pure hard computing. It gives us absolute control over the classifier logic. The output of this preprocessing is the number of the class which the input object belongs to. The task is thus solved during the first step and the use of a classifier is not necessary.

Figure 1. General scheme of a classifier
Adapted from Lecun et al. (1998).

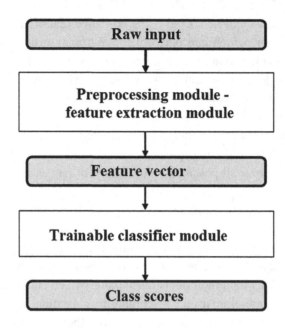

Ideal classifier means pure soft computing. It gives us better possibility of adaptation to a new problem area. In this case, a classifier which is sufficiently "intelligent" is used in order that all input objects are correctly ranked without any preprocessing, i.e. it is able to independently deduce all key features of the input objects.

Figure 1 also shows a relationship between the two extreme approaches: ideal preprocessing vs. ideal classifier. It is obvious that the first extreme corresponds to a rule-based classifier and it does not belong to the category of soft-computing. In contrast, the second extreme describes pure soft-computing solutions. Classifiers which are described in publications usually lie between these both extremes. It means that they work in two steps: preprocessing and own classification.

Systems with a high quality preprocessing can use a trivial classifier applying measurements such as Hamming distance in the second step (Hamming, 1950): Let us have two binary matrices **A** and **B** of the same type. Then the Hamming distance between these two matrices is calculated by the Equation (1). The Hamming distance corresponds to the number of elements whose values are different in these two matrices.

$$d = \sum_{i=1}^{m} \sum_{j=1}^{n} \left| a_{ij} - b_{ij} \right| \tag{1}$$

In contrast, systems with an intelligent classifier during preprocessing need only basic adaptation of a pattern, such as standardization of sizes. The classifier is then expected to independently abstract from the problem and to detect key features of objects to their correct classification. An example of such a highly sophisticated classifier can be a neural network Neocognitron (Fukushima, 1988).

Both approaches have their advantages and disadvantages. Methods that rely on preprocessing require having prior knowledge of key properties of objects to be able to create an algorithm for their extraction. It can be very difficult. Thus, due to the fact that the used classifier is trivial, it is possible to have full control over the decision logic. In addition, no large training sets are needed. Ideally, no training set is needed.

The advantage of the methods that are based on quality classifiers lies in their simplicity and universality. Ideally, there is no need to know anything about the nature of the problems and there is also no need to deal with some way of their solutions. On the other hand, the method of a solution proposed by the classifier remains hidden within the classifier and there is no possibility to guarantee that the system will correctly respond, expect all inputs respectively. In addition, a large training set and much time for adaptation is needed.

According to the available literature, real applications often use a hybrid method, but they significantly differ in how much they rely on data preprocessing and how much they rely on an independent judgment of a sophisticated classifier. However, both methods can achieve very good results. Different approaches are described for example in (Abdleazeem & El-Sherif, 2008), where complex preprocessing methods are used and in (Lecun, Bottou, Bengio, & Haner, 1998), where preprocessing is practically limited only to normalization of the input bitmap size.

Generality of these approaches: In case different types of data can be displayed as 2-dimensional bitmaps, it can be assumed that some procedures (preprocessing, classification), working for a certain class of problems (such as text recognition), can be applied to objects coming from a completely different problem domains (e.g. control of technological processes). In (Deng & Yu, 2011) is mentioned the use of a system for working with text (LeCun, Cortes, & Burges, 2014) and simultaneously with an audio recording of speech. Figure 2 and Figure 3 show an image and a numerical expression of one particular section of OHLC data (Lai, Yu, & Wang, 2004). The example illustrates the possibility of transferring n-dimensional data into a two-dimensional shape. Then it is possible to apply to such patterns the same procedures as if these patterns were characters or words written in a special alphabet. The intuitive concept of a "pattern" corresponds to the two-dimensional shapes. In case the transfer into 2D space is not possible, it is necessary to design special narrowly focused classification methods working with n-dimensional inputs

Figure 2. Displaying multidimensional data in a table

2010.06.02	8:15	1.22220	1.22260	1.22140	1.22210	107
2010.06.02	8:20	1.22220	1.22230	1.22150	1.22170	76
2010.06.02	8:25	1.22160	1.22170	1.27990	1.22090	71
2010.06.02	8:30	1.22110	1.22110	1.22910	1.21970	85
2010.06.02	8:35	1.21980	1.22160	1.22970	1.22140	78
2010.06.02	8:40	1.22150	1.22220	1.22140	1.22190	61
2010.06.02	8:45	1.22180	1.22190	1.22030	1.22120	84
2010.06.02	8:50	1.22130	1.22180	1.22070	1.22160	71
2010.06.02	8:55	1.22150	1.22260	1.22140	1.22200	61
2010.06.02	9:00	1.22220	1.22270	1.22120	1.22200	91
2010.06.02	9:05	1.22210	1.22220	1.22030	1.22090	53
2010.06.02	9:10	1.22080	1.22200	1.22050	1.22190	87
2010.06.02	9:15	1.22180	1.22390	1.22140	1.22350	90
2010.06.02	9:20	1.22340	1.22500	1.22350	1.22430	87
2010.06.02	9:25	1.22440	1.22450	1.22330	1.22430	77

or methods for two-dimensional inputs generalize so that they could operate even in an *n*-dimensional space.

The advantage of soft-computing techniques is their ability to extract rules from such problems which do not have a domain expert, who would be able to specify the rules correctly. Another advantage is the speed when applying these rules. Thanks to the speed, complex classification and optimization problems could be satisfactorily solved in much shorter time than through traditional (rule-based alias hard-

Figure 3. Displaying multidimensional data in a bitmap

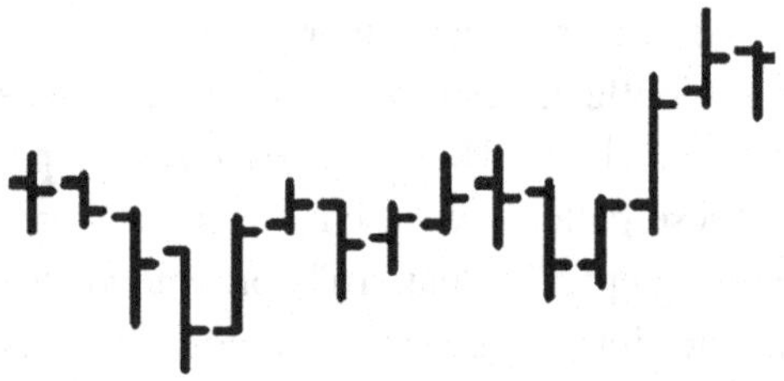

computing) methods. On the other hand, the disadvantage of soft-computing methods is the fact that their decision logic is not "under control", i.e. they can accidentally provide unexpected (incorrect) results. This feature almost eliminates a separate use of soft-computing methods in areas with a possible risk of damage property, health or life. In such critical cases, using artificial intelligence systems seems to be a more interesting possibility only to examine classification tasks such as searching for dependencies between patterns. It would be ideal to know the procedure how to extract decision-making rules from a soft-computing system, verify them, or edit and use them as a hard-coded system. For example, boosting appears to be a very promising method (Freund & Schapire, 1999), which allows to obtain very sophisticated classifiers through linear combination of so-called weak classifiers. In case these weak classifiers were designed so that their internal states were decodable, it would be possible to extract the solution algorithm from the resulting classifier.

Soft-computing methods can be divided into two groups according to the way to form a set of classes. (Bishop, 2006):

- **Classification Under Supervision:** Classification classes are explicitly created before the start of the classification process.
- **Self-Organization:** Classification classes are dynamically created during the classification process by variability of input patterns and variability of patterns defined within each class.

In reality, there can be a case where both approaches combine. Classification is supervised to pre-defined classes. Patterns that do not fit into any of the predefined classes are assigned to one or more "garbage" classes that can be dynamically created.

Furthermore, it is possible to divide soft-computing methods into two groups according to the process of adaptation (Bishop, 2006):

- Supervised learning.
- Unsupervised learning.

Supervised techniques involve the participation of a teacher or expert, who is responsible for 'teaching' or 'instructing' the classifier. This 'teacher' presents the algorithm with a set of inputs and informs the algorithm of the category or class to which it should be assigned to. The teacher also instructs the algorithm on how far a generated output is from the expected answer. This helps the learning algorithm alter its parameters in order to improve its classification performance. After training, the classifier is expected to classify previously unseen, but similar, inputs to the correct classes. The Back propagation algorithm used on neural networks is a prime example of such a methodology (Fausett 1994).

In contrast, *unsupervised classifiers* are not presented with prior knowledge during training. The algorithm is expected to examine the input parameters and to assign them to different classes based on similarity measures and clustering factors. Our proposal is based on an idea that the more similar patterns are, the closer their location in the space is (the smaller their distance is). Between similarities and distances thus exists an inverse dependence. During self-organization (Ciskowski & Zaton, 2010) a large group of patterns is usually presented to the system and the system is required to classify individual patterns by itself (e.g. to assign classes to individual patterns). We use not only standard tools for self-organization (cluster analysis, PCA, ICA), but modern tools belonging to artificial intelligence (SOM (Kohonen, Oja, Simula, Visa, & Kangas, 2002), Sammon map (Sammon, 1969), ART (Fausett, 1994) etc.) as well. Before calculation, some of the algorithms are required to specify the number of classes (cluster) where data should be distributed. Others (ART1) (Fausett, 1994) need only to specify the required degree of similarity between objects of one class and the number of classes determine separately during adaptation. Self-organizing methods are particularly used in cases, where we have a set of patterns - objects in n-dimensional space and we do not know how to properly measure their similarity (to classify them). Using self-organization, such objects can be viewed in 2D or 3D space (Kohonen, Oja, Simula, Visa, & Kangas, 2002).

Neural networks have emerged as an important tool for classification. The recent research activities in neural network classification have established that neural networks are a promising alternative to various conventional classification methods. The advantage of neural networks lies in the following theoretical aspects. First, neural networks are data driven self-adaptive methods so they can adjust themselves to the data without any explicit specification of functional or distributional form for the underlying model. Second, they are universal functional approximators so neural networks can approximate any function with arbitrary accuracy (Curram & Mingers, 1994; Hornik, 1991; Anastassiou, 2011). Since any classification procedure seeks a functional relationship between a group membership and the attributes of the object, accurate identification of this underlying function is doubtlessly important. Third, neural networks are nonlinear models, which makes them flexible in modeling real world complex relationships. Fourth, neural networks are able to estimate the posterior probabilities, which provide the basis for establishing classification rule and performing statistical analysis (Richard & Lippmann, 1991). On the other hand, the effectiveness of neural network classification has been tested mostly empirically. A number of performance comparisons between neural and conventional classifiers have been made by many studies (Curram & Mingers, 1994; Muniz et al., 2010). In addition, several computer experimental evaluations of neural networks for classification problems have been conducted under a variety of conditions (Patuwo, Hu, & Hung, 1993; Subramanian, Hung, & Hu, 1993).

Tasks of speech or text recognition are often used as a reference for assessing performance of various detection methods. There are dedicated databases TIMIT (LDC, 2014) for speech, (LeCun, Cortes, & Burges, 2014) for digits, (LDC, 2014) for handwritten English text and (IFN/ENIT, 2014) for handwritten Arabic text, which can be used for testing and comparing the obtained results via various classification methods. At present, there are a lot of classification methods which provide very good results. Some methods remain at the academic level and their performance is compared through test databases, the others are successfully used in practice. Relevant examples are Face Detection function in cameras, face recognition on CCTV cameras records, handwriting or speech recognition. Usually, these are methods that are associated with a given problem and the whole decision logic is designed and programmed by rules exactly. The processing power of current processors allows to solve complex tasks in a commercial environment as well as to use algorithms with a high degree of complexity. Soft-computing methods are applicable to such problems where there is no way of solving them, even with the use of brute force.

ROBUSTNESS AND INVARIANCE

In recognition systems, it is very important that they do not deal with small details, work only with determining properties of objects respectively. This refers either to a robust behaviour (random errors in an input vector do not interfere the output vector), or an invariant behaviour (the system completely ignores even large deviations if they have the same cause). Robust behaviour is achieved so that the whole system incorporates such elements which ignore extreme values and, if possible, perceive slightly each individual value. Much more interesting is the requirement for invariance of the system against some operations. The most common is the requirement for invariance against a shift in space or time, rotation in space, scaling in space or time, and change of scaling of a signal. Simply speaking, the degree of invariance of a classifier is the measure of its quality. It predicts how much the classifier is able to focus only on such properties of input objects that are crucial for its proper classification. In practice, there are used approaches of so-called key feature extraction (Trier, Jain, & Taxt, 1996; Abdleazeem & El-Sherif, 2008; Cruz, Cavalcanti, & Ren, 2010). The purpose of these methods is to filter out an individual classifier from disturbing "details" which litter the input objects. An example of such a method for extracting key features is provided in Figure 4. Instead of a bitmap with a number, the classifier is presented with histograms of vertical and horizontal projections, which are partially resistant to a shift or a tilt of digits. An explicit definition of

Figure 4. Histograms of horizontal and vertical projections - one of the methods for extracting key features
Adapted from Trier, Jain, and Taxt (1996).

functions to achieve robust / invariant behaviour is a demanding procedure requiring non-trivial knowledge of a problem domain. The fact that the proposed method will only work for specific types of tasks makes it even worse.

ARTIFICIAL INTELLIGENCE BASED METHODS

A lot of machine learning methods in pattern recognition tasks are successfully used. Contemporary classification systems widely use the theory of hidden Markov models (Chafik & Cherki, 2013) or the Neocognitron (Fukushima, 1988). No matter how often surprisingly good are the published results, no really widely applicable system for automatic digitization of more 'arbitrary' data has been designed yet. For example, digitization of text data can only be considered a process whose output is text, not a scanned image of the original. Despite the fact that the potential of artificial intelligence in classification and pattern recognition tasks seems to be high, artificial intelligence often loses out to traditional hard-computing methods, which still seems to be a cheaper and more reliable alternative.

This provides a field for design and exploration of new approaches that could improve and accelerate digitization of incomplete and inaccurate data or data containing noise for the purpose of classification and pattern recognition.

This chapter is focused on an analysis of the selected methods, which are widely used in pattern recognition tasks and represent a basis of state-of-the-art of the work. We have studied those methods from the theoretical point of view in order to decide which of them would be the most suitable for the purposes of classification and pattern recognition. The following priorities have been identified:

- Good Performance.
- Universality: The proposed classifier should classify data from any problem domain without cooperation with experts who usually analyse data in order to choose its characteristic features.
- Possibility of reverse engineering, which is the possibility of an extraction inner parameters of the classifier (i.e. from the adapted neural network).

Statistical Classifiers: Hidden Markov Models (HMM)

The Markov models (Rabiner, 1989) were initially introduced and studied in early 1970's (Baum & Petrie, 1966), but stay popular over years and are still used in the state of the art works (Fink, 2014). The Hidden Markov Models are widely used in application such as the speech recognition (Aymen, Abdelaziz, Halim, & Maaref, 2011), time-series analysis (Bai & Wang, 2011) or handwritten characters recognition (Álvaro, Sánchez, & Benedí, 2014).

We can describe the Markov model as a final-state automata with set of N distinct states $S = \{s_1, \ldots s_N\}$, where transition from one state to another (possibly the same one) is done with some defined probability taken from the transition probability matrix (2):

$$A = \{a_{ij}\} = \begin{bmatrix} a_{11} & \cdots & a_{1N} \\ \vdots & \ddots & \vdots \\ a_{N1} & \cdots & a_{NN} \end{bmatrix}, a_{ij} \geq 0, \sum_{j=1}^{N} a_{ij} = 1 \tag{2}$$

Each of the states from $\{s_1, \ldots s_N\}$ corresponds to some physical (observable) event. Once the Markov model is defined, we can ask it some state-in-time probability questions. Considering the Markov model in Figure 5, we can ask the probability that the observable sequence of states will be $O = \{s_2, s_1, s_2, s_3, s_2, s_2\}$ providing, that the actual state is s_1. The state transition probability matrix will be defined as following (3):

$$A = \begin{bmatrix} a_{11} & a_{12} & a_{13} \\ a_{21} & a_{22} & a_{23} \\ a_{31} & a_{32} & a_{33} \end{bmatrix} = \begin{bmatrix} 0.2 & 0.3 & 0.5 \\ 0.1 & 0.6 & 0.3 \\ 0.4 & 0.6 & 0.0 \end{bmatrix} \tag{3}$$

Figure 5. Example of a Markov chain with 3 states

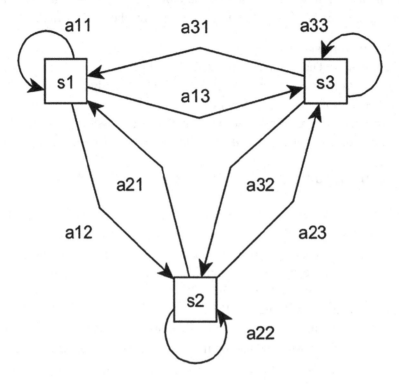

Now we can express and evaluate the O's probability as:

$$P\left(O \,/\, Model\right) = P\left(s_2\middle|s_1\right) \cdot P\left(s_1\middle|s_2\right) \cdot P\left(s_2\middle|s_1\right) \cdot P\left(s_3\middle|s_2\right) \cdot P\left(s_2\middle|s_3\right) \cdot P\left(s_2\middle|s_2\right)$$
$$= a_{12} \cdot a_{21} \cdot a_{12} \cdot a_{23} \cdot a_{32} \cdot a_{22} = 0.3 \cdot 0.1 \cdot 0.3 \cdot 0.3 \cdot 0.6 \cdot 0.6 = 9.72 \cdot 10^{-4}$$

To step forward from the Markov model described above to a hidden Markov model, we need to introduce new set $V = \left\{v_1, \cdots, v_M\right\}$ of M observation symbols. Unlike the Markov model, where we can see the inner states $\left\{s_1, \cdots, s_N\right\}$ of the model, in the hidden Markov model the states are not visible (are hidden). So we can only see the observation symbols $\left\{v_1, \cdots, v_M\right\}$, which have a different probability distribution in every state s_j. We can express the observation symbol probability distribution as follows (4):

$$b_j\left(k\right) = P\left(v_k\middle|s_j\right), j \in \left[1; N\right], k \in \left[1; M\right] \tag{4}$$

We also have to define the initial state distribution, i.e. distribution of states in which the hidden Markov model is found at the start (5).

$$\Pi = \left\{\pi_1, \cdots, \pi_N\right\}, \pi_i \geq 0, \sum_{i=1}^{N} \pi_i = 1 \tag{5}$$

where π_i is the probability that the hidden Markov model is in state s_i right after the initialisation. We can use the hidden Markov model for generation of some sample observation sequence $O = \left\{o_1, \cdots, o_P\right\}$ using Algorithm 1.

Linear Neural Classifiers: Hebbian Network

Hebbian learning theory can be summarized in the following rule: "Cells that fire together, wire together." (Doidge, 2007) The rule seeks to explain "associative learning", in which simultaneous activation of cells leads to strengthening their links. The main advantage of Hebbian algorithm is its simplicity and thus its speed. The basic variant of the algorithm only needs the operations of addition and multiplication of integers. In addition, we can consider as an advance the repeatability of the calculation (calculations in the Hebbian algorithm are not burdened with randomness). This allows relatively easy to study the behaviour on specific training sets. In addition, there is a possibility that discovered regularities will be applicable for some other types of networks.

For a description of the learning process, we consider the trivial model network with one input and one output neuron connected with a single connection (see Figure 6). In complex networks, these rules apply to all such triplets (input, output, connection), Figure 7.

Algorithm 1. Generating an observation sequence using the HMM

Choose the initial state $q_1 = s_i$ according to the distribution Π
Set p = 1
Repeat
    Choose $o_p = v_k$ according to the symbol probability distribution in the state q_p
    Transit to a new state q_{p+1} according to the probability matrix A
    Increment p
Until p > P.
End.

Figure 6. Trivial neural network considered in description of the learning process

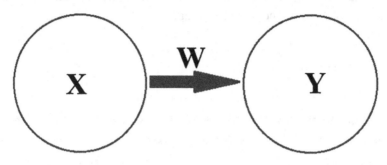

Figure 7. General topology of classifier; weights of connections w_{11}-w_{ij} are modified in accordance with the Hebbian learning rule.

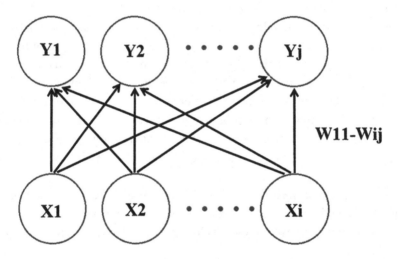

Neural networks are taught in so-called cycles. During each such cycle, all the training patterns are presented to the network one time. We derive formulas for calculating the value of weight w after the submission of the n-th pattern:

At the start, all weights w are initialized by value of I ($I = 0$ according to (Fausett, 1994)): $w_n = I$, $n = 0$. After the presentation of each (the n-th) pattern, the current value of w is raised by the product of the appropriate input and output: $w_n = w_{n-1} + x_n y_n, n > 0$. Therefore, we can express the weight value w at the end of the first cycle, e.g. after a presentation of the m patterns (6):

$$w_m = I + \sum_{i=1}^{m} x_i y_i \qquad (6)$$

where the expression (7)

$$\sum_{i=1}^{m} x_i y_i \qquad (7)$$

means a change of the w after one cycle.

Since the set of patterns presented to the network in each cycle is always the same, we can label the sum as C (e.g. change of the w after one learning cycle). The weight value at the end of the first cycle can be then written as $w_1 = I + C$. To calculate the value of w after a p-th cycle, we can use the expression:

$$w_p = I + pC.$$

Back Propagation Neural Networks

The very general nature of the Back propagation training method means that a Back propagation net (a multilayer, feedforward net trained by Back propagation) can be used to solve problems in many areas. (Fausett, 1994) describes the network in detail. It is simply a gradient descent method to minimize the total squared error of the output computed by the net. The training of a network by Back propagation involves three stages: the feedforward of the input training pattern, the calculation and Back propagation of the associated error, and the adjustment of the weights. After training, application of the net involves only the computations of the feedforward phase.

A multilayer neural network with one layer of hidden units (the Z units) is shown in Figure 8. The output units (the Y units) and the hidden units also may have biases (as shown). The bias on a typical output unit Y_k is denoted by w_{0k}; the bias on a typical hidden unit Z_j is denoted w_{0j}. These bias terms act like weights on connections from units whose output is always 1.

The neurons in the network use an activation function to compute their response to the input. One of the most common activation functions is the binary sigmoid (8).

$$f(x) = \frac{1}{1 + \exp(-x)} \qquad (8)$$

with

$$f'(x) = f(x)\left[1 - f(x)\right] \qquad (9)$$

Figure 8. A Back propagation network architecture

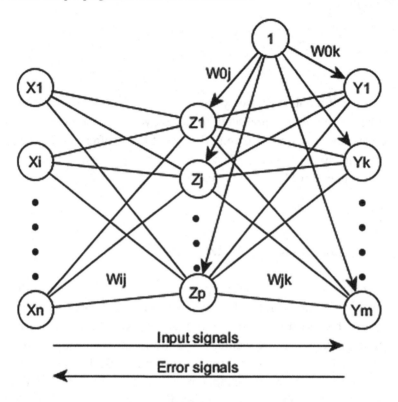

During feedforward, each input unit X_i receives an input signal and broadcasts it to all of the hidden units $Z_1, \cdots, Z_p$. Each hidden unit in turn computes its activation (10)

$$z_j = f\left(w_{0j} + \sum_i x_i w_{ij}\right) = f\left(y\_in_k\right) \tag{10}$$

to each output unit. Each output unit (Y_k) computes its activation (11)

$$y_k = f\left(w_{0j} + \sum_j z_j w_{jk}\right) = f\left(z\_in_j\right) \tag{11}$$

which forms the output of the network.

During training, each output unit compares its computed activation y_k with its target value t_k to determine the associated error for that pattern with that unit. Based on this error, the factor δ_k $(k = 1, \ldots, m)$ is computed (12).

$$\delta_k = \left(t_k - y_k\right) f'\left(y\_in_k\right) \tag{12}$$

δ_k is used to distribute the error at output unit Y_k back to all units in the previous layer (the hidden units that are connected to Y_k. It is also used (later) to update the weights between the output and the hidden layer. In a similar manner, the factor δ_j ($j = 1,\ldots,p$) is computed for each hidden unit Z_j (13).

$$\delta_j = \left(\sum_k \delta_k w_{jk}\right) f'\left(z\_in_j\right) \tag{13}$$

It is not necessary to propagate the error back to the input layer, but δ_j is used to update the weights between the hidden layer and the input layer. After all of the δ factors have been determined, the weights for all layers are adjusted simultaneously. The learning rate parameter $\alpha \in (0,1]$ is used to regulate the network's sensitivity. The adjustment to the weight w_{jk} (from hidden unit Z_j to output unit Y_k) is based on the factor δ_k and the activation z_j of the hidden unit Z), (14).

$$\Delta_{w_{jk}} = \alpha \delta_k z_j \tag{14}$$

The adjustment to the weight w_{ij} (from input unit X_i to hidden unit Z_j) is based on the factor δ_j and the activation x_i of the input unit, (15).

$$\Delta_{w_{ij}} = \alpha \delta_j x_i \tag{15}$$

The bias weights are adjusted in the same way bearing in mind that the bias value is 1, (16).

$$\Delta_{w_{0j}} = \alpha \delta_j, \Delta_{w_{0k}} = \alpha \delta_k \tag{16}$$

Neocognitron

The neocognitron originally proposed in (Fukushima, 1988) is an example of a hierarchical net in which there are many layers, with a very sparse and localized pattern of connectivity between the layers. The neocognitron is trained using supervised learning. The neocognitron was designed to recognize handwritten characters - specifically, the Arabic numerals 0, 1, ..., 9. The purpose of the network is to make its response insensitive to variations in the position and style in which the digit is written. The structure of the net is based on a physiological model of the visual system (Hubel & Wiesel, 1962).

The architecture of the neocognitron (see Figure 9) consists of several layers of units. The units within each layer are arranged in a number of square arrays. A unit in one layer receives signals from a very limited number of units in the previous layer; similarly, it sends signals to only a few units in the next layer. The input units are arranged in a single 19 x 19 square array. The first layer above the input layer has 12 arrays, each consisting of 19 x 19 units. In general, the size of the arrays decreases as we progress from the input layer to the output layer of the net. The layers are arranged in pairs, an *S*-layer followed by a *C*-layer. The S arrays are trained to respond to a particular pattern or group of patterns. The *C* arrays then combine the results from related *S* arrays and simultaneously thin out the number of units in each array. The motivation for the multiple copies of the arrays in each layer will become clearer when we consider the training of the net. For now, we simply note that each array (within a layer) is trained to respond to a different pattern of signals (or feature of the original input). Each unit in a particular array "looks for" that feature in a small portion of the previous layer. Training progresses layer by layer. The weights from the input units to the first layer are trained and then frozen. Then the next trainable weights are adjusted, and so forth. The weights between some layers are fixed, as are the connection patterns, when the net is designed.

Figure 9. Architecture of neocognitron
Based on Fukushima and Kunihiko (1980).

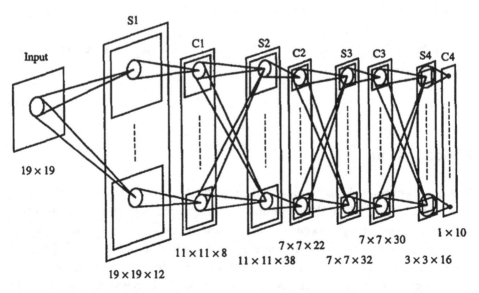

Boosting

The two most popular methods for creating ensembles are boosting (Schapire, 1999) and bagging (Breiman, 1996). Boosting is reported to give better results than bagging (Quinlan, 1996). Both of them modify a set of training examples to achieve diversity of weak learners in the ensemble. As alternative methods we can mention randomization based on a random modification of base decision algorithm (Dietterich, 2000) or Bayesian model averaging, which can even outperform boosting in some cases (Davidson & Fan, 2006).

Boosting has its roots in a theoretical framework for studying machine learning called the "PAC" learning model, due to Valiant (Valiant, 1984). Kearns and Valiant (Kearns & Valiant, 1988), (Kearns & Valiant, 1994) were the first to pose the question of whether a "weak" learning algorithm which performs just slightly better than random guessing in the PAC model can be "boosted" into an arbitrarily accurate "strong" learning algorithm. Schapire (Schapire, 1990) came up with the first provable polynomial-time boosting algorithm in 1989. A year later, Freund (Freund, 1995) developed a much more efficient boosting algorithm which, although optimal in a certain sense, nevertheless suffered from certain practical drawbacks. The first experiments with these early boosting algorithms were carried out by Drucker, Schapire and Simard (Drucker, Schapire, & Simard, 1993) on an OCR task.

Boosting is a general method for improving the accuracy of any given learning algorithm. The *AdaBoost* algorithm, introduced in 1995 by Freund and Schapire (Freund & Schapire, 1997), solved many of the practical difficulties of the earlier boosting algorithms. Pseudo code for AdaBoost is given below (Algorithm 2). The algorithm takes as input the training set $(x_1, y_1), \ldots, (x_m, y_m)$ where each x_i belongs to some domain or instance of the space X, and each label y_i belongs to some label set Y. AdaBoost calls a given weak or base learning algorithm repeatedly in a series of rounds $t = 1, \ldots, T$. One of the main ideas of the algorithm is to maintain a distribution or set of weights over the training set. The weight of this distribution on i-th training example on round t is denoted $D_t(i)$. Initially, all weights are set equally, but on each round, the weights of incorrectly classified examples are increased so that the weak learner is forced to focus on the hard examples in the training set. The weak learner's job is to find a weak hypothesis $h_t : X \rightarrow \{-1, +1\}$ appropriate for the distribution D_t. The goodness of a weak hypothesis is measured by its error (17):

$$\in_t = \Pr_{i \sim D_t}\left[h_t\left(x_i\right) \neq y_i\right] = \sum_{i:h_t(x_i) \neq y_i} D_t\left(i\right) \qquad (17)$$

Notice that the error ϵ_t is measured with respect to the distribution D_t on which the weak learner was trained. In practice, the weak learner may be an algorithm that can use the weights D_t on the training examples. Alternatively, when this is not possible, a subset of the training examples can be sampled according to D_t, and these (unweighted) resampled examples can be used to train the weak learner. It follows the pseudocode of the boosting algorithm AdaBoost (Freund & Schapire 1999).

The most basic theoretical property of AdaBoost concerns its ability to reduce the *training error*. Let us write the error ϵ_t of h_t as $\frac{1}{2} - \gamma_t$. Since a hypothesis that guesses each instance's class at random has an error rate of 1/2 (on binary problems), γ_t thus measures how much better than random are h_t's predictions. Freund and Schapire (Freund & Schapire, 1997) prove that the training error (the fraction of mistakes on the training set) of the final hypothesis H is at most (18):

$$\prod_t \left[2\sqrt{\epsilon_t (1-\epsilon_t)} \right] = \prod_t \sqrt{(1 - 4\gamma_t^2)} \leq \exp\left(-2\sum_t \gamma_t^2\right) \qquad (18)$$

Algorithm 2. AdaBoost

Given set of m examples $((x_1,y_1),...,(x_m,y_m))$ where $x_i \in X$, $y_i \in Y = -1,+1$}
Initialize: $D_1(i)=1/m$ for all I, t=1
Repeat
  Repeat
    Generate a new weak classifier C_t
    Learn C_t with D_t and get it's hypothesis $h_t: X \rightarrow \{-1,+1\}$
    Calculate the h_t's error ϵ_t according to (17)
  Until $\epsilon_t < E_{max}$

Calculate $\beta_t = \frac{1}{2} \ln\left(\frac{1-\epsilon_t}{\epsilon_t}\right)$

Calculate the weights summary: $Z_t = \sum_{i=1}^{m} D_t(i)$

Update the weight distribution:

$$D_{t+1}(i) = \frac{D_t(i)}{Z_t} \times \begin{cases} e^{-\alpha_t}, h_t(x_i) = y_i \\ e^{\alpha_t}, h_t(x_i) \neq y_i \end{cases} = \frac{D_t(i)\exp\left(-\alpha_t y_i h_t(x_i)\right)}{z_t}$$

  Increment t
Until end condition

The final hypothesis is: $h_{fin}(x) = sign\left(\sum_{t=1}^{T} \beta_t h_t(x)\right)$

End.

Based on Freund and Schapire (1995).

Thus, if each weak hypothesis is slightly better than random so that $\gamma_t \geq \gamma$ for some $\gamma \geq 0$, then the training error drops exponentially fast. AdaBoost is adaptive in that it adapts to the error rates of the individual weak hypotheses. This is the basis of its name "Ada" is short for "adaptive." (Freund & Schapire, 1999)

Freund and Schapire (Freund & Schapire, 1997) showed how to bound the generalization error of the final hypothesis H in terms of its training error, the sample size m, the VC-dimension d of the weak hypothesis space and the number of boosting rounds T. The VC-dimension is a standard measure of the "complexity" of a space of hypotheses. See, for instance, (Blumer, Ehrenfeucht, Haussler, & Warmuth, 1989). Specifically, they used techniques from (Baum & Haussler, 1989) to show that the generalization error, with high probability, is at most (19):

$$\widehat{P}_r\left[H\left(x\right) \neq y\right] + \tilde{O}\left(\sqrt{\frac{Td}{m}}\right) \tag{19}$$

where $\widehat{P}_r$ denotes empirical probability on the training sample. This bound suggests that boosting will overfit if it runs for too many rounds, i.e., as T becomes large. In fact, this sometimes does happen. However, in early experiments, several authors (Ranawana & Palade, 2006), (Kohonen, Oja, Simula, Visa, & Kangas, 2002), (Quinlan, 1996) observed empirically that boosting often does not overfit, even when run for thousands of rounds. The basic version of AdaBoost is designed for binary problems. However, there are variations AdaBoost.M1 and Adaboost.M2, which can work with multi classification problems. These two algorithms differ as follows:

- How they compute the D_t on each round.
- How they compute the final hypothesis h_{fin}.

AdaBoost.M1

AdaBoost.M1 uses a simple rule shown in Algorithm 3.

The initial distribution is initialized uniformly over S, so $D_1\left(i\right) = \dfrac{1}{m}$ for all i. To compute distribution D_{t+1} from D_t, h_t and the last weak hypothesis, we multiply the weight of i-th example by:

- Some number $\alpha \in \left[0,1\right)$ if h_t classifies x_t correctly (example's weight goes down).
- 1 otherwise (example's weight stays unchanged).

Algorithm 3. AdaBoost.M1

The used nomenclature is the following:

m - Number of learning examples

t - Number of iterations (i.e. number of weak classifiers in the ensemble)

T_{max} - Limit of iterations (i.e. max. size of the ensemble)

Given set of m examples $((x_1,y_1),...,(x_m,y_m))$ with labels $y_i \in Y = \{1,..., k\}$

Initialize: $D_1(i)=1/m$ for all I, t=1

Repeat

  Repeat

    Generate a new weak classifier C_t

    Learn C_t with D_t and get it's hypothesis $h_t:X \rightarrow Y$

    Calculate the h_t's error ϵ_t according to (17)

  Until $\epsilon_t < E_{max}$

Calculate $\beta_t = \epsilon_t / 1 - \epsilon_t$

Calculate the weights summary: $Z_t = \sum\limits_{i=1}^{m} D_t(i)$

Update the weight distribution:

$$D_{t+1}(i) = \frac{D_t(i)}{Z_t} \times \begin{cases} \beta_t, h_t(x_i) = y_i \\ 1, h_t(x_i) \neq y_i \end{cases}$$

  Increment t

Until $t > T_{max}$

The final hypothesis is: $h_{fin}(x) = \max_{y \in Y} \sum\limits_{t:h_t(x)=y} \log \frac{1}{\beta_t}$

End.

Based on Freund and Schapire (1996)

The weights are then renormalized by dividing by the normalization constant Z_t. Effectively, "easy" examples that are correctly classified by many of the previous weak hypotheses get lower weight, and "hard" examples which tend often to be misclassified get higher weight. Thus, AdaBoost focuses the most weight on the examples which seem to be hardest for WeakLearn.

The important theoretical property about AdaBoost.M1 is stated in the theorem (18). This theorem shows that if the weak hypotheses consistently have error only slightly better than 0.5, then the error of the final hypothesis $H(x)$ drops to zero exponentially fast. For binary classification problems, this means that the weak hypotheses need be only slightly better than random. However, for multiclass problems, the requirement of AdaBoost.M1 is much stronger: As the expected error of a hypothesis which randomly guesses the label is $1 - \frac{1}{k}$, where k is the number of possible labels, AdaBoost.M1 requirement for $k > 2$ might be hard to meet.

AdaBoost.M2

The second version of AdaBoost attempts to overcome this difficulty by extending the communication between the boosting algorithm and the weak learner. First, we allow the weak learner to generate more expressive hypotheses whose output is a vector in $[0,1]^k$, rather than a single label in Y. Intuitively, the y-th component of this vector represents a "degree of belief" that the correct label is y. The components with values close to 1 or 0 correspond to those labels considered to be plausible or implausible, respectively. While we give the weak learning algorithm more expressive power, we also place a more complex requirement on the performance of the weak hypotheses. Rather than using the usual prediction error, we ask that the weak hypotheses do well with respect to a more sophisticated error measure that we call the *pseudo-loss*. Unlike ordinary error which is computed with respect to a distribution over examples, pseudo-loss is computed with respect to a distribution over the set of all pairs of examples and incorrect labels. By manipulating this distribution, the boosting algorithm can focus the weak learner not only on hard-to-classify examples, but more specifically, on the incorrect labels that are hardest to discriminate. We will see that the boosting algorithm AdaBoost.M2, which is based on these ideas, achieves boosting if each weak hypothesis has pseudo-loss slightly better than random guessing. More formally, a mislabel is a pair (i, y) where i is the index of a training example and y is an incorrect label associated with example i. Let B be the set of all mislabels: $B = \{(i, y): i \in \{1,\ldots, m\}, y \neq y_i\}$

A mislabel distribution is a distribution defined over the set B of all mislabels. On each round of boosting, AdaBoost.M2 Algorithm 4 supplies the weak learner with a mislabel distribution D_t. In response, the weak learner computes a hypothesis h_t of the form $h_t: X \times Y \rightarrow [0, 1]$. Intuitively, we interpret each mislabel (i, y) as representing a binary question of the form: "Do you predict that the label associated with example x_i is y_i (the correct label) or y (one of the incorrect labels)?" With this interpretation, the weight $D_t(i, y)$ assigned to this mislabel represents the importance of distinguishing incorrect label y on example x_i. A weak hypothesis h_t is then interpreted in the following manner. If $h_t(x_i, y_i) = 1$ and $h_t(x_i, y) = 0$, then h_t has (correctly) predicted that x_i's label is y_i, not y (since h_t deems y_i to be "plausible" and y "implausible"). If $h_t(x_i, y_i) = h_t(x_i, y)$, then h_t's prediction is taken to be a random guess (values for h_t in $(0, 1)$ are interpreted probabilistically). This interpretation leads us to define the pseudo-loss of hypothesis h_t with respect to mislabel distribution D_t by the formula (Freund & Schapire, 1997) (20):

$$\epsilon_t = \frac{1}{2}\sum_{(i,y)\in B} D_t\left(i,y\right)\left(1 - h_t\left(x_i,y_i\right) + h_t\left(x_i,y\right)\right) \qquad (20)$$

It can be verified that the pseudo-loss is minimized when correct labels y_i are assigned the value 1 and incorrect labels $y \neq y_i$ assigned the value 0. Further, note that pseudo-loss 0.5 is trivially achieved by any constant-valued hypothesis h_t. The weak learner's goal is to find a weak hypothesis h_t with small pseudo-loss. Thus, standard "off-the-shelf" learning algorithms may need some modification to be used in this manner, although this modification is often straightforward. After receiving h_t, the mislabel distribution is updated using a rule similar to the one used in Ada-Boost.M1. The final hypothesis $H(x)$ outputs, for a given instance x, the label y has maximizes a weighted average of the weak hypothesis values $h_t(x, y)$.

The following theorem gives a bound on the training error of the final hypothesis. Note that this theorem requires only that the weak hypotheses have pseudo-loss less than 1/2, i.e., only slightly better than a trivial (constant-valued) hypothesis, regardless of the number of classes. Also, although the weak hypotheses h_t are evaluated with respect to the pseudo-loss, we of course evaluate the final hypothesis $H(x)$ using the ordinary error measure.

Suppose the weak learning algorithm *WeakLearn*, when called by AdaBoost. M2 generates hypotheses with pseudo-losses $\epsilon_1, ..., \epsilon_T$, where ϵ_T is as defined in (20). Let $\gamma_t = 1/2 - \epsilon_t$. Then the following upper bound holds on the error of the final hypothesis h_{fin} (21) (Freund & Schapire, 1997):

$$\frac{\left|\left\{i : h_{fin}\left(x_i\right) \neq y_i\right\}\right|}{m} \leq \left(k-1\right)\prod_{t=1}^{T}\sqrt{1-4\gamma_t^2} \leq \left(k-1\right)\exp\left(-2\sum_{t=1}^{T}\gamma_z^2\right) \tag{21}$$

Diversity of Classifiers

The success of an ensemble system - that is, its ability to correct the errors of some of its members - rests squarely on the diversity of the classifiers that make up the ensemble. If all classifiers provided the same output, correcting a possible mistake would not be possible. Therefore, individual classifiers in an ensemble system need to make different errors on different instances. If each classifier makes different errors, then a strategic combination of these classifiers can reduce the total error. Specifically, an ensemble system needs classifiers whose decision boundaries are adequately different from those of others. Such a set of classifiers is said to be diverse. Classifier diversity can be achieved in several ways.

- To use different training datasets to train individual classifiers, where training data subsets are drawn randomly, usually with replacement, from the entire training data. To ensure that individual boundaries are adequately different, despite using substantially similar training data, weaker or more unstable clas-

Algorithm 4. AdaBoost.M2

The used nomenclature is the following:

m – number of learning examples

t – number of iterations (i.e. number of weak classifiers in the ensemble)

T_{max} – limit of iterations (i.e. max. size of the ensemble)

Given set of m examples $((x_1,y_1),...,(x_m,y_m))$ with labels $y_i \in Y = \{1,...,k\}$

Given $B = \left\{ (i,y) : i \in \{1,\cdots,m\}, y \neq y_i \right\}$

Initialize: $D_1(i,y) = \dfrac{1}{|B|}$ for (i, y) ∈ B, t=1

Repeat

  Repeat

    Generate a new weak classifier C_t

    Learn C_t with D_t and get it's hypothesis h_t:X → Y

    Calculate the h_t's pseudo-loss ϵ_t according to (20)

  Until $\epsilon_t < E_{max}$ $Z_t = \sum_{(x,y) \in B} D_t(i,y)$

  Calculate $\beta_t = \epsilon_t / 1 - \epsilon_t$

  Calculate the weights summary:

  Update the weight distribution:

$$D_{t+1}(i,y) = \frac{D_t(i,y)}{z_t} \cdot \beta_t^{\left(\frac{1}{2}\right)\left(1 + h_t(x_i,y_i) - h_t(x_i,y)\right)}$$

  Increment t

Until $t > T_{max}$

The final hypothesis is: $h_{fin}(x) = \max_{y \in Y} \sum_{t=1}^{T} \left(\log \frac{1}{\beta_t} \right) h_t(x,y)$

End.

Based on Freund and Schapire (1996)

sifiers are used as base models, since they can generate sufficiently different decision boundaries even for small perturbations in their training parameters.

- To use different training parameters for different classifiers. For example, a series of Multilayer Perceptron (MLP) neural networks can be trained by using different weight initializations, number of layers / units, error goals, etc. Adjusting such parameters allows one to control the instability of the individual classifiers, and hence contribute to their diversity.

- To use entirely different type of classifiers, such MLPs, decision trees, nearest neighbor classifiers, and support vector machines can also be combined for added diversity.

- To use different features, or different subsets of existing features. In fact, generating different classifiers using random feature subsets is known as the random subspace method

Each individual classifier in an ensemble system allows to generate different decision boundaries. If proper diversity is achieved, a different error is made by each classifier, strategic combination of which can then reduce the total error. Figure

Figure 10. Combining an ensemble of classifiers for reducing classification error and/or model selection
Adapted from http://shareengineer.blogspot.cz/2012/09/ensemble-learning-and-model-selection.html.

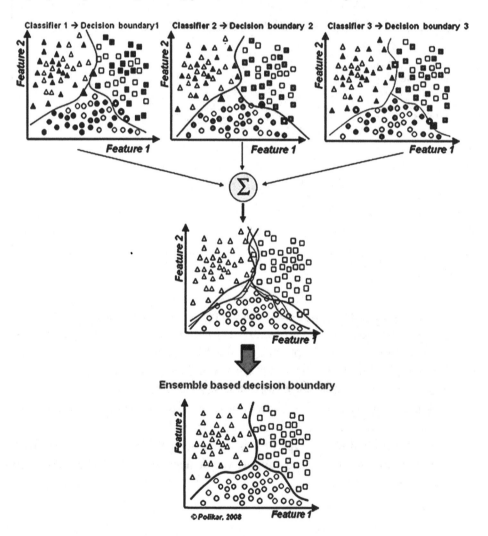

10 graphically illustrates this concept, where each classifier - trained on a different subset of the available training data - makes different errors (shown as instances with dark borders), but the combination of the (three) classifiers provides the best decision boundary.

CONCLUSION

In this chapter we have briefly analysed five selected methods of the pattern recognition. All the analysed methods give promising results and they are widely used in state-of-the-art works. Advantages and weaknesses of the analysed algorithms are shown in Table 1.

The method of hidden Markov models is designed especially for applications of pattern recognition that evolve over time (time series analysis, continuous written text). If we want to focus more on the recognition of individual patterns, therefore the method based on hidden Markov models appears inappropriate. Neural networks and boosting are good candidates to combine them for the proposal of a classifier. In (Kocian, 2015), the author has used a linear Hebbian network and multi-layered Back propagation network from the set of neural networks and AdaBoost.M1 from the methods of boosting. The reasons for choosing AdaBoost.M1 were as follows.

Table 1. Advantages and weaknesses of the analysed algorithms

Methods	Advantages	Weaknesses
Hidden Markov models	Not relevant	Computationally intensive. Not suitable for individual patterns
Linear neural classifiers	Simple to implement, quick in operation. Internal logic is visible	No diversity. Worse performance in comparison to the Back propagation networks
Back propagation neural networks	Good performance on any type of patterns. ood diversity.	Internal logic is not visible. More complex in comparison to the linear classifiers
Neocognitron	Can handle rotated patterns	Very complex, not suitable for boosting. Internal logic is not visible.
AdaBoost.M1	Simple to implement. Tends to form more compact ensembles than in the case of AdaBoost.M2.	not relevant
AdaBoost.M2	An ability to boost weak classifiers only slightly better than a random guess.	AdaBoost.M2 tends to form bigger ensembles than the Adaboost.M1. The implementation of the algorithm is more complicated than in the case of Adaboost.M1.

Kocian, 2015.

It needs minimum requirements for the quality of weak classifiers and it is resistant against overfitting, which corresponds to the idea of a system that does not require any deep knowledge of the problem domain. Based on the previous analysis, the author (Kocian, 2015) proposed and developed such classifier, which is able to suppress the effect of the weaknesses of the used neural networks as well as Ada-Boost.M1 for the purpose of classification.

ACKNOWLEDGMENT

The research described here has been financially supported by the University of Ostrava grant SGS17/PrF/2015. Any opinions, findings and conclusions or recommendations expressed in this material are those of the authors and do not necessarily reflect the views of the sponsors.

REFERENCES

Abdleazeem, S., & El-Sherif, E. (2008). Arabic handwritten digit recognition. *Int. J. Doc. Anal. Recognit.*, *11*(3), 127–141. doi:10.1007/s10032-008-0073-5

Álvaro, F., Sánchez, J. A., & Benedí, J. M. (2014). Recognition of on-line handwritten mathematical expressions using 2D stochastic context-free grammars and hidden Markov models. *Pattern Recognition Letters*, *35*(1), 58–67. doi:10.1016/j.patrec.2012.09.023

Anastassiou, G. A. (2011). Multivariate sigmoidal neural network approximation. *Neural Networks*, *24*(4), 378–386. doi:10.1016/j.neunet.2011.01.003 PMID:21310590

Aymen, M., Abdelaziz, A., Halim, S., & Maaref, H. (2011). Hidden Markov Models for automatic speech recognition. *Communications, Computing and Control Applications (CCCA), 2011 International Conference on* (pp. 1-6). IEEE.

Bai, J., & Wang, P. (2011). Conditional Markov chain and its application in economic time series analysis. *Journal of Applied Econometrics*, *26*(5), 715–734. doi:10.1002/jae.1140

Baum, E. B., & Haussler, D. (1989). What size net gives valid generalization? *Neural Computation*, *1*(1), 151–160. doi:10.1162/neco.1989.1.1.151

Baum, L. E., & Petrie, T. (1966). Statistical Inference for Probabilistic Functions of Finite State Markov Chains. *Annals of Mathematical Statistics*, *37*(6), 1554–1563. doi:10.1214/aoms/1177699147

Bishop, C. M. (2005). *Neural Networks for Pattern Recognition.* New York: Oxford University Press.

Bishop, C. M. (2006). *Pattern Recognition and Machine Learning (Information Science and Statistics).* New York: Springer-Verlag New York, Inc.

Blumer, A., Ehrenfeucht, A., Haussler, D., & Warmuth, M. K. (1989). Learnability and the Vapnik-Chervonenkis dimension. *Journal of the ACM, 36*(4), 929–965. doi:10.1145/76359.76371

Breiman, L. (1996). Bagging predictors. *Machine Learning, 24*(2), 123–140. doi:10.1007/BF00058655

Chafik, S., & Cherki, D. (2013). Some Algorithms for Large Hidden Markov Models. *World Journal Control Science and Engineering, 1*(1), 9–14.

Ciskowski, P., & Zaton, M. (2010). Neural pattern recognition with self-organizing maps for efficient processing of forex market data streams. In *Articial Intelligence and Soft Computing* (pp. 307–314). Berlin: Springer-Verlag. doi:10.1007/978-3-642-13208-7_39

Cole, D. (2014). The Chinese Room Argument. In E. N. Zalta (Eds.), *The Stanford Encyclopedia of Philosophy.* Retrieved July 30, 2015, from http://stanford.library.usyd.edu.au/entries/chinese-room

Cruz, R. M., Cavalcanti, G. D., & Ren, T. I. (2010). Handwritten digit recognition using multiple feature extraction techniques and classier ensemble.*17th International Conference on Systems, Signals and Image Processing,* (pp. 215-218). Rio de Janeiro, Brazil.

Curram, S. P., & Mingers, J. (1994). Neural networks, decision tree induction and discriminant analysis: An empirical comparison. *The Journal of the Operational Research Society, 45*(4), 440–450. doi:10.1057/jors.1994.62

Davidson, I., & Fan, W. (2006). When efficient model averaging out-performs boosting and bagging. In Knowledge Discovery in Databases: PKDD 2006 (pp. 478-486). Springer Berlin Heidelberg. doi:doi:10.1007/11871637_46 doi:10.1007/11871637_46

Deng, L., & Yu, D. (2011). Deep convex net: A scalable architecture for speech pattern classication. In *Proceedings of the Interspeech,* (pp. 2285-2288).

Dietterich, T. G. (2000). An experimental comparison of three methods for constructing ensembles of decision trees: Bagging, boosting, and randomization. *Machine Learning, 40*(2), 139–157. doi:10.1023/A:1007607513941

Doidge, N. (2007). *The brain that changes itself: Stories of personal triumph from the frontiers of brain science*. New York: Penguin Books.

Drucker, H., Schapire, R., & Simard, P. (1993). Boosting performance in neural networks. *International Journal of Pattern Recognition and Artificial Intelligence*, *7*(4), 705–719. doi:10.1142/S0218001493000352

Fausett, L. V. (1994). *Fundamentals of Neural Networks*. Englewood Cliffs, NJ: Prentice-Hall, Inc.

Fink, G. A. (2014). *Markov Models for Pattern Recognition*. London: Springer Science & Business Media. doi:10.1007/978-1-4471-6308-4

Freund, Y. (1995). Boosting a weak learning algorithm by majority. *Information and Computation*, *121*(2), 256–285. doi:10.1006/inco.1995.1136

Freund, Y., & Schapire, R. (1999). A short introduction to boosting. *J. Japan. Soc. for Artif. Intel.*, *14*(5), 771–780.

Freund, Y., & Schapire, R. E. (1995). A desicion-theoretic generalization of on-line learning and an application to boosting. In *Computational learning theory* (pp. 23–37). Springer Berlin Heidelberg. doi:10.1007/3-540-59119-2_166

Freund, Y., & Schapire, R. E. (1996). Experiments with a new boosting algorithm. In *Proc. International Conference on Machine Learning, ICML.*Morgan Kaufmann.

Freund, Y., & Schapire, R. E. (1997). A decision-theoretic generalization of on-line learning and an application to boosting. *Journal of Computer and System Sciences*, *55*(1), 119–139. doi:10.1006/jcss.1997.1504

Fukushima, K. (1988). Neocognitron: A hierarchical neural network capable of visual pattern recognition. *Neural Networks*, *1*(2), 119–130. doi:10.1016/0893-6080(88)90014-7

Fukushima, & Kunihiko. (1980). Neocognitron: A Self-Organizing Neural Network Model for a Mechanism of Pattern Recognition Unaffected by Shift in Position. *Biological Cybernetics, 36*(4), 193-202.

Hamming, R. (1950). Error detecting and error correcting codes. *The Bell System Technical Journal*, *29*(2), 147–160. doi:10.1002/j.1538-7305.1950.tb00463.x

Hornik, K. (1991). Approximation capabilities of multilayer feedforward networks. *Neural Networks*, *4*(2), 251–257. doi:10.1016/0893-6080(91)90009-T

Hubel, D., & Wiesel, T. (1962). Receptive fields, binocular interaction, and functional architecture in the cat's visual cortex. *The Journal of Physiology*, *160*(1), 106–154. doi:10.1113/jphysiol.1962.sp006837 PMID:14449617

IFN/ENIT. (2014). *IFN/ENIT-database*. Retrieved July 30, 2015, from http://www. ifnenit.com/

Kearns, M., & Valiant, L. (1994). Cryptographic limitations on learning Boolean formulae and finite automata. *Journal of the ACM*, *41*(1), 67–95. doi:10.1145/174644.174647

Kearns, M. J., & Valiant, L. G. (1988). *Learning Boolean formulae or finite automata is as hard as factoring*. Harvard University, Center for Research in Computing Technology, Aiken Computation Laboratory.

Kocian, V. (1915). *Artificial Intelligence Algorithms for Classification and Pattern Recognition*. (Unpublished doctoral dissertation). University of Ostrava, Ostrava, CZ.

Kohonen, T., Oja, E., Simula, O., Visa, A., & Kangas, J. (2002). Engineering applications of the self-organizing map. *Proceedings of the IEEE*, *84*(10), 1358–1384. doi:10.1109/5.537105

Lai, K. K., Yu, L., & Wang, S. A. (2004). Neural network and web-based decision support system for forex forecasting and trading. In Data Mining and Knowledge Management (pp. 243-253). Berlin: Springer-Verlag.

LDC. (2014). *Linguistic Data Consortium*. Retrieved July 30, 2015, from https:// www.ldc.upenn.edu/

Lecun, Y., Bottou, L., Bengio, Y., & Haner, P. (1998). Gradient-based learning applied to document recognition. *Proceedings of the IEEE*, *86*(11), 2278–2324. doi:10.1109/5.726791

LeCun, Y., Cortes, C., & Burges, C. (2014). *The MNIST database*. Retrieved July 30, 2015, from http://yann.lecun.com/exdb/mnist/

Muniz, A. M., Liu, H., Lyons, K. E., Pahwa, R., Liu, W., Nobre, F. F., & Nadal, J. (2010). Comparison among probabilistic neural network, support vector machine and logistic regression for evaluating the effect of subthalamic stimulation in Parkinson disease on ground reaction force during gait. *Journal of Biomechanics*, *43*(4), 720–726. doi:10.1016/j.jbiomech.2009.10.018 PMID:19914622

Patuwo, E., Hu, M. Y., & Hung, M. S. (1993). Two-Group Classification Using Neural Networks. *Decision Sciences*, *24*(4), 825–845. doi:10.1111/j.1540-5915.1993. tb00491.x

Quinlan, J. R. (1996). Bagging, boosting, and C4. 5. In AAAI/IAAI, (vol. 1, pp. 725-730).

Rabiner, L. R. (1989). A tutorial on hidden Markov models and selected applications in speech recognition.*Proceedings of the IEEE, 77*(2), 257-286. doi:10.1109/5.18626

Ranawana, R., & Palade, V. (2006). Multi-Classifier Systems: Review and a Roadmap for Developers. *Int. J. Hybrid Intell. Syst., 3*(1), 35–61. doi:10.3233/HIS-2006-3104

Richard, M. D., & Lippmann, R. P. (1991). Neural network classifiers estimate Bayesian a posteriori probabilities. *Neural Computation, 3*(4), 461–483. doi:10.1162/neco.1991.3.4.461

Sammon, J. W. (1969). A nonlinear mapping for data structure analysis. *IEEE Transactions on Computers, 18*(5), 401–409. doi:10.1109/T-C.1969.222678

Schapire, R. E. (1990). The strength of weak learnability. *Machine Learning, 5*(2), 197–227. doi:10.1007/BF00116037

Subramanian, V., Hung, M. S., & Hu, M. Y. (1993). An experimental evaluation of neural networks for classification. *Computers & Operations Research, 20*(7), 769–782. doi:10.1016/0305-0548(93)90063-O

Trier, O. D., Jain, A. K., & Taxt, T. (1996). Feature Extraction methods for Character recognition – A Survey. *Pattern Recognition, 29*(4), 641–662. doi:10.1016/0031-3203(95)00118-2

Turing, A. M. (1950). Computing Machinery and Intelligence. *Mind, 59*(236), 433–460. doi:10.1093/mind/LIX.236.433

Valiant, L. G. (1984). A theory of the learnable. *Communications of the ACM, 27*(11), 1134–1142. doi:10.1145/1968.1972

Zadeh, L. A. (1994). Soft Computing and Fuzzy Logic. *IEEE Software, 11*(6), 48–56. doi:10.1109/52.329401

KEY TERMS AND DEFINITIONS

Artificial Neural Network: An Artificial Neural Network (ANN) is the information-processing paradigm that is inspired by the way biological nervous systems. Its key element is the structure of the information processing system. It is composed of a large number of highly interconnected processing elements (neurons) working in unison to solve specific problems.

Boosting: Boosting is a general method of converting rough rules of thumb into highly accurate prediction rule.

Classifier: A classification problem occurs when an object needs to be assigned into a predefined group or class based on a number of observed attributes related to that object. A classifier is a computer based agent which can perform a classification task.

Diversity of Classifiers: Individual classifiers in an ensemble system need to make different errors on different instances. If each classifier makes different errors, then a strategic combination of these classifiers can reduce the total error. Such a set of classifiers is said to be diverse.

Pattern Recognition: Pattern recognition is a branch of machine learning that focuses on the recognition of patterns and regularities in data.

Soft Computing: Soft computing is a partnership of distinct methods. The dominant aim of soft computing is to exploit the tolerance for imprecision and uncertainty to achieve tractability, robustness and low solutions cost.

Chapter 4
Modeling and Language Support for the Pattern Management

Zdenka Telnarova
University of Ostrava, Czech Republic

ABSTRACT

Patterns are mentioned usually in the extraction context. Little stress is posed in their representation and management. This chapter is focused on the representation of the patterns, manipulation with patterns and query patterns. Crucial issue can be seen in systematic approach to pattern management and specific pattern query language which takes into consideration semantics of patterns. In the background we discuss two different approaches to the pattern store and manipulation (based on inductive database and PANDA project). General pattern model is illustrated using abstract data type implemented in Oracle. In the following chapters the introduction to querying patterns and simple scheme of the architecture PBMS is shown.

DOI: 10.4018/978-1-5225-0565-5.ch004

INTRODUCTION

Sophisticated data processing tools (pattern recognition, data mining, knowledge extraction, etc.) were designed and developed because of reduce user interference in the process of extracting knowledge artefacts from the data. These knowledge artefacts denoted as patterns are characterized by a high degree of diversity and complexity. The problem of storing and manipulating patterns has limited attention in comparison with attention to the knowledge extraction techniques. So far patterns have not been exhaustively treated in terms of their storing, retrieving and querying. There is a leg of management systems that can provide support for general pattern definition and manipulation.

Like data also patterns can be modelled, stored, manipulated and queried. Patterns can be seen in the similar way as entity in data modelling. In reality there is innumerable amount of entities and process of data modelling is focus on finding them in connection with its specific domain. Modelling patterns is also finding specific types of patterns in connection with knowledge extracting techniques. For example, patterns can be modelled as association rules, clusters, time series data, etc. To be able to manipulate patterns with their generic structure we have to incorporate all kinds of patterns. These ideas were introduced in (Rizzi, Bettin et al. 2003) and also for some kinds of pattern indication for implementation were shown (Catani, Maddalena & Mazza 2005). Another approach to the manipulation of patterns was developed in inductive databases. Inductive databases do not work with generic patterns but focuses on specific pattern categories. Some object – relational databases also solve problem of specific kind of patterns, mainly for pattern's extraction from time series data.

The goal of the chapter is to describe three approaches mentioned above and introduce the design of solution based on enlargement object - relational approach to the idea of generic pattern structure.

BACKGROUND

In general, a pattern can be defined as a compact and rich in semantics representation of raw data (Catania, Maddalena, & Mazza, 2005). Patterns can be generated from different application context. Usually patterns are extracted by using some data mining tools or other pattern recognition tools. Raw data from which the patterns are extracted change with high frequency. The question is whether existing patterns still represent the data source. It is clear that any tool for providing manipulation with patterns not only in terms of changing pattern information can be useful for users.

Several approaches have been provided for pattern management. In this chapter we can mention Inductive Database approach which is based on integrated architecture, which means that raw data and patterns are stored together, and PANDA framework relying on separated architecture where raw data and patterns are logically stored and managed by two distinct systems.

Inductive database in this context can be defined as a database that contains inductive generalization about the data, in addition to the usual data. The inductive database concept has been suggested in several papers, for example (Mannila 1997).

Inductive Database

The schema of the inductive database (Boulicaut, Klemettinen & Mannila 1998) is a pair $R = (\mathbf{R}, Q_R, e, V)$, where $\mathbf{R}$ is a database schema, Q_R is a collection of patterns, V is a set of result values and e is the evaluation function that defines pattern semantics. This function maps each pair $(\mathbf{r}, \theta_i)$ to an element of V, where $\mathbf{r}$ is a database over $\mathbf{R}$ and θ_i is a pattern. The instance of the schema $\mathbf{R}$ of the inductive database is a pair $(\mathbf{r}, s)$ and consists of database $\mathbf{r}$ over the schema $\mathbf{R}$ and subset $s \subseteq Q_R$.

Having inductive database user can select specific data from that database as well as select specific subset of patterns. Pattern can be considered as intensional fact similar to the derived fact in deductive databases. Unlike deductive databases where fact can be derived from existing facts and deductive rules as an instance of the database, inductive database facts denote generalizations that can be learned from data.

For formulating queries we can create expression based on relational algebra with modification for referring to the patterns and the value of evaluation function on the patterns. In the context of object-relational databases evaluation function is a method that encodes the semantics of the patterns.

PANDA Framework

This framework is based on a separated architecture. We consider two spaces: source space (space of raw data) and a pattern space (Terrovitis & Vassiliadis 2003) . There always exist relationships among the members of the source space and the members of the pattern space. The cardinality of these relationships is many-to-many, pattern can correspond to more data items and data can correspond to more patterns.

Characteristics of data space and pattern space according to (Terrovitis, Vassiliadis, 2003).

We assume that each data item is characterized by a finite number of dimensions (call N), we have domain of each dimension call dom(x). If $A_1, \ldots, A_N$ are the dimensions of the data items, the source space is defined as dom (A_1) x ....x dom (A_N) and call it D^N. And actually stored data, respectively active source space is denoted D^N_A

Each pattern is characterized by a finite number (call M) of dimensions or features. We can call dom(x) the domain of each dimension. If B_1, ..., B_M are the dimensions of patterns, the pattern space is defined as dom (B_1) x ....x dom (B_M) and call it D^M. And active pattern space is denoted D^M_A

Relationship among Data and Patterns

is characterized in general as many-to-many relationship (no function) f_{DP}: $D^N \rightarrow D^M$. We can observe some more characteristics on this relationship like:

- Participation measures for the relationship, it means how large subset of D^N, resp. D^M is involved into relationship.
- Importance measures for a data item, it means how many patterns are related to the particular data item.
- Importance measures for a pattern, it means how many data items are related to the particular pattern.

When we take onto consideration separate architecture (stored patterns separated from data) the idea about Patter_Base Management Systems occurs (PBMS). Patterns can be managed the same way as data are managed. We present here PANDA project architecture of PBMS according to (Catania, Maddalena, Mazza, 2005). PBMS is a system for handling (storing/processing/retrieving) patterns defined over raw data in order to efficiently support pattern matching and to exploit pattern-related operations generating intensional information. The architecture stands on three layers. Raw Data Layer includes raw data can be managed by DBMS or can be stored in files or any other physical mean outside a DBMS. Pattern Layer includes patterns that are managed by PBMS as a separate system outside of the DBMS. Intermediate Layer maps patterns to their corresponding data. This layer is responsible for matching raw data with patterns according to their relationships.

We assume raw data managed by common DBMS, patterns managed by PBMS and query language which can provide us by information from data and patterns. How does PBMS work? What is based on? PBMS according to (Terrovitis, Vassiliadis, 2003) is based on this structure:

- Pattern layer which is populated with patterns. On the view of abstraction pattern layer is on the same level of abstraction as scheme of database and patterns on the abstraction level of database tuples.

- Type layer is an abstraction type like abstract (built-in and user defined) defined type for patterns.
- Class layer holds built-in and user-defined definition of collection of semantically related patterns.

ABSTRACT PATTERN TYPE

Definition of Pattern Type

A pattern type *PT* is a quintuple

[*N, SS, D, MS, MF*],

where

N = Unique identifier of the pattern type,
SS = Structure Scheme - distinct complex type,
D = Domain - is a set type,
MS = Measure Schema – a tuple of atomic types,
MF = A Mapping Formula - a predicate over *SS* and *D*.

Each pattern is instance of a specific pattern type. Structure schema depends on specific pattern type as is shown later for several specific pattern types. There is different structure for association rule, cluster, time series, etc. Definition below comes from the same quoted work.

Definition of Pattern

A patter *p* over a pattern type *PT* is a quintuple

[*PID, S, AD, M, MF*],

where

PID = A unique identifier,
S = Structure (instance of Structure Scheme),
AD = The Active Domain, a relation which instantiates the set type of Domain,
M = Measure – valid values of the respective structure and measure schema of *PT,*
MF = Mapping formula – predicate instantiating the respective mapping formula of *PT.*

As we mentioned Structure Scheme depends on specific patter type. It occurs useful to define pattern class as a collection of semantically related patterns which are instances of specific pattern type. For example we can have pattern class AssociationRule as collection of all instances of the specific pattern type Association Rule.

Definition of Class of Patterns

A pattern class is a triplet

[*Name, PT, Extension*],

where

Name = A unique identifier of the class,
PT = A pattern type,
Extension = A finite set of the patterns with pattern type *PT*.

SPECIFIC PATTERN TYPES

Though we consider pattern types as a general concept some of concrete types depending of pattern recognition algorithm can be shown. Let us mention only a few of them like Association Rule, Interpolating Line, Time Series, cluster, etc.

Pattern Type Association Rule

N: Association Rule,
SS: TUPLE (head: SET(STRING), body: SET(STRING)),
D: BAG (transaction: SET(STRING)),
MS: TUPLE (confidence: REAL, support: REAL),
MF: $\forall$ x(x$\in$ head $\vee$ x $\in$ body x $\Rightarrow$ transaction).

Confidence describes what percentage of the transactions including the head also includes the body. Support describes what percentage of the whole set of transactions include the body.

Instance of the Pattern Association Rule

PID: 1,

S: (head = {'Programing with PL/SQL'}, body= {'Databases', 'Programing with SQL'}),

AD: 'Select name AS transaction FROM subjects',

M: (confidence = 0.75, support = 0.55),

MF: {transaction: $\forall$ x (x $\in$ {'Programing with PL/SQL'} $\vee$ x $\in$ { 'Databases', 'Programing with SQL'} $\Rightarrow$ x $\in$ transaction)}.

This pattern describes situation when student that assigns for Databases and Programing with SQL also assigns Programing with PL/SQL with confidence 0.75 and support 0.55. (Telnarova, Z. & Schenk, J., 2015)

Pattern Type Cluster

N: Cluster (two dimensional),

SS: TUPLE (center: TUPLE (x: REAL, y: REAL), radius(r: REAL)),

D: BAG (a: INTEGER, b: INTEGER),

MS: precision: REAL,

MF: $(BAG.a - TUPLE.center.x)^2 + (BAG.b - TUPLE.center.y)^2 <= TUPLE.radius.r^2$.

Instances of the Pattern Cluster

Let us have customers and know their age and incomes. Via cluster analysis we have obtained clusters, each cluster contains customer with similar age and income. For example, we can obtain the clusters shown in Box 1.

The actual patterns for data from BAG can be described this way.

Box 1.

Cluster 1		Cluster 2	
Age	**Income**	**Age**	**Income**
30	33	43	60
31	31	47	60
29	29	45	59
30	27	49	61

PID: Cluster1:

S: (TUPLE(center(x: 30, y: 30), radius(r: 3)),
AD: 'Select age, income FROM customers',
M: Precision: 1,
MF: $(age - 30)^2 + (income - 30)^2 <= 32$.

PID: Cluster2:

S: (TUPLE(center(x: 45, y: 60), radius(r: 2)),
AD: 'Select age, income FROM customers ',
MF: Precision: 0.75,
MF: $(age - 45)^2 + (income - 60)^2 <= 22$.

MAPPING FORMULA

Mapping formula express relation between the pattern and the source data. Mapping formula has to enable identification of the data that are represented by patter and identification of the pattern that are related to the data. The mapping formula must express variety of relations between patterns and data. It must on pattern type level relates the structure schema with the domain, respectively on the pattern level the structure with active domain. The form of mapping formula must correspond with query language that uses the formula for receiving information and knowledge from patterns and data.

Formally the mapping formula can be defined as an expression

pm (dv, pv)

where *mp* is a predicate called the mapping predicate, *dv* are variable names from the domain *D*, *pv* are variable names from the structure schema *SS*.

As we mentioned above mapping formula is a predicate. This predicate is defined using first order logic containing logical connectives and at least two constructor functions – the tuple and the set constructor.

The mapping formula is not a query but the mapping formula is used to construct the query that returns all data from the specific dataset that can be approximately represented by the pattern. To evaluate the query all the free variables of the predicate take value from the active domain by the pattern.

IMPLEMENTATION OF THE ABSTRACT MODEL IN ORACLE

To be able to store patterns in pattern base it is necessary to create a structure of the pattern base. Pattern base can be modeled by simple meta-meta model shown on Figure 1. Patter_type is a general structure - entity which instances are specific types of patterns. Specific types can be added to pattern base according to the situation when some other specific type occurs in reality. This new instance of pattern_type creates specification for particular pattern it means concrete structure of attributes and their domains. For example Association Rule can be instance of patter_type and this specification concretizes the structure of the entity pattern.

Pattern_type entity is abstract entity that is specified only by definition of attributes and description of their meanings through informal text specification. Pattern entity (as an instance of pattern_type entity) has formal declaration according to concrete specification belongs to specific pattern_type. Figure 2 shows example of data type model for abstract data type in Oracle for patter_type Association Rule.

N: AssociationRule,
SS: TUPLE (head: SET(STRING), body: SET(STRING)),
D: BAG (transaction: SET(STRING)),
MS: TUPLE (confidence: REAL, support: REAL),
MF: $\forall$ x (x$\in$ head $\vee$ x$\in$ body $\Rightarrow$ x $\in$ transaction).

Figure 1. Meta-meta model for pattern

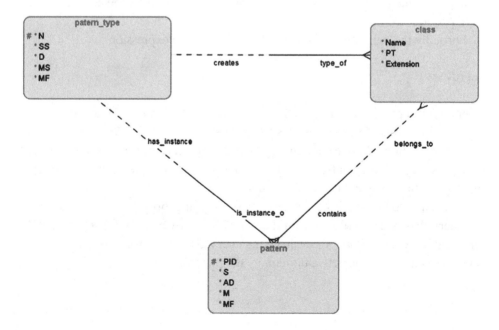

Figure 2. Model of abstract data type in Oracle

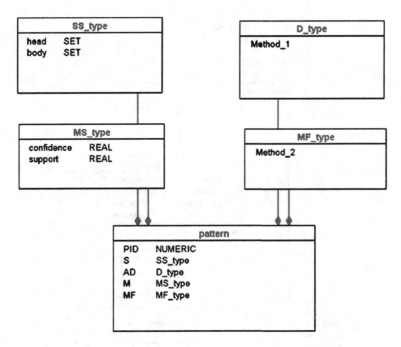

Method_1 is implementation of selecting data from specific database, Method_2 is implementation of mapping formula (predicate over *SS* and *D*).

Figure 3 is an example of data model for generation of schema for storing patterns. This model is based on Oracle abstract data type collection (set of strings for head and body) and object (Method_1 and Method_2).

Implementation of Mapping Formula

For implementation of mapping formula in Oracle we can use abstract data type of Oracle, where mapping formula is coded as a method of abstract data type object using PL/SQL language.

Oracle Methods are functions/procedures declared in the object type definition to implement behavior of the object of that type. There are written in PL/SQL or virtually any other languages (Java, C...). Oracle uses these types of methods:

1. **Member Method:** Which is defined on object instance's data. Member methods are used to access an object instance's values.

Figure 3. Data model uses Oracle abstract data types

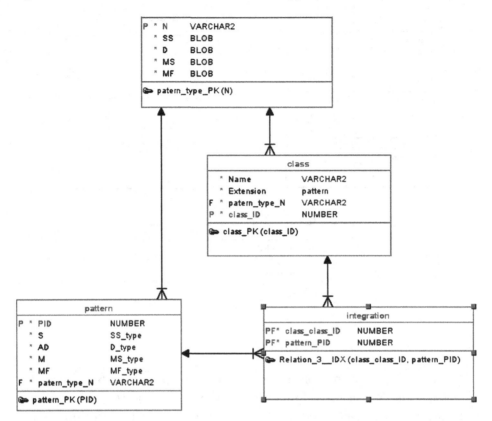

Example:

```
CREATE TYPE demo_typ2 AS OBJECT (a1 NUMBER,
        MEMBER FUNCTION get_square RETURN NUMBER);
CREATE OR REPLACE TYPE BODY demo_typ2 IS
        MEMBER FUNCTION get_square
        RETURN NUMBER
        IS
BEGIN
            RETURN SELF.a1 * a1;
END get_square;
END;
```

Member methods have a built-in parameter named SELF that denotes the object instance currently invoking the method. SELF can be explicitly declared, but that is not necessary. It is simpler to write member methods that reference the attributes and methods of SELF implicitly without the SELF qualifier (Oracle 2015, https:// docs.oracle.com).

2. **Static Method:** Which is invoked on the object type, not its instances. This method can be used to the operations that are global to the type (e.g. initialization).

Static methods differ from member methods in that the SELF value is not passed in as the first parameter. Methods in which the value of SELF is not relevant should be implemented as static methods. Static methods can be used for user-defined constructors.

Example Creating an Object Type with a STATIC Method:

```
CREATE TYPE atype AS OBJECT(
    a1 NUMBER,
    STATIC PROCEDURE newa (
    p1        NUMBER,
    tabname   VARCHAR2,
    schname   VARCHAR2));
CREATE TYPE BODY atype AS
    STATIC PROCEDURE newa (p1 NUMBER, tabname VARCHAR2, schname
VARCHAR2)
    IS
    sqlstmt VARCHAR2(100);
    BEGIN
    sqlstmt:= 'INSERT INTO '||schname||'.'||tabname|| ' VAL-
UES (atype(:1))';
    EXECUTE IMMEDIATE sqlstmt USING p1;
    END;
END;
CREATE TABLE atab OF atype;
BEGIN
    atype.newa(1, 'atab', 'HR');
END;
```

3. **Constructor Method:** Which is a built-in constructor function, like in C++. Every object type has a constructor method implicitly defined by system. This method returns a new instance of the user-defined object type and sets up the values of its attributes. The name of constructor method is the same as the name of the object type.

Example:

```
CREATE TABLE people_tab OF person_typ;
INSERT INTO people_tab VALUES (
    person_typ(001, 'Zdenka Telnarova', '5562290800'));
LANGUAGE SUPPORT FOR PATTERN
```

There are two different approaches to query patterns. It is based on the form of mapping formula:

- Predicate form of mapping formula,
- Mapping formula is expressed by procedure/function or method of Abstract Data Type (ADT).

If the mapping formula is a method of ADT or procedure/function then evaluating formula means call the method. In case mapping formula is a predicate we deal with the declarative representation of the formula and module that computes the formula by logic program is needed.

Tasks for query language:

- **Pattern Matching:** If new pattern is loaded into set of patterns the question is whether this pattern is already found in the storage. Another question is what data corresponds to new loaded pattern.
- **Deduce New Pattern Based on Existing Patterns:** Can be composed with part-of relationship.
- **Meta Querying:** Query deals not only with patterns but also with pattern type. This idea is very new. It was mentioned in (Terrovitis, Vassiliadis, 2003) and introduced binary pattern operators.

Three Fundamental Pattern Operators

Assume raw data as a point sets in the data space (Terrovitis & Vassiliadis, 2003). Two given patterns p_A and p_B can satisfy exactly one of following:

1. p_A subsumes p_B, it means that image (set of points in data space) of p_A is a superset of the image of p_B,
2. p_A and p_B are disjoint, it means that their images in the data space have no common points or
3. p_A and p_B intersect, it means that their images in the data space have at least one common and one not common point.

Intuitive Interpretation of the Operation

Ad 1: A pattern p_A subsumes pattern p_B when there are not equivalent and data represented by p_B are also represented by p_A. For example if the formula predicate of p_A is $x > 0$ and p_B is $x > 1$ then we can say that p_A subsumes p_B.

Ad 2: Two patterns are disjoint if they do not have any common item in the data space. It means that intersect of the items of these patterns is empty.

Ad 3: Intersection require that at least a common data item exists and there is at least one data item that corresponds to the first pattern but does not correspond to the second pattern.

For more information about operation with patterns see (Terrovitis & Vassiliadis, 2003). There is also formal definition of this operation and other operation like pattern equivalence.

Pattern Predicates

Patterns have specific properties that can be express by pattern predicates. Some of that predicates were introduced in (Catania, Maddalena, Mazza, 2004).

Identity is a property which expresses that two different patterns have the same identifier. Formally

$p_1 = p_2$ if $p_1.pid = p_2.pid$

where

p_1, p_2 = Patterns,
$p_1.pid, p_2.pid$ = Identifiers of $p_1, resp.$ p_2.

Intensional subsumption is a property expressing that two patterns have the same structure but one represents a smaller set of raw data.

Formally:

$p_1 \leq^i p_2$ if $p_1.s = p_2.s$, $p_1.d \subseteq^i p_2.d$ and $p_1.f \leq^i p_2.f$

where

$\leq$ = Symbol for subsumption
p_1, p_2 = Patterns,
$p_1.s$, resp. $p_2.s$ = Structure of p_1, resp. p_2,

$p_1.d$, resp. $p_2.d$ = Domain of p_1, resp. p_2,
$p_1.f$, resp. $p_2.f$ = Mapping formulas of p_1, resp. p_2.

Extensional subsumption is a property expressing that two patterns have the same structure but one represents a smaller set of raw data through the considered formula.
Formally:

$$p_1 \leq^e p_2 \text{ if } p_1.s = p_2.s, \ p_1.d \ \lceil_{p1.f} \subseteq^i p_2.d \ \lceil_{p2.f}$$

where

p_1, p_2 = Patterns,
$p_1.s$, resp. $p_2.s$ = Structure of p_1, resp. p_2,
$d \ \lceil_f$ = The set of data items satisfying the formula.

Goodness is a property where measures of the one pattern are better than measures of the other.

- **Temporal Validity (ω_T):** Let us have the pattern p_1 and temporal value t, than $\omega_T (p_1, t)$ is true if p_1 is temporally valid at time t.
- **Semantic Validity (ω_S):** Let us have p of type pt, a data source D, measure function μ_m for pt and some conditions $v_1, \ldots v_n$. Predicate ω_S is true if p is semantically valid with respect to D and $v_1, \ldots v_n$.

Query Operators

Let us remain the definition of the class of patterns.
A pattern class is a triplet

[*Name, PT, Extension*]

where

Name = A unique identifier of the class,
PT = A pattern type,
Extension = A finite set of the patterns with pattern type *PT*.

Pattern class is a collection of semantically related patterns which are instances of specific pattern type. In PBMS framework queries are created and executed over the classes of patterns. Query operators against patterns come out from relational operators like projection, selection, join, etc. Some modifications had to be done in terms of specific structure the class of patterns has.

Each query composed from query operator has input and output. Input of the query is one or more classes and output is a set of patterns that satisfy the query.

Projection

is an operation where the structure and measures of the patterns in class are reduced according the specification. The modification lies in adding attributes characterizing pattern measure.

$$\pi_{(l\_s,\, l\_m)}(c)$$

where

π = A symbol for projection,
c = A pattern class,
l_s = Non empty list of attributes, subset of attributes from pattern structure,
l_m = A list of attributes occurring in the pattern measure.

Selection

is an operation that allows select only those patterns from the certain class that satisfy specific condition. The modification occurs in selection predicate which can contain attributes not only from the structure, but also from the active domain or measure.

$$\sigma_F(c)$$

where

σ = A symbol for selection,
F = A selection predicate,
c = A class.

Join

is an operation which combine patterns from two different classes satisfying the condition for the join. In addition to relational algebra join operation incorporates composition function that defines the pattern type of the result. Adding composition function creates the main modification in comparison with relational algebra.

$$c_1 \, x_{F, \, cf} \, c_2$$

where

$x =$ Symbol for join,
$c_1, c_2 =$ Two different classes,
$F =$ A join predicate,
$cf =$ A composition function.

Important property of the patterns is their temporality. That is why temporal operator which can work within querying with temporality is so important.

Pattern Constructors

Pattern constructors are methods how to create new patterns from new data sets. These methods are primarily methods of data mining or other pattern recognition techniques but it can be also part of Pattern Base Management Systems. These constructors are based on pattern operations mentioned above.

Intersection constructor creates new pattern from patterns p_A and p_B. This new patter consists of new *pid* generated by system, new structure $\{S_A, S_B\}$, new relation $ad_{A\cup B}$ that contains all data specified in the data fields.

Union constructor creates new pattern which gets new *pid* from the system. The structure is a set composed from structure components of initial patterns, the pattern data is the union of the data of initial patterns.

SOLUTIONS AND RECOMMENDATIONS

The issue of storying, manipulation and querying patterns is very important one. The way how to store and manipulate patterns is similar but not equal to way of manipulating data structures like relations or object classes. Patterns have several specific properties that have to be considered. Nowadays we can observe two different kind of manipulation with patterns. One is based on separate storing raw data and patterns the other deals with common storage space. No one is prepared now for routine using. In spite of the fact that a lot of work have been done in general definition and design of the pattern model as a general structure there is lag of Pattern Base Management System for management of patterns.

One of the possible architecture was proposed by PSYCHO (Catania, Maddalena, & Mazza, 2005). Simple scheme is shown on Figure 4. This architecture is based on extra layer in the system which is responsible for manipulating with patterns. This layer is named Middle Layer and deal with PBMS engine. On the physical layer there is pattern base. Pattern base consists of pattern types, patterns and class definitions. PBMS engine consists of four modules.

- PDL (Pattern Definition Language) creates and modifies patterns types and class definition.
- PML (Pattern Modification Language) extracts patterns from pattern base, updates them or inserts patterns into pattern base.
- PQL (Pattern Query Language) executes queries. Queries can be divided into two parts: non cross-over queries which are put only on patterns (for example compare two patterns) or cross-over queries where data source (stored in database) are required to execute the query.
- Formula Handler deals with the declarative representation of formulas, integrity constraints, etc.

Figure 4. PBMS architecture based on PSYCHO

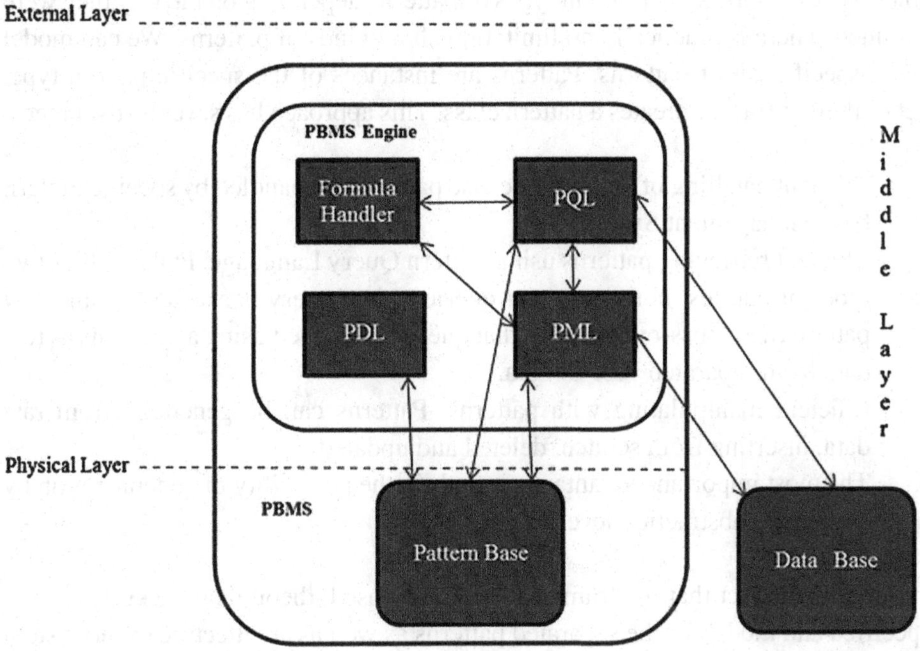

For the future research there are also two different ways how to continue. Either work with patterns as an entity implemented into object relational or object database or work with patterns as a construct implemented into pattern base. We recommend and try to implement proposed model and architecture based on separation the patterns from data source. As we discus above a lot of work has been done in this field but so far there is no exists working Pattern Base Management System which can solve our problem with manipulating of patterns. By implementation of the proposed model we can have a strong tool which can be used for variety of pattern types.

CONCLUSION

In this chapter we presented two different approaches to the patterns store, manipulating and retrieving. The first is based on inductive database which works in the platform of one integrated architecture. It means that raw data and patterns are stored together.

The second one (so called PANDA framework) relies on separated architecture where raw data and patterns are logically stored and managed by two distinct systems. Although inductive database approach is mentioned only in very brief way, framework with separated data and patterns is discussed in more details.

We presented general pattern model based on pattern types. This approach enables users to work with different types of patterns depending on the way they were obtained. There is practically no limitation about kinds of patterns. We can model every specific set of patterns. Patterns are instances of the specific pattern type. Set of these instances creates a pattern class. This approach has several advantages:

- Efficient handling of patterns because patterns are handled by specific Pattern base Management System.
- Efficient retrieving patterns using Pattern Query Language. PQL enables two types of queries: non cross-ever queries when query is executed using only patterns and cross-over queries that query is executed using as patterns as raw data from separated base of data.
- Efficient manipulating with patterns. Patterns can be generated from raw data, inserting from scratch, deleted and updated.
- The most important advantage grounds in the possibility of generalization by meta-meta abstraction level.

In spite the fact that the framework was proposed, theoretical background was specified and model for the separated patterns as well as architecture of the system were designed there is no any PBMS which can help users manipulate patterns.

We have described implementation using ADT in Oracle. Using this approach, we can preserve generality of the model. We can create pattern type as ADT where unique identifier, Structure Scheme, Domain and Measure Schema are attributes of ADT and Mapping Formula is the method of this ADT. We can handle patterns similarly to handle tables based on ADT. Using this way, we do not have specific operators for manipulating patterns as we describe in the chapter LANGUAGE SUPPORT FOR PATTERN.

In future we would like to focus on pattern language (based on relational algebra and relational calculus) with the goal to create query language for retrieving and comparing patterns with conservation of the generality of the model.

REFERENCES

Boulicaut, J. F., Klemettinen, M., & Mannila, H. (1998). Querying inductive database. In PKDD98, (LNAI), (vol. 1510, pp. 194-202). Springer-Verlag.

Catania, B., Maddalena, M., & Mazza, M. (2004). A Framework for Data Mining Pattern Management. In *Proceedings of ECML/PKDD*. doi:10.1007/978-3-540-30116-5_11

Catania, B., Maddalena, M., & Mazza, M. (2005). A prototype system for pattern management. In *Proceedings of the 31st International Conference on Very Large Data Bases (VLDB05)*.

Mannila, H. (1997). Inductive databases and condensed representation for data mining. In *Proceedings of the International Logic Programming Symposium*.

Oracle 11g. (n.d.). Retrieved April 10, 2015, from https://docs.oracle.com/en/

Rizzi, S., Bettino, E., Catania, B., Gollfarelli, M., Halkidi, M., Terrovitis, M., . . . Vrachnos, E. (2003). Towards a logical model for patterns. In *Proceedings of 22nd International Conference on Conceptual Modeling (ER03)* (LNCS), (*Vol. 2813*, pp. 77-90). Springer.

Telnarova, Z., & Schenk, J. (in press). The Logical Model for Pattern Representation. *International Conference on Numerical Analysis and Applied Mathematics (ICNAAM.)*

Terrovitis, M., & Vassiliadis, P. (2003). *Architecture for Pattern_Base Management Systems*. Retrieved May 13, 2015, from http://citeseerx.ist.psu.edu

Terrovitis, M., Vassiliadis, P., Skiadopoulos, S., Bertino, E., Catania, B., Maddalena, A., & Rizzi, S. (2004). Modeling and Language Support for the Management of Pattern-Base. In *Proceedings of the 16th International Conference on Scientific and Statistical Database Management (SSDBM04)*. IEEE Computer Society. doi:10.1109/SSDM.2004.1311218

KEY TERMS AND DEFINITIONS

Abstract Data Type (ADT): In object-relational databases ADT helps to model object properties of modeled domain.

Mapping Formula: In the pattern base context mapping formula describes the relationship between the source space (space of raw data) and pattern space. Mapping formula carries semantics for patterns.

PANDA Framework: Generic framework for the comparison of both simple and arbitrarily complex patterns defined over raw data and over other patterns.

Pattern: Consistent and recurring characteristic or trait that helps in the identification of a phenomenon or problem, and serves as an indicator or model for predicting its future behavior.

Pattern Base Management System: System for storing, manipulating and retrieving patterns as well as obtaining information and knowledge from pattern base with relation to database.

Pattern Type: General definition of the set of patterns with the same characteristics. This definition contains unique identifier of the pattern type, Structure Scheme, Domain, Measure Schema and Mapping Formula.

PDL: Pattern Definition Language is used for general definition of the set of patterns.

PML: Pattern Manipulation Language is used for manipulation (like inserting, deleting and updating) with patterns.

PQL: Pattern Query Language enable users to obtain information and knowledge from Pattern Base (non cross-over queries) and from Pattern Base in relation to Data Base (cross-over queries).

PSYCHO: Prototype System for Pattern Management.

Chapter 5
Trading Orders
Algorithm Development:
Expert System Approach

Bronislav Klapuch
University of Ostrava, Czech Republic

ABSTRACT

The chapter puts into the business of financial markets area in greater detail at FOREX currency market. It describes the main methods used for in currencies trade. The main goal of this paper is to explain the principle of creating an Automated Trading System (ATS) with the MQL4 language. The chapter shows concrete architectural elements of the program on the demonstration examples and it is a guide for the development of an ATS. The main benefit is creation of the original trading system, which optimizes an ATS usage on the base of historical data in practice. Optimization of the trading parameters is based on the equity performance in the historical periods.

DOI: 10.4018/978-1-5225-0565-5.ch005

INTRODUCTION

This chapter combines two worlds, in which I am living in. It connects the world of informatics and the world of financial markets. Informatics accompanied me since the early nineties, while with financial markets I met later – in 2007.

The issue of trading the financial instruments is so wide, that it could be written hundreds of books and yet it doesn't embrace everything. Perhaps, it would be best to have a focus on the one particular part. So, I am going to introduce the basics of financial markets and the programming too.

The essential part of preparation for the creation of trading algorithms is to understand different market operating aspects including actually established methods, that help us to forecast market trends with the best probability. Here are introduced the main ones. Then we can finally proceed to do, what we have really discussed in detail – creation of an automated trading systems by programming.

For our purposes we will focus on the currency FOREX market and programming in MQL4.

Individual instruments here are called "currency pairs" or in an abbreviation "couples". We will not talk here about the "commission charges" or "rolling positions". The reason is not that we are not able to program it, but I want to avoid excessive generalization. The development platform for the MQL4 programming language is directly the trading platform Metatrader which is a common tool widely used by many of the world brokers. It will be shown here not just the program construction, but also MQL4 orders. We will create here a simple trading system.

BACKGROUND

The Automated Trading Systems (ATS) are currently primarily used by banks and various financial investment institutions. They created systems for their own needs, with which operate large teams of developers on. Such systems are usually very rugged and their advantage is the relative high safety. There is a movement of huge amount of money, thus it is required completely different approach to a small individual speculator.

There are some commercial programs for traders, which are offered on the Internet at different prices. Unfortunately, nothing, and neither the cost, does not indicate, whether they are a really profitable systems or scam. As profitable or better said "non-loss ATS" we call systems, that in the long term view, the order of days or weeks, its activities the capital on the trading account increases and not vice versa.

The last group of programs are freely distributable creations of enthusiasts, who create them with own efforts. However, the most of these programs reached only a certain stage of development and are not suitable for a real profitable business use.

The prerequisite for the functional profitable system is in fact a personal experience with markets, where we can profitably trade manually. Only then we can put own experience into a program, which algorithmically does just what we otherwise do manually.

Freely available programs are often partly creations of failed traders or first beta-profit programs that are no longer freely available, when they reach the certain stage of profitability.

Accordingly, there is not just intention to create a comprehensive guide for creating of trading programs, but we also can find specific, functional, original program, which is profitable under the certain conditions. Also, we would like to show, how we can discover these profitability conditions.

THE PRINCIPLES OF TRADING ON THE STOCK, COMMODITY, AND CURRENCY MARKET

Under the term "Trading" we understand a simply trading on stock exchanges and similar markets. In our terminology we can call the retailer in this case "trader". Such trader is actually a speculator, who expects a price movement in a particular direction. If the price goes indeed in his direction, he gains. Otherwise he lost. Sometimes we hear in this context the term "investment" and "investor". Let's explain the difference between the investment and the speculation.

Investment and Speculation

Investment means injecting capital into a trade for a longer period. It means usually for more than a six months and we expect a dividend yield or a continuous appreciation of the deposit value. There it is generally higher capital appreciation, than inserting on a savings account at the bank. But there is also a higher risk that the investment value vice versa decreases. Investor buys businesses. He has interest in the financial results and dividends.

Speculation is a transaction entered into in anticipation of predicted revenues and due this coupled with some risk. Speculation is mostly short-term trade, where we expect price development up or down and profit on the price movements in the direction which we expected.

Such speculative trade can take place even within a minute or less. Speculator deals with a risk (Beneš, 1993).

Trades take place in various markets. Stock transactions take place on the stock exchanges, commodities are traded on commodity exchanges. Currencies can be traded for example also in currency FOREX market. Trades mediates "broker", which is a licensed corporation for which we have a merchant account and that makes our trade commands on the market.

STOCKS, COMMODITIES, CURRENCIES, CFDS, OPTIONS: DESCRIPTION OF INDIVIDUAL MARKETS

Stocks

Shares – we are not dealing here with form of shares in the meaning of (Beneš, 1993) a type of security with whom are connected the shareholder rights to participate under the law and the Articles of Association on its management, profit and liquidation balance upon dissolution of the company. For our purposes, we will proceed only from the basic stocks concepts as a proportion of company ownership units.

Stock index portfolio is composed from predefined number of shares. The stock index is an indicator characterizing the development of courses on the stock market. The stock index of leading shares is represented by joint stock companies quoted on the relevant stock exchange. Their weight in the index is derived for example according to the basic capital, stock market capitalization and others. The basic principle of determining the amount of stock index results from the ratio between the current value of the selected set of weighted shares and the value of certain fixed date fixed in the past. (Beneš, 1993)

Commodities

Commodities are goods that are traded on markets and it is uniquely defined by its quantity and quality. (Beneš, 1993) For simplified example - oil is named (OIL), gold (GOLD), corn (CORN)... But it is not always as simple as this example.

CFD

Trading "Contracts for Difference" (CFD) is a trading where a trader speculates on the movements of mutual exchange rates between currencies or the movements of derivative instruments such as gold. This method allows a trading to buy or sell a certain amount of instruments without expending funds on the basis of a deposit (margin) which guarantees the settlement of traded instructions in the event that the exchange rate change in a way that is disadvantageous for the trader. Derivative trading is highly standardized and subject to very strict rules. The transaction unit is one LOT. The purchase or sale of one LOT at FOREX market means buying or selling 100,000 units of one currency for another one. In the case of commodities and other instruments can be the LOT size different. Of course, you can trade a higher nominal value or to sell or buy one LOT a multiple. (XTB-Trader 2008) A financial derivative is a designation for financial transactions derived from traditional financial instruments. This is e.g. options, financial futures, swaps, etc. (Beneš, 1993)

- **Options:** Options are another sophisticated tool for trading. In this case it is speculation at future price basically of anything. This tool certainly deserves a detailed description because it is quite difficult to understand. However, we will not discuss it here. For further explanation can be used for example the source (Beneš, 1993).
- **FOREX:** The FOREX market (Foreign Exchange) is the currency market which has not designated settlement place. The market wchich was originally designed for an interbank transaction in currencies, is currently used by a broad spectrum of traders using FOREX brokers.

FUNDAMENTAL AND TECHNICAL ANALYSIS

What we call as fundamental analysis is the usage of messages, for example periodic announcement of the results, that have a direct or indirect impact on the value of a financial instrument. These impulses are usually different for individual markets. For shares may be an impulse for example publication of financial results, a change in the management. In the case of shares, we see the long-term economic data and the assumption of revenue in the coming period, the ratio between assets and liabilities or the assumption of dividends.

Important fundamental news are different for commodities. For example, the price of oil can react to the announcement of the quota mining limit, publication of weekly inventory status, a political stability in the regions, where oil is extracted. The price of the crops often reacts to the change of the weather, the price of precious metals to the economic situation.

Currency react to the announcement of changes in central bank interest rates. Fundamental analysis examines developments in particular financial results. Currency reacts to a change in the political situation and the economic status of countries, that affect a particular currency.

Technical analysis is based on monitoring the sentiment of the previous season and using statistical methods primarily determines more or less likely direction of development of the share price, commodity, or a currency pair.

Technical Analysis (TA) is the study of price movements. The main idea of TA lies in the fact that we predict the future direction and level of movement prices on the base of historical price movements. In other words, we watch the behavior of prices in the charts.

INDICATORS OF TECHNICAL ANALYSIS

We can identify trends and patterns of price behavior that can help us to find good trading opportunities. The most important term TA is a term trend. If we can find and identify the trend and will trade in the direction of the trend, we have quite a big chance that we'll make. We understand the trend of price movement in a particular direction, ie upwards or downwards. The trend is a not small change in prices, but the longer-term price movement pointing up or down. Such a trend can take from several tens of minutes after several months. It depends on what time frame (TF) business. If the price does not change much and moves only in a specific area, we call this phenomenon "chop" and also that "the market goes sideways."

If technical analysis based on the monitoring of price movements in history, it is obvious that the main work tool trader's chart. The best known and most commonly used charts are the bar chart and the candlestick chart.

In classic the bar chart you will find many bars illustrate bid and demand. Each line is characterized by 4 prices: OPEN, HIGH, LOW and CLOSE. Distances between HIGH and LOW price are called RANGE.

Comparison of these five values is used to determine the probability of price movement in the future and many private traders use analysis of individual bars for a very lucrative business. In each comma is a lot of information, and smart marketers use this to creation of various trading strategies and methods.

- **OPEN:** Opening price at which to buy and sell currency pairs on the beginning of the trading day or period of time, given that comma shows. In the bar chart shows the horizontal point from the left column of the chart is the candle body candles placed between OPEN and CLOSE. Candlewick, ie vertical lines delimit HIGH (above) and low (bottom).
- **HIGH:** The highest price that buyers reached during the day. This value is not that interesting as OPEN and CLOSE prices, but if HIGH price within a specified time period as high as CLOSE signals a major buyer's commitment to obtain a given currency at any price. Thus, we can also count on the fact that prices will rise above in the next trading period.

- **LOW:** The lowest price which sellers achieved during the day. Like the HIGH or LOW price is not very interesting, unless consistent with price CLOSE. In this case it is a very negative day and is a strong likelihood that the next day, prices will continue their sharp decline.
- **CLOSE:** Closing price. In the bar graph is shown in horizontal line to the right of the column.

The candlestick graphs originated in 17th century Japan as an aid for trade rice. The body of the candle, which is higher than the open-close of a different color (usually white or green) from the candle, which is lower than the open-close (which is usually black or red).

For every trader is paramount to detect and identify trends. It is a widespread adage "the trend is my friend". Trades made in the direction of the trend are likely to be successful. Trendlines (TrendLines (TL)) are essential building blocks in determining the strength and direction of the trend.

THE USE OF INDICATORS IN TECHNICAL ANALYSIS

- **Moving Averages:** Important single indicator, mainly used to identify trends, predict future prices and determine the appropriate time to enter the trade. Bollinger bands are used to determine market volatility. Determine the area of standard deviations, making it easier to track possible changes in price.
- **MACD:** The indicator to identify moving averages that indicate a new trend. MACD indicator is basically a composition of two moving averages. One way the use of force is tracing the trend. The greater the deviation from the histogram MACD zero line, the more we can infer that it is a force larger trends.
- **Stochastic Indicator:** Helps us determine when the market is overbought or oversold. Like other so-called. "Oscillators" it is usable especially in the market with no clear trend.
- **RSI Relative Strength Index:** Like the stochastic indicator is relatively well helps determine overbuying or overselling market.
- **Williams% R:** Also an indicator for determining the pre-sold and overbought area
- **Pivot Points:** Used to identify important support and a resistance. These are calculated based on the price level high, low, open, close price, mostly on the previous day, but also, for example, the previous week or month.

- **Elliot Wawes:** Ralf Nelson Elliot wave theory developed trendujícího market. According to this theory, the price ranges pětivlnovém cycle.
- **Money Management (MM):** A way to work with capital for risk reduction.

For a successful business it needs to take care of his business. Since this unavoidable risk of loss, we should his capital intended for trading divide so as to adverse developments in prices does not threaten its ability to further trading. So if we have a trading account some capital, it should be based on the quantity to determine the amount of risk that we intend to take. If we would have risked too much, although we could have a greater possibility of profit, but also when we encounter a few losing trades, we will soon have nothing to risk. Correct level of risk is indeed subjective, but there are also experiences rooted principles in their own interest should be followed. On the other hand, if we lying on trading account capital untapped, correctly set money management will help with the evaluation.

Stoploss, TakeProfit ...

In the terminology of trading we are certainly not avoiding terms such as stop-loss (SL) or ProfitTake or TrailigStop (TS), Ask, Bid, the price for Maket, the price for Limit and more.

- **Stops (SL):** A tool restricting loss. When the price in another direction than we originally anticipated, SL automatically close our position. Although we lost, but only in so far as we are willing to take risks.
- **TakeProfit (TP):** The price that you can set, and when it reaches the market, trade is closed and we collect profits. Sometimes the term is referred to as *ProfitTake (PT)*.
- **TrailingStop (TS):** Automatically shifted SL. Set your size TS, and that after reaching a specified price movement in our direction gradually moves SL. This tool is standard equipment trading platform. But we can program the more sophisticated tools of this type, which can slide SL based on various other indicators. Anyways TS programmatic issues on the side of our computers, so if we fall out internet connection, of course, stop scrolling SL at our open trade specific work, as well as other program matters that are performed on our computer.
- **Ask, Bid, the Currency Pair:** If we see the GBPUSD exchange rate = 1.5884. We know exactly what that means? The first part of "GBP" base currency. In our case we are the British pound. The second part, "USD" is reversed or quotation currency. In our case it will be the US dollar.

When buying exchange rate tells us how much we have to pay troops quotation currency, we could buy one unit of the base currency. When selling the exchange rate tells how many units of the currency quotation we get when we sell 1 British pound.

In fact, we'll see two numbers. The first number is BID (offer), and the second number is ASK (demand). For our purposes we need to understand that the higher price is ASK and lower the BID (I alphabetically it goes way behind). We always get the less favorable. The difference between the bid and ask price is called the spread. For some brokers, such as forex, this spread is only normal fee for the execution of a particular trade. The stock and commodity markets usually pay well known. Commission, which is the fee for a shop that is either a percentage, calculated from the size of the business, or fixed. Alternatively, a combination of both, or is computed differently.

- **Pip:** The smallest increase in prices, which can make currency pair. It is also known as a point. For example, one pip = 0.0001 for EURUSD or USDJPY to 0.01.
- **PIP VALUE:** The course of the currency pair is expressed as a decimal number. Currency pairs are growing about the smallest value - move - 1 point or PIP. If the bid price, for example GBPUSD moves from 1.5130 to 1.5131, it just moves on a PIP. The value of a pip depends on the currency cross currency pair, ie according to the second currency in a currency pair symbol. The value of one pip for the pair GBPUSD is $ 10 for a standard lot.
- **One LOT:** A standardized unit of volume, which represents the volume of currency in the amount of 100,000 units of the base currency (the first currency in a currency pair symbol).

Leverage, Margin

Leverage (leverage effect) means that a business must pay for only a fraction of the value of trade (initial margin). A relatively small change in the exchange rate value of the basic causes far greater percentage change in the return on capital invested in the store when it is closed.

Derivatives trading enables the use of high financial leverage (leverage), which allows to conclude transactions, for example, 100 times higher than the balance on the account of the investor. Such high lever means that, in case of the exchange rate we favorable direction earn hundred times more than in the case of purchase without the use of leverage.

Here it must be remembered that the leverage we can bring as fast profit and loss.

Risk Reward Ratio (RRR)

When you open a particular position should evaluate the potential profit in proportion to the risk. These measurable (in the region one of the few) data. Thus, the ratio between the amount of the limited risk-taking, for example, a tool called stop-loss (SL) and the amount of the expected profit, which we put so. ProfitTake (PT). Buy If, for example EURUSD currency pair at a price of 1.2500 SL and placed on the price of 1.2490, at 1.2530 PT, we RRR = 1: 3

Business Direction: Long, Short

Just as soon as you can buy and then sell (long), it is possible for (not all) of brokers to perform the opposite operation - to sell first, and then close the position by buying and speculate on the price movement flow down (short). The possibility of using short instructions can be in different markets is limited. Some stores do not permit such exchanges; in others it is necessary to provide for a particular loan broker. For derivative financial instruments, however, use short steps routine directly and without restriction. The same is true for most, if not all forex brokers.

Trading Environment for Programming and Testing

To access the market monitoring and trading orders are used a lot of software trading platforms. Some are on the web interface, while others require a custom application on a computer trader. These applications often offer the ability to create custom scripts, indicators or automated systems. One of the most widespread trading platform is "Metatrader". The user can choose whether to enter the information manually, or if your computer has it routine work and he only follows that everything happens according to his wishes. There is facing another option: Leave everything on the computer, or combine its own strategy carried out manually, with strategies, which takes place the computer itself. Combining these options will still appear as the golden mean.

DESCRIPTION OF THE USE OF SOFTWARE "METATRADER"

Trading Platform "Metatrader" is created by MetaQuotes Software Corp. The individual brokers platform distributes its clients with various modifications name and settings. To demonstrate use a version of "X-Trader", which is used by clients of XTB. Metatrader is composed of parts placed with a broker (back office) and partly placed with a client, that is with us (front end). For programming their own applications, we are interested in the version designed for the PC.

Trading Platform "Metatrader" is created by MetaQuotes Software Corp. The individual brokers platform distributes its clients with various modifications name and settings.

The trading platform is free to download on the broker's website. Installer works in different languages, so you can choose and Czech, to run the program itself is the chosen language, which is set by the operating system on your computer. Thus far, we have set Czech, the Czech localization. The program is intended for use in the MS Windows operating system. With certain restrictions, to use the program in Linux using an emulator "wine". Into this environment, however, we must add files, fonts, and font file MFC42.DLL. The restriction is certain possibilities for testing strategies - the inability to set the time interval testing. Other features that I had the opportunity to verify the correct functioning even in the emulated environment. Just maybe I suggest not allow the online update system.

After installation program can run. We get the opportunity to open a new "demo" account, or we can use already existing account whether real or demo. I recommend for the development and testing of any scripts, indicators or automated strategies using a demo account.

- **Syntax of MQL4:** If we control the programming language C, the programming language MQL4 toy. Generally, it is easier, but includes features that work closely with the market, and it is different. But first we learn about the editor "MetaEditor", which is part of a complete trading platform MetaTrader, which already have installed. We may alternatively use any text editor, e.g. Notepad, but MetaEditor is equipped, besides help to the language MQL4, a built-in compiler source code. In the upper left of the window for editing code. We can also open multiple windows with source code. The main task of the bottom window is displayed compilation result. Here we highlight the compiler syntax error in translation. Another important Func this window is help on the individual functions. The most we can get, in the last upper right window. Individual tabs give us the opportunity:
  - ○ Open individual files from the source directory structure,
  - ○ View the structure of the standard features of the language by browsing register,
  - ○ Search for help using crawlers.
- **Script:** Scripts are used for one-time capacity. An example could be a script that closes all startup or for example only profitable position.
- **Indicator:** Indicators can graphically display moments of technical analysis so that they are more readable for humans. One can then easily adjusted place

to open or close positions. In the history of trading it was invented many indicators that the various markets have explanatory power better or worse. Some are well known, others are unknown. We can create your own indicators that we were able to visualize our business strategy. As an example, I cite the source.

- **Expert Advisor (EA):** "Expert Advisor" in an environment MetaTrader synonymous general "Automated Trading System" (AOS). It is there to automatically send instructions to open or close the trading orders algorithmised in response to events in the rate of the selected instrument.

- **Own Program Writing:** Can be programmed differently. Even using inappropriate methodologies can lead to a successful conclusion. Mostly there is a relatively small amount of code. However, there cannot resist to use my years of experience in software development, testing and project management. I believe that things should be done properly from the start. This not only helps to prevent potential errors in the program, but also to significant inefficiencies in the creation of the work. Moving like this: Select the iterative method of programming. Simply, this means that we gradually add code to the individual functional parts. It is unnecessary to describe them here at length about some of the specific methodology and procedural framework. Sufficient to indicate different phases and iterations that lead to the creation of a functional program that reliably done what he should.

First, we create a proposal the main functionality of the program. This essential part of the program, inspect, we have not made a typo or somewhere not forget to write semicolon or close parenthesis. After all, for syntax errors warn us embedded compiler. Then we perform testing. With a script or indicator we have no other option than to start our work environment trading platform. Here I strongly recommend you to check whether you are using a live account (I mean real account.). We might be unpleasantly surprised if our program does not work according to our ideas. For testing in the AOS platform MetaTrader integrated test system that will be described in detail later. Testing will tell us whether our proposal is correct, and if we continue, or modify their original idea. When testing a program often leads to unexpected behavior of the program. As I mentioned, reveals compiler syntax errors. Worse it is with finding runtime errors which occur perhaps only because the program is not doing what it should. In this case, I recommend tuning the program frequently used command "Comment ()" or "Print ()", which lists, in the first case to display the graph window, in the second case to the logo program, you have chosen comments, or the current values of variables. After completing this course, our debugging tools from the code removed, as some now useless comments.

Only after satisfactory testing continue creating other elements. Other elements may be, for example, various filters or any graphic elements, where we can win with colors, but do not have a major impact on the functionality of the program. Inserting each new member shall be considered as a new phase or iteration. At the end of each iteration definitely re-test the entire program, and will focus primarily on the newly created part. The testing may vary. It depends on what the testing, and especially since we expect the program itself. Other range testing will be with a simple script, the other will be at the test indicator, and another test at AOS. It is quite laborious and inefficient write the entire program at once, and only in the end find that the expected results will not come for some reason, we could detect it much earlier. It is also advisable for the sake of individual functional elements to separate and identify commentary. Finding mistakes in long code is confusing endless suffering. And we try to prevent the continuous testing.

DESIGN AND CONSTRUCTION OF ATS

When designing ATS, we are faced with the question of what a program has to do.

In most cases, if not in all, the objective is profitable trading system. This kind of system we cannot create even if we are brilliant in the computer programming, if we do not have the IDEA. I write that word by UPPER letters, because it is the base of the ATS. It is not written here, how we get the idea. On this subject was written hundreds of books. The best ideas are simple.

ATS Custom Design

Let us look at our project a little more broadly. It is technically simple to sit next to computer and just start writing code. For the complicated ATS we should be not just the programmers but also software architects, project managers and testers. Let us take our idea now and create a basic prototype which can make us sure, that our assumptions are correct.

For example, we want to develop a trend strategy with using so-called crossing two moving averages. The strategy is based on a system which buy orders occurs, when the faster moving average crosses the slower one from below. Analogously for sale, the faster moving average crosses the slower one from above. This is a classic strategy, but even today it does not lose its charm.

When is our prototype created, let us get into a testing and an optimization. It is important to find out, while the prototype is in testing, if the base idea is correct and profitable at least in certain market conditions. To achieve positive results, we also need further conditions and parameters, which we can find by the parameters optimization. In our example the parameters are the length of each period of moving averages.

In case that we will find out that our ATS does not show any profitability, it is useless to continue with this ATS.

If we found the conditions for successful profitable operation of our ATS and its limitations, so we can continue in the next phase of the project. We propose "Filters" when we try to limit opening trades with a small probability of profit. In our case we were decided that "we take" just trades that are only in the direction of our higher trend.

For purpose there is supposed, we can put two moving averages, one with higher period. If there is the purchasing signal, the system will only respond to those where if the low moving average than the control and of course with the sell signal by contrast. It is not necessary to repeat that after such intervention into the code is performed testing and optimization again to find out if our step was correct.

It is time to start with our programming in real. Let us to write our prototype. It is enough list declaration of global externally adjustable variables ShortMA and LongMA and a major part – "start()". Declaration of other global variables and constants of external adjustable variables determines the program context, the "init()" and "deinit()" we can leave empty yet.

```
int start()
{
//
 double Sma1, Lma1, Sma2, Lma2;
 int ticket, total;
Sma1 = iMA(NULL, 0, ShortMA,0,MODE_EMA,PRICE_CLOSE,1);
 Lma1 = iMA(NULL, 0, LongMA,0,MODE_EMA,PRICE_CLOSE,1);
 Sma2 = iMA(NULL, 0, ShortMA,0,MODE_EMA,PRICE_CLOSE,2);
 Lma2 = iMA(NULL, 0, LongMA,0,MODE_EMA,PRICE_CLOSE,2);
```

We have found the value of the size of the moving average (MA) for a shorter period and for the longer period. This is for the previous candle and for the candle before her.

```
 if (iVolume(Symbol(),0,0) > 1) return (0);
//Buy Order
 total=OrdersTotal();
 if(total<1)
 {
 if((Sma1>Lma1) && (Sma2<Lma2)) // condition for open BUY order
```

Then we can continue with a typing of the basic condition for the purchase, thus command "BUY". The following code is executed with the conditions, that the value of the long period MA of right previous candle is higher than lower period MA. A candle before is must be to maintain the conditions contrary. Then follow the instruction "OrderSend()", which provide the actual execution of the trade. The other things, we can see around, are the treatment and check if the trade order was sent in order.

```
{
 ticket=OrderSend(Symbol(),OP_BUY, Lots, Ask, 3, 0,
Ask+TakeProfit*Point, Label, MagicN, 0, Blue);
 if(ticket>0)
 {
 if(OrderSelect(ticket,SELECT_BY_TICKET,MODE_TRADES))
Print("Buy order opened: ",OrderOpenPrice());
 }
 else Print("Error opening Buy order: ",GetLastError());
 return(0);
 }
// Sell Order
 if((Sma1<Lma1) && (Sma2>Lma2)) // podmínka otevření SELL
 {
 ticket=OrderSend(Symbol(),OP_SELL, Lots, Bid, 3, 0, Bid
TakeProfit*Point, Label, MagicN, 0, Red);
 if(ticket>0)
 {
 if(OrderSelect(ticket,SELECT_BY_TICKET,MODE_TRADES))
Print("Sell order opened: ",OrderOpenPrice());
 }
 else Print("Error opening Sell order: ",GetLastError());
 return(0);
 }
 }
//
 return(0);
}
```

Such prototype is actually a functional program. We fold it, optimizing and testing. If we can get a positive result, there is great hope that the final ATS will be profitable.

From the test report, we will find that our prototype has an interesting result. It'll looks absolutely great. But do not celebrate yet, we cannot optimize future data.

Filters Implementation

When we have programmed and tested a functional prototype, then it is the turn to solve the performance of our system. As we know, optimization has created "equity graph" for us, a chart which corresponds to the size of our bank account value, a beautiful rising diagonal line. But it is a modeled environment that uses data that applies to the past and not the future. Such filters can be used more gradually, and it could be found out only by testing whether the results of our automated system are better, or rather the opposite.

Let us therefore try to take only trades, that are in the direction of the trend. If there is the upward trend, we only trades "long" and when there is downward trend, we take trades such "short".

We have added a program to the next moving average. Its size we let up to user.

```
extern double SuperLongMA = 204;
```

The actual moving average is placed in "start ()".

```
double SLma1;
SLma1 = iMA(NULL, 0, SuperLongMA,0,MODE_EMA,PRICE_CLOSE,1);
```

But we must not forget the most important thing - to put it as a condition for instruction

```
"SELL" or "BUY".
if((Sma1>Lma1) && (Sma2<Lma2) && (Sma1>SLma1))
// condition for opening BUY
```

Condition for instruction SELL certainly will add separately. Now, of course, follows compilation and testing.

ATS Testing and Optimization

In previous chapters, we continually encountered the terms "testing" and "optimization".

Without these two concepts we would not indeed much worthwhile programmed. Without feedback we would not know, which way to proceed and that the settings are for our program in a certain period best. Fortunately, there is a tool for testing and optimizing incuded in the platform MetaTrader4. To open it, use a menu or the keyboard shortcut Ctrl-R. It will appear as another window under our existing ones. We can add the necessary data:

- **Strategy:** We choose our AOS, which we want to test.
- **Symbol:** Select a currency pair, whose data we need.
- **Model:** We have a choice of three options. If our strategy is simple or we will test only a short period of time, we can choose the most demanding complete test.

But let us equate, that testing can take many hours. Also, our computer system resources will be maximized. Therefore, if you need only approximate results and if possible immediately, choose one of the other options.

- **Use Date:** After snags, we can choose the length of time that has run through our testing. It is certainly useful to conduct testing in several different time periods. In order to ensure that our system is sufficiently robust and behaves correctly as this week, for example, in May last year.
- **Visual Display:** It will help us to monitor the response of our ATS on the chart, where we can test the speed adjust as it is necessary. By doing this graph, as well as the normal, which is shown in real time, we can also insert indicators. View of the plotted points reveals the reaction system, the place where the individual instructions were opened or closed. Monitoring thus created a chart, so we are able to detect defects on the system or to discover new opportunities.

Under the menu Properties strategy, we find adjustable ATS values. Values, that are both general settings, such as account size testing or its currency, but mainly optional parameters, that we have in the program labeled as "extern". In this part we will be quite a lot of work and in optimization.

Symbol Properties are frequently in the contrary, more or less informative sections, where we learn the details of the selected currency pair.

- The entry period test setup timeframe (TF), thus choosing the time frame in which our test run. We will use such TF, which we intend to use later as in real traffic (Klapuch 2011).

COMBINED TRADING SYSTEM

Now it is the turn of a different perspective on quality testing. Each ATS is intended for other uses therefore it is tested in several sections of various lengths of historical data. First, it is advisable to pass the greatest period of time. Test equity curve is usually non-linear.

The curve will select the areas that are significantly profitable, and sections that are unprofitable. We consider being profitable in the equity curve graph sections with rising and loss segments characterized by curve downward. When you look at historical chart on the course of prices, you will realize that most of the state of the market. Most often there are differences in volatility, the market is moving a trend or not "going to parties". So take advantage of these data, we have prepared for similar situations in the future. Let us optimize for these states recognized market value adjustment of these optimizations can be saved. When we notice on the chart similar signs of market status in the future, change the settings on our ATS respective values corresponding period. For example, when we find that the price is in trend fits probably get more value TP when the price goes contrary "to the side" Download TP to a lower value or use a strategy that just like the situation requires. It pays to have the appropriate tools at the right time.

Now, let us analyze our ATS. Turn off automatic size adjustment of the contract, we do not distorted results and perform a subsequent test and optimize a longer period. Do store the records, including the settings of the optional variables. Now, however, most of this test will use equity chart. Let us divide it into sections that are profitable, and sections that are either unprofitable or neutral. (Klapuch 2011)

To be able to individual sections designated in equity chart work, assign them to a real period in the price chart, we can shape according to the price chart in the future adhere to a reasonable adjustment of ATS.

Each of the selected areas now optimize and test separately, to then you will be able to select for each season the most appropriate setting. Results of optimization and testing may be stored in a table similar to the following. The table contains test results, and especially optimized values for optimal settings in the monitored chart.

Since it is a complex set of data, clearly not here to say that the parameters in certain market behaviors or zoom. The ideal is to set all the variables in the corresponding period, which corresponds to the current state of the market.

As we have said earlier, it is a matter of setting AOS largely intuitive. Particularly the identification of areas, that we have assigned to individual patterns of behavior chart, is quite challenging. Therefore, let us equate that system performance will practice a little lower.

But we can work with the size of the contract. If it is bind to the percentage of account size, we could also achieve interesting results. Consider then again the whole period that we have tested the size of the contract 0.1 LOT during initial deposit of $ 10,000. Now, the size will change dynamically. The other values we will let the same as for the overall assay.

As we could see, based on the contract size setting results after optimization really different. We must therefore choose the optimal benefit / risk ratio. Personally, I tend more to the cautious scenario, and I would rather avoid declines over 50% of the bill. We must also take account of the fact that they are optimized values. The actual performance of our ATS will be probably lower. This possible reduction in performance we can remedy by changing the optional variable in each period. However, it is a realistic assessment of individual risk, whether we accept a riskier option rather safer option, even at the cost of smaller profit. (Klapuch 2011)

EVALUATION APPROACH TO MANUAL VERSUS AUTOMATED TRADING SYSTEMS

Between the traders, there are two major directions. It is a discretionary trading, i.e. manual trading, where a trader based on their own experience and intuition to give instructions to the platform directly, or most of them create their own system of rules that, if possible, adheres to a disciplined manner. The second group of traders are supporters of ATS, whose experience is inserted into similar systems of rules and algoritmize them, or use systems which was programmed for them by someone else (Klapuch 2011).

REFERENCES

Beneš, V. (1993). *Bankovní a finanční slovník*. Prague: Svoboda - Libertas. (in Czech)

Klapuch, B. (2011). *Trading Orders Algorithm Development*. (Unpublished master thesis). University of Ostrava, Ostrava, Czech Republic.

XTB X-Trade Brokers Dom Maklerski Spolka Akcyjna, organizační složka. (2008). *Manual XTB-Trader*. Retrieved September, 09, 2010, from http://www.xtb.cz/ob-chodni_systemy/xtb_trader/navod_k_obsluze/XTB-TraderManual.pdf

KEY TERMS AND DEFINITIONS

Automated Trading Systems (ATS): A computer program that creates orders and automatically submits them to a market center or exchange. Automated trading systems and electronic trading platforms can execute repetitive tasks at speeds with orders of magnitude greater than any human equivalent.

Foreign Exchange (FOREX): Refers to the foreign exchange market. It is the over-the-counter market in which the foreign currencies of the world are traded. It is considered the largest and most liquid market in the world.

MetaQuotes Language 4 (MQL4): Integrated programming languages designed for developing trading robots, technical market indicators, scripts and function libraries within the MetaTrader software.

Chapter 6
Analysis and Classification Tools for Automatic Process of Punches and Kicks Recognition

Dora Lapkova
Tomas Bata University in Zlin, Czech Republic

Michal Pluhacek
Tomas Bata University in Zlin, Czech Republic

Zuzana Kominkova Oplatkova
Tomas Bata University in Zlin, Czech Republic

Roman Senkerik
Tomas Bata University in Zlin, Czech Republic

Milan Adamek
Tomas Bata University in Zlin, Czech Republic

ABSTRACT

This chapter deals with the pattern recognition in the time series. The data was obtained from the measurement of the force profiles via strain gauge sensor. This pattern recognition should help to classify different techniques of the professional defence (direct punch, direct and round kicks) and gender of the attacker. The aim is to find a suitable feature sets from the measured raw data which has to be transferred in appropriate way; in the case of this research spectral analysis or discrete cosine transformation were used. Based on the previous experience of authors, artificial neural networks with Levenberg-Marquardt training algorithm were selected as a classifier. In these experimentations, students from the Faculty of Applied Informatics, Tomas Bata University in Zlin participated. The results were successful and higher level than expected accuracy of 85% was achieved. The future plans include involving more participants and repeating the simulations to confirm the proposed technique.

DOI: 10.4018/978-1-5225-0565-5.ch006

INTRODUCTION

The field of pattern recognition is very extensive. This chapter will introduce pattern recognition in time series produced by measurements of the force exerted by punches and kicks. Punches and kicks are part of basic knowledge in professional defence, which is a field primarily focused on the legal protection of personal interests. It covers various areas - theory and practice of defence, attack and prevention, scientific disciplines such as tactics (e.g. skill in the counter attack), strategy (precautionary action) and operation (behaviour after a conflict situation). Moreover, it includes the knowledge of somatology and the chosen parts of crisis management, especially the phases of the conflict and solutions to conflict situations (Lapkova et al., 2012).

The kick and punching techniques are the most important and effective techniques in unarmed professional defence with significant force delivery. Various kick techniques are the subject of research investigation mostly for the needs of martial arts. (Gianino, 2010, Liu et al. 2000, Pieter and Pieter 1995).

The request for automatic recognition system arises with the complex situations every day. Such a system should help with the classification of persons during e.g. complex expert opinion for needs of legal proceedings. This chapter introduces an idea of classification gender, trained / untrained persons based on measured force profile dependent on the time. The importance of the impact force profile is discussed. Based on analysis, suitable set of features and / or any transformation applied on them are proposed to find out if it is possible to distinguish between classes during the automatic recognition. To uncover whether there are certain unique characteristics for professional defence techniques the artificial neural network (ANN) was chosen as a suitable classifier. According to the knowledge of authors, the research with the same approach of the measurement and obtaining of the feature set have not been applied yet. The reason for selection of ANN is a general experience of researchers who verified this technique as suitable for pattern recognition in time series. Also some statistics on the data sets will be performed out to help the data analysis.

In this long-term research, the participants from Tomas Bata University, Faculty of Applied Informatics, Czech Republic, were asked to perform a set of different punch and kick techniques on a measuring station. The impact force profiles were stored for further analysis.

Firstly, kick and punch techniques are explained. In the following paragraph, measuring devices, the method of data storage and experiment setup for measurement are described. Artificial neural network theory is depicted in the next section. Problem definition and consequent analysis are followed by result section. The conclusion summarizes the punch and kick techniques classification.

PUNCH AND KICK TECHNIQUES

During the data collecting, participants were asked to perform several punch and kick techniques - direct punch, direct kick and round kick.

Direct punch is based on energy which is transferred through arms, particularly through closed fist (Figure 1). This type of punch is delivered by the arm following a direct line. The aim is to stop the attacker and increase distance between the defender and an attacker. In the following experiment, the punch was delivered by the back hand (Lapkova et al., 2014 a).

The direct (Figure 2) and round kicks (Figure 3) are used to stop and keep the attacker in distance where the attacker cannot touch us. Another way of usage is to destabilize an attacker.

During the direct kick (Figure 2), a sole or a heel are the hit areas. This kick is made directly and by the shortest way to the target.

Figure 1. Direct punch

Figure 2. Direct kick

Figure 3. Round kick

Compared to direct kick, the round kick (Figure 3) uses an instep together with a part of shank as hit areas. The direct kick is considered to be stronger than the round kick.

MEASURING STATION

The sensor for measurement and collecting data is connected through the strain gauge into the computer which is used for data storage. The strain gauge type TENZ2334 is an electronic appliance that converts signals into suitable data format that can be stored in the computer memory. The core of the appliance is a single-chip microcomputer that controls all of the activities. The strain gauge sensor (L6E-C3-300kg - Figure 4) is connected to this appliance via four-pole connector XLR by four conductors. The number of values measured by the sensor calculates the averages of around 600 measurements per second while the data is immediately stored in the memory of a device with a capacity of 512 kB (Lapkova et al., 2012).

The mentioned above strain gauge sensor was placed on the measuring station according to the following schematic (Figure 5c). The whole measurement position is depicted in Figure 5a and schematically in Figure 5b. It consists of punching bag, punching bag base with strain gauge sensor, strain gauge TENZ2334 (the same as for the strain gauge sensor SRK-3/V) and camera for recording of the motion of measured persons.

During the measurement the target was positioned in such manner that the centre of the strain gauge sensor was in the height of 70cm for the cases of kicks and in the shoulder height of person who performed the punch. The person was made to stay at the same place for the whole experiment. Any unnecessary movement (e. g. lunge etc.) would lead to data distortion.

Figure 4. Strain gauge sensor L6E-C3-300kg

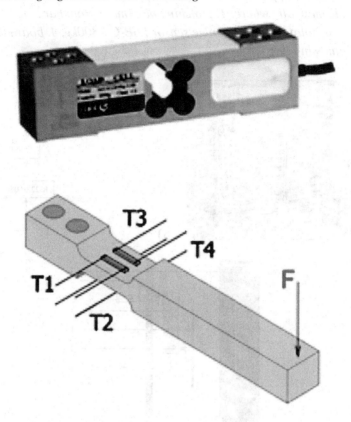

Compared to previous research, the advantage of this strain gauges sensor is his dimensions. The previous strain gauge sensor of the type SRK-3/V had the diameter 58 mm. The space was unsuitable mainly for the untrained and mid-trained persons. They were not able to hit the sensor in the middle because the diameter was too small. The standard deviation was marked.

For the current research, the strain gauge sensor L6E-C3-300kg was selected because of its dimensions 200x200x5mm. It is easier to hit it. Another advantage was observed in no dependence of the place where the pressure is given in the panel. The strain gauge sensor L6E-C3-300kg (Figure 4) works as propped bending beam. During force delivery the biggest deformation of sensor is in places with the thinnest walls – there are metal film of strain gauges which change their electrical resistance depending on deformation (Lapkova et al., 2014 a). Strain gauges are plugged in Wheatstone bridge which allow to convert difference of resistance to electrical signal which is possible to process further for analysis and / or classification task.

Figure 5. a) Measuring position, b) measuring position schematically, c) measuring station schematically where: 1. punching bag (made from hardened vinyl filled with foam), 2. template, 3. strain gauge sensor L6E-C3-300kg, 4. board (200 x 200 x 5 mm), 5. punching bag base

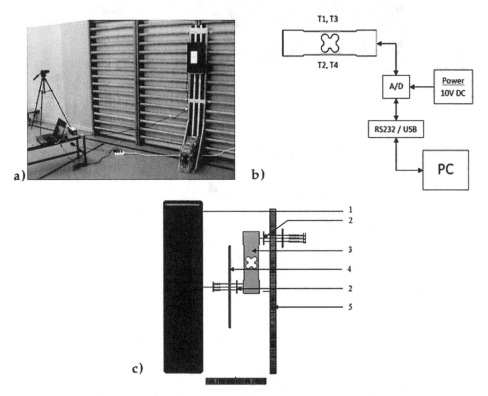

PARTICIPANTS OF THE EXPERIMENT

The research collects data for future extensive dataset and experiments in wider scale. Some persons were used on both tested measurement stations, some only on the second station. The results carried out through the second sensor are presented in this chapter. Currently, 220 participants took part in the experiment; 192 men and 28 women. All participants were in the age from 19 to 28. Most of participants come from our faculty (Faculty of Applied Informatics, Tomas Bata University in Zlin, Czech Republic). Unfortunately, the amount of women studying here is not as high as the number of men. Therefore, some experiments used only a subset from the collected data to have balanced training and testing sets of women and men.

Based on previous training and experience the participants were divided into following categories:

- **Untrained:** These people have never done any combat sport, martial art or combat system. They have no theoretical knowledge of the striking technique. The technique was presented to these people before the experiment for safety reasons. Noted further as *UTM or M1* (for men) and *UTW or W1* (for women).
- **Mid-Trained:** These people have the theoretical knowledge of striking techniques and do attend the Special physical training course for at least six months. The course is focused on self-defense and professional defense. Noted further as *MTM or M2* (for men) and *MTW* (for women).
- **Trained:** These people have attended the Special physical training course for two or more years or practiced a combat sport or martial art for the same time period. Noted further as *TM* (for men) and *TW* (for women). In some experiments for distinguishing of kicks, a special group of men were taken into consideration; men who play football regularly, they use a special kicking technique. The group has a label *M3*.
- **Self-Trained:** These people did practice or still do practice (for less than 2 years) some combat sport, martial art or combat system. As there is no guaranty on the quality of the training they are separated into a separate category. Noted further as *STM* (for men) and *STW* (for women).

The exact numbers of participants in each group are given in Table 1.

The subset for some experiments and its exact numbers of participants in each group is given in Table 2.

Table 1. The number of participants and samples in groups

Group	Number of Participants	Number of Samples
UTM	81	729
MTM	58	581
SM	37	361
TM	16	149
UTW	12	111
MTW	8	90
SW	2	20
TW	6	69
Total number	220	2110

Table 2. The number of participants in groups

Group	Number of Participants
M1	44
M2	32
M3	18
W1	9

The last used subset consists of 20 participants, 12 men and 8 women. In this case, none of the participants have ever done any combat sport, martial art or combat system. They had no theoretical knowledge of the striking technique. The technique was presented to these persons before the experiment for safety reasons. They were untrained men *UTM* and women *UTW*.

ARTIFICIAL NEURAL NETWORKS

Artificial neural networks are inspired in the biological neural nets and are used for complex and difficult tasks (Hertz et al., 1991; Wasserman, 1980; Gurney, 1997; Fausset, 2003). The most often usage is classification of objects as also in this case. ANNs are capable of generalization and hence the classification is natural for them. Some other possibilities are in pattern recognition, control, filtering of signals and also data approximation and others.

There are several kinds of ANN. Simulations were performed with feedforward net with supervision and Levenberg-Marquardt training algorithm (Fausset, 2003). ANN needs a training set of known solutions to be learned on them. Supervised ANN has to have input and also required output. ANN with unsupervised learning exists and there a capability of self-organization is applied.

The neural network works so that suitable inputs (features) in numbers have to be given on the input vector. These inputs are multiplied by weights which are adjusted during the training. In the neuron the sum of inputs multiplied by weights are transferred through mathematical function like sigmoid, linear, hyperbolic tangent etc. to the output from a neuron unit - node.

These single nodes (Figure 6) are connected to different structures to obtain different structures of ANN (e.g. Figure 7a and Figure 7b), where

$$\sum \delta = TF\left[\sum \left(x_i w_i\right) + bw_b\right]$$

Figure 6. A node model, where TF (transfer function like sigmoid), x_1 - x_n (inputs to neural network), b – bias (usually equal to 1), $w_1 - w_n$, w_b – weights, y – output

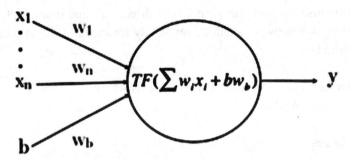

Figure 7. ANN models: a) with one hidden layer, b) with two hidden layers and more outputs

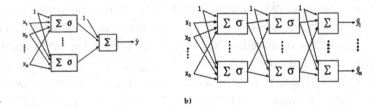

and

$$\sum = TF\left[\sum\left(x_i w_i\right) + bw_b\right];$$

TF means transfer function and logistic sigmoid function is used in this case.

EXPERIMENT DESIGN

In the past research, a direct kick and a round kick were classified via artificial neural networks (Lapkova et al., 2014c, 2014d). In these two cases, the artificial neural network was used to distinguish a gender and a training level of participants. In another paper (Lapkova et al., 2014a), authors achieved very good results in distinguishing between genders in the case of the direct punch.

This chapter summarizes the existing research and investigate the possibility of different set of input features for other classifiers used in future. The reason is to optimize the performance of classifiers as best as possible.

The chapter presents two experiments:

1. To distinguish between the techniques - direct kick and round kick.
2. To distinguish between genders, separately for cases of direct punch, direct and round kicks.

The following section shows the data analysis which has been done before experimentation with ANNs.

Data Analysis

For data analysis we used two pieces of software – Office Excel and MINITAB. MINITAB is software for statistical analysis and for creating graphs. Artificial neural networks were implemented in the Mathematica environment (currently also called Mathematica programming language produced by Wolfram Research company).

In this research, various dependencies are important for observing. The dependence of mean force on time for the punch is depicted in Figure 8a and Figure 8b. The Figure 8b is shortened part of the whole graph to depict the interesting part data recognition. These figures include all participants, the curves are the means calculated for each group: UTM, MTM, STM, TM, UTW, TMW, STW, TW.

Figures 9a and 9b show dependencies of mean force on time - men and women separately. The figures (Figures 10a, 10b, 10c, and 10d) compare dependencies of mean force dependent on time for each training level.

As can be visible from above figures, the data are very similar. In the case of Figure 10, women have always a weaker punch than men but in some category the difference is not as significant as authors would expect. Sometimes, to visualize only the mean force can lead to bad assumptions.

Figure 8. Dependence of mean force on time: a) whole graph, b) shortened graph

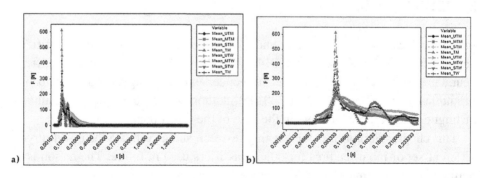

Figure 9. Dependence of mean force on time: a) men, b) women

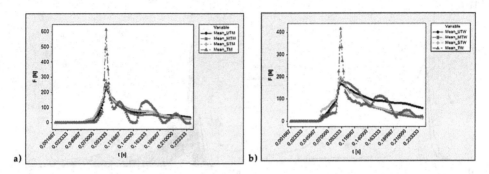

Figure 10. Dependence of mean force on time: a) untrained men and untrained women, b) mid-trained men and mid-trained women, c) self-trained men and self-trained women, d) trained men and trained women

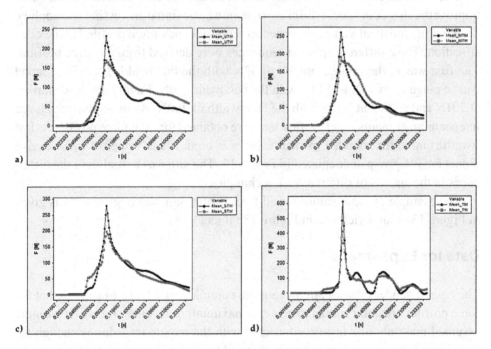

Data for Experiment 1

Also following figures for the case of round and direct kick classification designed in the experiment 1 can prove this. An example the mean force profiles for the W1 group are depicted in Figure 11a. The similarities of the main peak are clearly visible. However, the mean value may prove very misleading. In Figure 11b all collected

Figure 11. a) Mean force profiles – group W1, b) force profiles – round kick – group W1

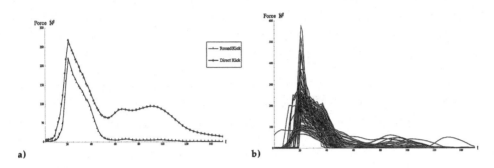

a)   b)

force profiles for the Round kick (W1 group) are depicted. There is high variety in the force profiles that makes the possibility of simple classification much harder. To improve the chance of successful classification a basic signal processing was applied.

A set of statistical values was used to represent each force profile for the classification. Three different spectral sequences were derived from the force profiles. The first was in the range from 3N to 53N with the bandwidth 10N. The second was in range from 73N to 133N with the bandwidth 20N. Finally the third starting at 201N and ending at 801N with the bandwidth of 200N. By this approach eleven integer number inputs for classification were obtained for each force profile. As last (twelfth) input the rounded median value was used. Mean values of these twelve inputs for W1 group are depicted in Figure 12. The aim was to highlight the differences in the signals of different kick techniques.

The example of input values for all force profile samples in group W1 is given in Figure 13a round kick and in Figure 13b direct kick.

Data for Experiment 2

The case of gender classification was more complicated. Figure 14a shows that the force profiles are quite similar except the maximum peak value. It may be wrongly assumed that only one feature connected with the maximum value is enough for distinguishing between round kick performed by men and women. In this case, the previously described transformation to spectral frequencies would not be enough. However, the true scale of the problem can be understood from Figure 14b where all collected force profiles for round kick are depicted (blue – men, red – women). It can be clearly seen that some kicks performed by men have lower maximum value than some kicks performed by women. Furthermore, the shapes of many force profiles seem to be very similar by naked eye. Such set of input features is not suitable

Figure 12. Mean classification input values – group W1

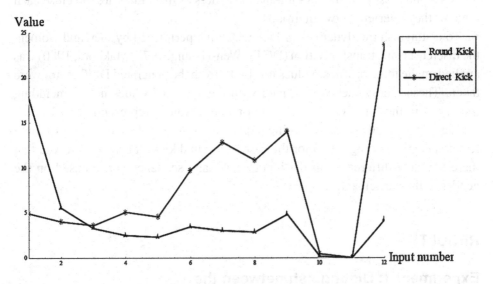

Figure 13. Classification input values: a) round kick – group W1, b) direct kick – group W1

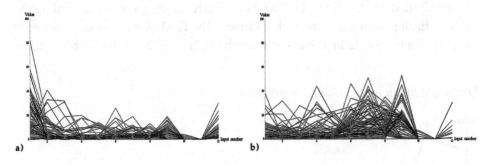

Figure 14. Force profiles for round kick: a) mean for men and women, b) all force profiles

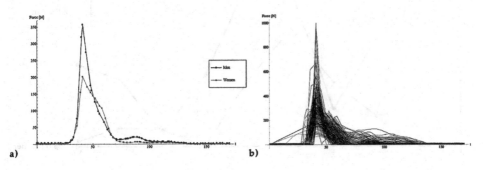

for ANN and most probably not for any classifiers as the values are too close each other or they interfere between groups.

To distinguish the dynamics of kick technique performed by men and women, the discrete cosine transformation (DCT) (Wen-Hsiung, 1977; Makhoul, 1980) was applied on the force profiles. Values no. 4 – 13 from the generated DCT vector were taken. These nine values were joined with the count of values no. 1 (including rounding) in the force profile. Thus ten numeric values representing each force profile were created and served as input data for the ANN. The mean value of input features is given in Figure 15 for the case of a round kick. It can be observed that there are clear differences in the input values and sequence shape based on the gender of the participant.

RESULTS

Experiment 1: Distinguish between the Techniques – Direct Kick and Round Kick

The simulations were performed with feedforward net with supervision and Levenberg-Marquardt training algorithm. The number of participants was given according the Table 2. Each person made the kick 10 times. The final number of kicks for each category can be visible in Table 4 in the column N_1+N_2. It can be visible that the

Figure 15. Mean input values – round kick

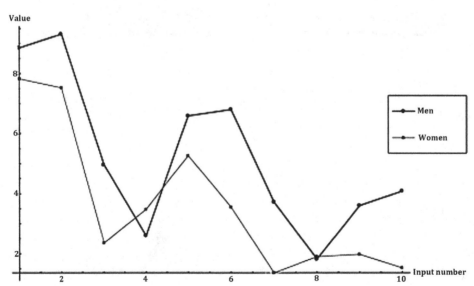

number of men was higher than number of women. The group of women was used only for basic comparison of gender. To generalize the results, the future plans will be aimed to have the same amount of men and women for each testing.

Two different methods of preparing the training and testing set were applied. Typically the set of samples was halved for this purpose. One halve was used as a training set. The other halve served as testing set. In the first approach (noted "a") all ten samples for halve of the participants in the group were used as the training set. The remaining samples were used for testing set. In the second approach (note "b") five samples for each participant served as training set and other five as the testing set.

Different settings of the number of iterations and number of neurons in the hidden layer were tested. The goal was to achieve a higher than 85% rate of successfully classified samples from the testing set. In this initial study the 15% fail rate was taken as acceptable mainly due to errors that occur during the physical measuring. However, the aim for future research is to improve the success rate significantly (up to 95% if possible).

The best results obtained for each group are presented in Tables 3 and 4. In Table 3, the final neural network setting for each training set is given alongside with Root Mean Square Error (RMSE) that is a typical measure of the quality of training process. Table 4 depicts the numbers of successfully classified samples (corresponding to results in Table 3). The obtained model was applied on training set and testing set to find out the absolute value of how many cases were classified correctly and how many incorrectly.

As can be visible from the Table 4, the results achieved at least 89% for the first strategy of training and testing sets creation and for both strategies if the women group is omitted. As mentioned above, the number of women was infinitesimally

Table 3. Final neural network setting and RMSE

Group	RMSE	Nodes in Hidden Layer	Training Iterations
M1a	0.197889	3	60
M1b	0.202538	3	60
M2a	0.172885	2	60
M2b	0.189389	3	20
M3a	2.02E-15	3	40
M3b	0.127763	2	40
W1a	0.255196	7	60
W1b	0.246739	2	30

Table 4. The number of successfully classified samples

Group	$N_1 + N_2$	RMSE	N_3	$N_{3\%}$	N_4	$N_{4\%}$
M1a	440	0.197	422	95.909	399	90.681
M1b	440	0.202	418	95	407	92.5
M2a	320	0.172	310	96.875	287	89.687
M2b	320	0.189	308	96.25	285	89.062
M3a	180	2.02E-15	180	100	165	91.666
M3b	180	0.127	177	98.333	170	94.444
W1a	80 + 100	0.255	76	95	91	91
W1b	90	0.246	83	92.222	74	82.222

Where:

N_1 – number of samples in the training set.

N_2 – number of samples in the testing set.

Note: Except W1a it applies that $N_1 = N_2$.

N_3 – number of successfully classified samples from the training set.

N_4 – number of successfully classified samples from the testing set.

small amount in this experiment. The percentage of the successfully classified items is higher than the specified goal. On the other hand, it is visible, that the division of samples for training and testing had an impact to the final classification success. It could be caused by the insufficient amount of participants.

Experiment 2: To Distinguish between Genders, Separately for Cases of Direct Punch, Direct and Round Kicks

As in the experiment 1, the training and testing sets were created by dividing participants from each gender group into halves. Thus the ANN is trained on force profiles of different participants than it is tested afterwards. The aim was to achieve the highest % of successfully classified samples from the testing set. An extensive tuning experiment was designed to investigate the effect of different number of nodes in the hidden layer and number of training iterations. The number of nodes in hidden layer was set up from 1 to 10 by step 1 and the number of training iterations was set up from 4 to 320 by step 20. The feedforward artificial neural network with Levenberg – Marquardt training algorithm was applied for simulations. The % of successfully classified samples from testing set was observed. The results of tuning experiments are summarized in Table 5 (direct punch), Table 6 (round kick) and Table 7 (direct kick).

The best results and corresponding number of nodes in hidden layer and number of training iterations are given in bold numbers; direct punch - 80 training iterations

Table 5. ANN tuning experiment results: Direct punch

N. / It.	40	60	80	100	120	140	160	180	200	220	240	260	280	300	320
1	57	57	57	57	57	57	57	57	57	57	57	57	57	57	57
2	48	52	52	53	52	53	53	53	52	50	54	57	57	56	56
3	65	65	65	66	65	65	64	64	64	63	63	64	63	63	63
4	63	66	65	65	67	67	67	67	69	69	69	67	67	67	67
5	62	64	60	56	57	57	56	64	64	64	64	63	63	61	61
6	59	59	61	61	60	59	55	53	52	51	51	51	51	51	51
7	65	65	63	62	62	63	67	65	63	62	62	62	63	63	65
8	50	53	54	56	56	56	56	56	55	54	54	53	54	53	54
9	66	66	**71**	71	66	67	68	69	67	66	68	63	62	61	62
10	55	55	56	56	58	58	59	58	57	59	52	50	49	49	49

Table 6. ANN tuning experiment results: Round kick

N. / It.	40	60	80	100	120	140	160	180	200	220	240	260	280	300	320
1	85	85	85	85	85	85	85	85	85	85	85	85	85	85	85
2	82	79	78	78	80	75	76	76	76	76	76	76	76	76	76
3	82	82	82	83	81	81	83	83	83	83	83	83	83	83	83
4	80	82	84	84	84	84	83	84	83	81	81	80	80	81	81
5	79	78	79	79	76	81	82	82	82	82	82	81	81	80	80
6	78	80	84	83	86	**87**	86	84	84	84	84	84	84	84	84
7	78	77	75	73	76	78	79	79	79	80	81	81	81	81	80
8	82	82	81	80	77	78	78	78	78	77	77	78	71	71	69
9	80	79	77	80	80	82	78	77	77	77	77	77	77	77	76
10	72	74	75	73	71	75	65	67	67	67	67	68	68	69	68

and 9 hidden nodes gives 71% success. The kicks produced better results; round kick – 140 training iterations and 6 nodes in a hidden layer gives 87% success, similarly for the direct kick – 60 training iterations and 1 hidden node achieved 86% success.

The best performing combinations of number of nodes in the hidden layer and the number of training iterations were analysed in more details, similarly as in the Experiment I. In the cases when the equal % successfully classified samples were observed the combination with less number of nodes in the hidden layer was selected. The structure with the less number of nodes is better from the complexity

Table 7. ANN tuning experiment results: Direct kick

N. / It.	40	60	80	100	120	140	160	180	200	220	240	260	280	300	320
1	74	**86**	86	86	86	86	86	86	86	86	86	86	86	86	86
2	85	86	86	86	86	86	86	86	86	86	86	86	86	86	86
3	82	82	82	82	82	82	82	82	82	82	82	82	82	82	82
4	83	83	84	84	83	79	82	84	84	84	84	84	84	84	84
5	71	72	73	85	84	82	84	83	84	84	84	84	84	84	84
6	77	79	77	75	80	82	78	77	77	77	78	79	78	76	76
7	73	77	77	79	79	80	79	78	77	79	77	78	77	76	76
8	78	83	83	83	83	83	83	83	82	80	80	80	79	80	77
9	81	82	82	85	84	85	85	85	86	85	85	85	85	86	84
10	74	73	74	76	77	79	81	82	84	85	86	85	85	85	86

and computational time point of view. The root mean square error (RMSE) was tracked and the number of successfully classified samples from both the training and testing sets were analysed. The final success percentage rates for both the training and testing sets for both kick techniques are given in Table 8.

Additional Statistics

The results from the experiments performed by ANN led to the idea that that some other features would be useful to implement. The following additional statistics was performed to find out suitable members for the input vector of features for classifiers.

The statistics was done by MINITAB which is useful software for statistical data analysis. In Table 9, results for each category of the direct punch measurement – especially mean of force, maximum force and standard deviation are shown. Table 10 is focused on maximum force and on standard deviation. As can be seen, the maximum values are more different between each group than the mean. Therefore, the future testing of ANN will use this additional input value and comparisons will be made.

Table 8. Success rate (%) overview

	Training Set [%]	Testing Set [%]
Direct punch	99	71
Direct kick	99	86
Round kick	100	87

Table 9. Results overview for each category: Direct punch

	Mean	St. Dev. of Mean	Coef. Var.	Maximum
UTM	23,148	48,08	240,59	233,76
MTM	17,522	44,512	313,25	260,37
STM	28,42	55,91	228,37	279,12
TM	27,75	88,92	499	612,7
UTW	15,17	36,157	265,72	169,9
MTW	20,76	45,779	254,28	192,09
STW	81,66	66,21	88,7	220,2
TW	40,78	78,56	256,9	415

Table 10. Maximum force for each category: Direct punch

	Maximum	St. Dev. of Maximum
UTM	233,76	82,23
MTM	260,37	122,96
STM	279,12	118,43
TM	612,7	202,9
UTW	169,9	33,87
MTW	192,09	31,21
STW	220,2	39,3
TW	415	223,6

As expected, the most visible differences are in the maximum value. These values are increasing as expected. If the kick is more trained, the maximum force is higher.

Table 11 and Table 12 show the same values for the direct kick.

Statistical data of the direct kick shows differences compared to the direct punch. The trend of the relation between the level of trained person and the level of maximal force is not obvious. In both groups of men and women, groups with higher maximal force are observed. Authors expected the insinuating dependency between the level of training and achieved maximal value of the force profile.

Table 13 and Table 14 shows the same values for the round kick.

As expected, group of self-trained men who plays football regularly has the highest maximal force. The differences between each category are higher than in the case of direct kick. It is surprising that also here the rule - the more trained the higher maximal force value - is not valid.

Table 11. Results overview for each category: Direct kick

	Mean	St. Dev. of Mean	Coef. Var.	Maximum
UTM	14,04	38,423	301,64	261,31
MTM	15,326	37,729	269,6	245,27
STM	20,904	45,13	182,5	269,89
TM	22,18	67,47	361,2	526,2
UTW	21,7	34,18	189,55	162,02
MTW	15,284	29,416	223,73	219,95
STW	29,91	38,8	142,48	157,89
TW	35,43	64,5	212,4	362,9

Table 12. Maximum force for each category: Direct kick

	Maximum	St. Dev. of Maximum
UTM	261,31	92,34
MTM	245,27	91,09
STM	269,89	106,34
TM	526,2	303
UTW	162,02	42,06
MTW	219,95	32,4
STW	157,89	15,75
TW	362,9	212,3

Table 13. Results overview for each category: Round kick

	Mean	St. Dev. of Mean	Coef. Var.	Maximum
UTM	30,799	83,32	289,8	410,2
UTM + football	34,03	84,7	256,71	386,2
MTM	24,867	81,54	349,93	455,4
MTM + football	23,601	80,6	360,27	470,9
STM	43,86	106,27	256,93	508,2
STM + football	79	172,69	239,4	766,1
TM	30,99	101,4	329,94	495,8
UTW	27,349	60,54	230,51	218,28
MTW	37,74	73,49	192,04	288,2
STW	34,5	63,44	198,7	215,29
TW	40,93	76,94	210,5	351,4

Table 14. Maximum force for each category: Round kick

	Maximum	St. Dev. of Maximum
UTM	410,2	211
UTM + football	386,2	185,7
MTM	455,4	196
MTM + football	470,9	181,4
STM	508,2	293,2
STM + football	766,1	257,7
TM	495,8	206,9
UTW	218,28	93,62
MTW	288,2	129,9
STW	215,29	29,88
TW	351,4	182,7

The question of the force dependence on the body weight and body height was studied too. But the results have not shown any marked dependence or tendency.

In all, it can be stated that for all techniques marked differences can be found between genders. Differences between groups based on the training level are not so demonstrable. The punches proved the expected dependency but the kicks did not. As mentioned above, the feature of maximum was useful for the direct punch. For the other techniques and also for the punch, authors will continue with analysis and looking for a suitable set of features that would increase the accuracy of the classifiers.

CONCLUSION

This chapter summarizes the existing research and investigate the possibility of different set of input features for other classifiers used in future. The reason is to optimize the performance of classifiers as best as possible. The chapter deals with the artificial neural networks design and testing in the task of different punch and kick techniques force profile classification together with the gender recognition. The goal of 85% successful classification rate was accomplished (in male categories) and except the case of direct punch classification where the rate was only 71% within the testing phase.

There have been however several difficulties during the training process. Firstly, the measured force profile had to be transferred into suitable feature set of the input vector. Employing the spectral analysis solved the first experiment. The second experiment had a worse position. The data preprocessing using discrete cosine transformation was suggested because the original measured data was not different between men and women. In both experiments, the aim was not only to find out if ANN is able to solve such a problem but also to find the suitable of ANN structure for future usage.

This brought a second difficulty, when the neural network exhibited very strong tendency to over fit, meaning that the higher success rate for training set lead to significantly worse success rate for the testing set. The finding of the balance between these two was the main issue during the neural network designing and learning process. The results presented in previous sections are very promising and encourage further research of neural network based classification of force profiles.

From promising results presented in this paper it can be stated that the ANN is a valid tool for this classification task as it managed to obtain better than 85% success rate for both experiments - gender and punch and kick techniques classification.

Nevertheless, the results obtained by ANN classification led to the idea to find additional suitable features. Some statistical data analysis was carried out. Based on the results, the maximal value of the force profile is useful only in the punch technique. The body weight or height did not show any marked importance for usage.

The results are based on measurements of persons (students) from the Faculty of Applied Informatics, Tomas Bata University in Zlin, Czech Republic. The future plans are to invite more people, not only from academic environment, to have a bigger representative sample and to confirm above described experiments. The following research will include implementing of artificial neural networks on more complex tasks like the classification of participant's gender and training level in one step and / or classification of higher number of different kick and striking techniques. Unfortunately, it needs to find appropriate persons from different levels of training.

ACKNOWLEDGMENT

This work was supported by Grant Agency of the Czech Republic - GACR P103/15/06700S, further by financial support of research project NPU I No. MSMT-7778/2014 by the Ministry of Education of the Czech Republic and also by the European Regional Development Fund under the Project CEBIA-Tech No. CZ.1.05/2.1.00/03.0089. Further, this work was supported by Internal Grant Agency of Tomas Bata University in Zlin under the project No. IGA/CebiaTech/2016/007.

REFERENCES

Blower, G. (2007). *Boxing: Training, Skills and Techniques*. Crowood.

Bolander, R. P., Neto, O. P., & Bir, A. C. (2009). The effects of height and distance on the force production and acceleration in martial arts strikes. *Journal of Sports Science and Medicine*. Available: http://www.jssm.org/combat/3/9/v8combat3-9.pdf

Fausett, L. V. (1993). *Fundamentals of Neural Networks: Architectures, Algorithms and Applications*. Prentice Hall.

Gianino, C. (2010). Physics of Karate: Kinematics analysis of karate techniques by a digital movie camera. *Latin-American Journal of Physics Education,4*(1).

Gurney, K. (1997). *An Introduction to Neural Networks*. CRC Press. doi:10.4324/9780203451519

Hertz, J., Kogh, A., & Palmer, R. G. (1991). *Introduction to the Theory of Neural Computation*. Addison – Wesley.

Lapkova, D., & Adamek, M. (2014a). Analysis of Direct Punch with a View to Velocity. In *Proceedings of the 2014 International conference on Applied Mathematics, Computational Science and Engineering*. Craiova: Europment.

Lapkova, D., Pluhacek, M., & Adamek, M. (2014b). Computer Aided Analysis of Direct Punch Force Using the Tensometric Sensor. In *Modern Trends and Techniques in Computer Science: 3rd Computer Science On-line Conference 2014* (CSOC 2014). Springer.

Lapkova, D., Pluhacek, M., Kominkova Oplatkova, Z., & Adamek, M. (2014c). Using artificial neural network for the kick techniques classification – An initial study. In *Proceedings 28th European Conference on Modelling and Simulation ECMS 2014*. Digitaldruck Pirrot GmbH.

Lapkova, D., Pluhacek, M., Kominkova Oplatkova, Z., Senkerik, R., & Adamek, M. (2014d). Application of Neural Networks for the Classification of Gender from Kick Force Profile – A Small Scale Study. In *Proceedings of the Fifth International Conference on Innovations in Bio-Inspired Computing and Applications IBICA 2014*. Springer International Publishing.

Lapkova, D., Pospisilik, M., Adamek, M., & Malanik, Z. (2012). *The utilisation of an impulse of force in self-defence*. In XX IMEKO World Congress: Metrology for Green Growth, Busan, Republic of Korea.

Liu, P. (2000). A kinematic analysis of round kick in Taekwondo. *ISBS-Conference Proceedings Archive, 1*(1).

Makhoul, J. (1980, February). A fast cosine transform in one and two dimensions. *IEEE Transactions on Acoustics, Speech, and Signal Processing, 28*(1), 27–34. doi:10.1109/TASSP.1980.1163351

Pieter, F., & Pieter, W. (1995). Speed and force in selected taekwondo techniques. *Biology of Sport, 12*, 257–266.

Wasserman, P. D. (1980). *Neural Computing: Theory and Practice*. Coriolis Group.

Wen-Hsiung Chen, , Smith, C., & Fralick, S. (1977, September). A Fast Computational Algorithm for the Discrete Cosine Transform. *IEEE Transactions on Communications, 25*(9), 1004–1009. doi:10.1109/TCOM.1977.1093941

KEY TERMS AND DEFINITIONS

Artificial Neural Networks: A technique of the soft computing area for solving complex tasks; in this case they are used for classification.

Kick: A part of basic knowledge in professional defence. The direct and round kicks are used to stop and keep the attacker in distance where the attacker cannot touch us.

Mid-Trained Men/Mid-Trained Women (MTM/MTW): Notation for the purpose of this research. These people have the theoretical knowledge of striking techniques and do attend the Special physical training course for at least six months.

Professional Defence: A field primarily focused on the legal protection of personal interests.

Punch: A part of basic knowledge in professional defence. Direct punch is based on energy which is transferred through arms, particularly through closed fist.

Self-Trained Men/Self-Trained Women (STM/STW): Notation for the purpose of this research. These people did practice or still do practice (for less than 2 years) some combat sport, martial art or combat system. As there is no guaranty on the quality of the training they are separated into a separate category.

Trained Men/Trained Women (TM/TW): Notation for the purpose of this research. These people have attended the Special physical training course for two or more years or practiced a combat sport or martial art for the same time period.

Untrained Men/Women (UTM/UTW): Notation for the purpose of this research. These people have never done any combat sport, martial art or combat system.

Chapter 7
Research on Processing the Brain Activity in BCI System

Jaromir Svejda
Tomas Bata University in Zlin, Czech Republic

Roman Senkerik
Tomas Bata University in Zlin, Czech Republic

Roman Zak
Tomas Bata University in Zlin, Czech Republic

Roman Jasek
Tomas Bata University in Zlin, Czech Republic

ABSTRACT

The basic idea of BCI (Brain Computer Interface) is to connect brain waves with an output device through some interface. Human brain activity can be measured by many technologies. In our research, we use EEG (Electroencephalography) technology. This chapter will deal with processing of EEG signal and its utilization in practical applications using BCI technology mentioned above. This chapter is organized as follows. Firstly, the basic knowledge about EEG technology, brain and biometry is briefly summarized. Secondly, research of authors is presented. Finally, the future research direction is mentioned.

DOI: 10.4018/978-1-5225-0565-5.ch007

INTRODUCTION

Linking the central nervous system with artificially created system is the main focus of authors' current research. Scientific research of this field began in 1970. First experimental implants, which were intended for people, appeared after years of experiments on animals in 1990. The original idea was designing appropriate compensations for damaged senses such as hearing, sight and movement; nowadays, scientific discipline called neuroprosthetics deals with this idea. With the recent progress in technologies, it was found that it is possible to assemble system without the necessity of direct connection with central nervous system. Electrical activity of neurons may be sensed by non-invasive method, which uses special electrodes. Pioneering researches show that real applications bring rather expansion of human funcionality than just its restoration.

Many laboratories and scientific teams around the world began to develop techniques, which deals with system control through the brain activity. This kind of technology is called BCI (Brain – Computer Interface) system and it is known as the interface between computer and the brain. (Pfurtscheller, 2000) One of the first comprehensively documented system based on BCI technology was BCI2000 platform. (Schalk, 2004)

Technology itself falls into several scientific disciplines. Firstly, there are several methods, which allow measurement of brain activity (ECoG, EEG, fMRI and BOL). It is obvious that most of knowledgement about human brain are based on medicine findings. Futher, signals or data have specific form; thus, it requires the utilization of methods from signal processing, physics and mathematics. Sample recognition should be processed by some artificial neural network. (Hazrati, 2010; Kaper, 2003; Lotte, 2007) Another key issue, which should not be neglected, is communication channel selection. It is important to use such communication channel, which is effective for data transfer. Last scientific discipline, which BCI technology uses, is algorithmisation. It can be use either for software or hardware part of the system.

The aim of whole BCI is the research on creation of new communication system, which translates human initiative into signals used to control external device. Many experts present states of signal processing and classification methods in (Blankertz et al, 2004). There are quite a few solvers in this specific field of study.

Brain activity is measured through BCI system. Further, specific properties of obtained signal are derived and transferred to signals, which are appropriate to control end device. Good example is Emotiv Corporation, which developed BCI interface for interaction between human brain and computer based on processing electromagnetic waves (EEG) from the human brain. (Emotiv, 2015)

Generally, interface offers wide range of possible branches in which BCI can be used; for example, in commercial sphere: interactive applications, intelligent adaptive environment, audio-visual art and design or automotive industry. Further usage is in medicine, robotics and last but not least usage is in scientific research. (Emotiv, 2015; Esfahani, 2011; Fabiani, 2004; Gao, 2003; Guger, 2003; Lal, 2004; Li, 2009; Del Pozo-Banos, 2014; Wolpaw, 2003)

Researches show that BCI system works well also in real time systems, where strict conditions have to be met. (Guger, 2000 - 2003)

Another possible area for utilization of BCI systems is in person identification. Genetic features in human electroencephalogram (EEG), which would be able to clearly identify individual subject, are the focus of scientific community since 1924, i.e. from early beginings of EEG signal acquisition performed by Hans Berger. Finding the right genotype – phenotype map would help to create a main and cheap tool for understanding and early diagnosis of many diseases; mainly those, which affect the brain. It would be taken as main tool, because it would be created on the base of quantitative measurement of EEG features, which are closer to gene function than traditional interpretation of congnitive testing. (Del Pozo-Banos, 2014)

Biometric systems, which use EEG as non-invasive and relatively saving "window" to the human brain, currently gaining interest of scientific community. However, the most of current scientific effort is focused on development of diagnostic and monitoring tools for diseases such as sleep apnea, schizophrenia or epilepsy; further focus is on creating so called Brain Machine Interface (BMIs), which assist to disabled people. (Del Pozo-Banos, 2014)

Potential of EEG signal for usage as one of biometric feature was proven n 2001 (Paranjape). This fact also proves other late publications, which describe mainly algorithms for biometric authentication. Each of yet developed algorithms solve mentioned issue in different way.

This chapter summarize current scientific knowledge in the field of control external system by using BCI technology. Further, it deals with possibilities of BCI system deployment in authentication systems.

RESEARCH BACKGROUND

Brain-Computer Interface

Brain-Computer Interface (BCI) is technology, which provides interconnection between brain and computer. This technology requires signals representing the brain activity and algorithm, which can process these signals so that they can be used in other specific applications; for example, control robot devices using brain activity or interaction with software application (Schalk, 2004). General principle of BCI technology is depicted in Figure 1.

Figure 1. General principle of BCI system

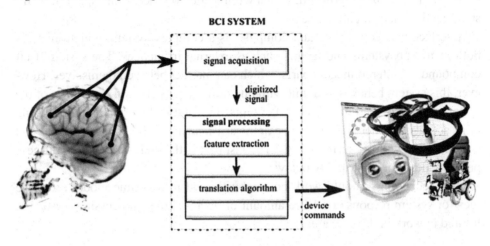

There are three basic approaches of sensing brain activity: invasive, partially invasive and non-invasive. Invasive methods require neurosurgery because of the need to perform implantation of sensors to gray cerebral cortex. With this method, it is possible to obtain brain signals in very good quality. However, the main disadvantage is propensity to expansion of scar tissue in the brain, which can lead to signal weakening or its loss.

Partially invasive systems are characterized by their division into the two main parts. The first is implanted inside the skull while the second is located entirely outside of the brain. A typical representative is ECoG (Electrocorticography) technology, which uses electrodes located directly on exposed surface of the brain. Electrodes location is performed using surgical intervention called craniotomy. Obtained signal is in better quality then in the case of non-invasive methods and it is also less sensitive to scar tissue formation.

Although the previous two approaches provide very precise signals, they still requires surgical intervention to either skull or brain. This issue absents in non-invasive methods, which includes EEG (Electroencephalography) or fMRI (functional magnetic resonance imaging) technology. On the other hand, it is necessary to be satisfied with significantly less accurate signals, which are usually affected by unwanted noises; in case of EEG technology they are caused by the passage of signal through the bone tissue.

Common technical applications usually use non-invasive methods of sensing the brain activity, especially devices based on EEG technology; therefore, the rest of this chapter deals with this kind of devices. Design of processing algorithm is complicated by nonstacionarity of EEG signal i.e. its characteristic properties vary with time. Moreover, these properties also depend on measured subject; thus, it is necessary to use such algorithm, which will be able to process the signal notwithstanding the issues mentioned above.

Interface between device and computer is a complex system, which includes both many subsystems and factors such as external influences. The system itself compounds of interconnected parts, which can interact between themselves. However, this system behaves as a unit with one or more properties. Description of the system can be divided into three larger units. The first is the brain and the sensing of its activity. Further is the interface or the artificial unit, which process inputs and communicate with its surroundings. The last part is the end device. Each of these parts are described separately below.

This technology should work both robustly and in real-time mode. From the view of system response on large amount of data and their processing, system is limited to work in discrete area.

EEG Technology

Basic functional unit of the brain is neuron. Human brain contains approximately from 10^{10} to 10^{11} neuronal cells. During its activities, these cells create electric and magnetic field (Paranjape, 2001). These fields are caused by the sum of electric signals coming from a flow of ions through neurons. The flow appears especially in cerebral cortex. Each electric activity of the brain is equivalent to specific external stimulus (eye blink, hand movement etc.).

Resulting electric field can be measured using electrodes located on the skull of the subject. Signal measured in this way is then called EEG (electroencephalogram). EEG record represents sum of electric activity in individual areas of the brain; thus, EEG is a record of temporal change of electric potential caused by brain activity. The record is obtained using standard non-invasive method for sensing brain activity of central neurvous system.

Deficiency of this method is summarization of neural signals. Each active synapse transmits electromagnetic pulse to the environment. Main source of signal for EEG devices is electrical activity of synapto-dendritic membranes located in surface layers of the cortex. Number of these pulses is in high orders. Moreover, their precise localization cannot be realized by just several electrodes located on the head of the subject.

Activity of EEG signal is usually sensed in four basic channels:

- Alpha (8 -13 Hz),
- Beta (14 - 30 Hz),
- Theta (4 - 7,5 Hz),
- Delta (0,5 - 4 Hz).

Signal, which is obtained from the sensor, is amplified and filtered using digital filter before its processing. The main reason is presence of unwanted artefacts in biological signal itself. Design of digital filter is significantly affected by the fact, that applied filter has to be computationally fast enough and also sufficiently accurate.

Electrodes on the skull are usually distributed according to standard positions, which are defined by international 10 – 20 system (Homan, 1987) or by its modification (MCN – Modiffied Combinatorial Nomenclature) (Oostenveld, 2001), which is intended for measuring more precise EEG signal from higher number of electrodes. Numbers from the title of the system refers to the fact that real distance between neighboring electrodes equals to 10% or 20% from the whole width or length of human skull. Both systems bring a methodics of naming positions of individual electrodes.

The name of each position consists of two parts. First part refers to specific parietal lobe using letters: F – frontal, T – temporal, C – Central, P – parietal and O – Occipital. There is no central lobe in the brain; thus, letter C is used for identifications purposes only. Letter markings use also a letter A, which refers to electrodes located on imaginary center line; more specifically, it is an area around auricle. Moreover, there are also defined positions with Pg (area around nasopharynx) and Fp (area around frontal region of the brain) mark. Second part specify brain hemisphere using numbers; even numbers (2, 4, 6, 8) indicate a position in the right hemisphere, while odd numbers (1, 3, 5, 7) are intended for determinating position in the left hemispehere.

MCN system describes new positions, which are always located exactly halfway between positions described in the original 10 – 20 system. Distances between these new positions are the same as they were in case of origin ones i.e. 10% from the whole distant between endpoints of subject's skull. New positions required several changes in the marking of individual locations. While the number part was extended only by the number 9 for the left hemisphere positions, the letter part required more significant changes. Positions are marked using two letters, which indicate two original positions between which the new position is located; for example, FC area is located between frontal (F) and central (C) area. The only exception is AF, which refers to area between Fp and F. Moreover, four locations from the original 10 – 20 system had to be renamed because of MCN system purposes. This change is related to positions T3, T4, T5 and T6 which were renamed to T7, T8, P7 and P8.

Electrical activity of the brain is measured from each electrode. Voltage level of this activity moves from units to hundreds µV. However, obtained signal is unsteady and its statistical properties depend on both specific subject and specific position of electrode.

Authors use device from Emotiv Corporation (Figure 2) to measure EEG signal for the purposes of their research. Distribution of electrodes of this device is depicted on Figure 3 according to methods described above.

Following biological artefacts has to be considered during signal processing:

- **Artefacts Caused by Eye Movements:** Eye generates electric dipole in its movement. Therefore, very high amplitude occurs in the measured signal. Athough it seems like disturbing element in the signal processing, it is well usable for the needs of BCI applications.
- **Artefacts of Heart Activity:** Signal with the frequency of heart contraction also occurs in EEG record. However, signal amplitude is very low. Signal waveform looks like a tip, which is one of the main factors pointing to epilepsy.
- **Artefacts Caused by Muscle Activity:** The cause is electric field generated by muscle contraction. It is probably the most common phenomenon occure in EEG records.

Figure 2. Emotiv EPOC neuroheadset

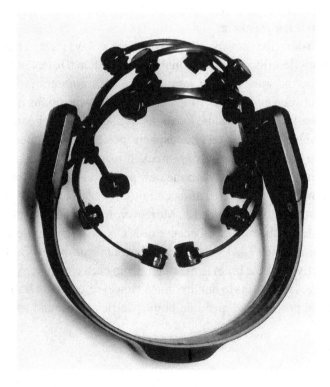

Figure 3. Electrode distribution on Emotiv EPOC neuroheadset device

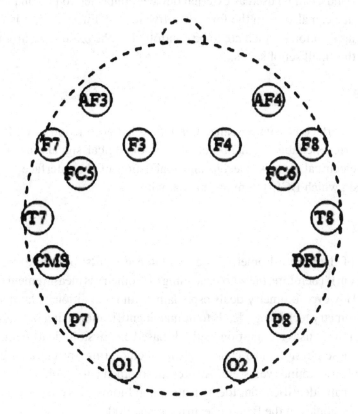

Brain

Brain is one of the most complex structure in known universe. In the context of complex systems, it is taken as organic nervous system. There are few commercially available devices intended for reliable measuring of brain activity. The most common and the user-friendliest method is non-invasive EEG technology. Other methods were also briefly metioned above. It is also possible to combine these methods to obtain higher accuracy of the measured signal.

Even if the wide spectrum of data obtained from the brain may be used in many realizations, it is not easy to understand of significance of the whole signal even in cases, where the proportion of noise is minimal. (Lotte, 2007)

External Device

The letter C from BCI abbreviation does not have to be taken as personal computer only. Currently, any device with the processor, which is possible to control by the set of commands, can be used as external devices connected to personal computer. Eternal device can also be in the form of software tool. First of all, it is necessary to add that applications, which are to be controlled by the brain, are currently often limited by the small set of states.

Interface

The whole interface is usually realized on the higher abstraction level. It connects seemingly irreconcilable elements: analogous biological signals and artificially generated electrical signals. Design and realization of the interface is given by specific task, which BCI system has to deal with.

Biometry

The bases of the term "Biometry" are two Greece words: bios (life) and metron (measurement). Therefore, the whole meaning of biometry is measurement of a living organism. However, biometry deals especially with recognition of human characteristics. Biometry technology leads to human identification using his unique body properties; thus, it uses recognition methods based on physiological characteristics. Currently, these physiological characteristics include fingerprint, hand geometry, handwriting, iris, retina, veins etc. At present, biometry technology becomes the basis of security identification. Identification and biometric systems are extensive and discussed topics in the field of security. (Rak, 2008)

Each living form in known universe consists of complex structure. The situation, where two or more organic structures would coincide with each other, is extremely unlikely. The identification process is based on the recognition of physical characteristics of a person; therefore, the most significance usage of biometric methods is in applications, where the unique identification is required. It is mainly about applications connected with either secure authorization to secure system or determination of correct identity. The most common usage of biometry is for access to buildings (respectively to the network with sensitive information), identity checks or data protection.

Verification means confirmation of accuracy. Firstly, sensing of necessary physiological characteristics and creation of reference profile is performed. Secondly, sensed sample is compared with template during verification process. Finally, the result of the whole process is agreement (access allowed) or disagreement (access rejected). That is all what biometry performs in verification process.

To compare with the sample, it has to be found a template in database according to the identifier assigned to a user and then comparison with actual measurement can be performed. Result is unambiguous and it should be immediate; thus, it requires direct connection with both database and sensor or with other computers.

The database of templates is initialized by sensing samples under administrate's access or during creation of new user account. The sensing should be performed more times to avoid future issues with verification.

Sensing the Biometrical Data

Hardware devices ensure scanning of analog real input (image, thermal, voice, chemical etc), which has to be converted to digital representation of binary data. This phase of biometric identification is the most vulnerable to errors. Firstly, a specific sensing device can cause inaccuracies due to the discretization of measured data. Secondly, the ambient noise (for instance dusty or scratched sensor) may affect the measured signal. Further, another issues may occur with authorized person, e.g. unintentional corruption of scanned sample of organic body. In the case of fingerprint, using of secondary thermalsensor, which is able to detect whether the object is alive, usually solves this issue or not.

The most common biometric properties, which are used for identification purposes, are listed below together with the brief description of what is measured. (Rak, 2008)

- **Fingerprint:** Structure of papillary lines and their details.
- **Handwriting Dynamics:** Differences in pressure and speed of writing.
- **Face Geometry:** Dimensions of specific face parts and distances between them.
- **Iris:** An image of the iris pattern.
- **Retina:** Vein structure on eye background.
- **Hand Geometry:** Palm and fingers dimensions.
- **Vein Structure on the Wrist:** Vein structure.
- **The Shape of the Ear:** Dimensions of visible part of the ear.
- **Voice:** Tone and timbre of the voice.
- **DNA:** String of deoxyribonukleon acid.

Data Representation

Database does not contain the scanned data in its entirety (for instance the whole pixel array of image), because it would consume too much memory. Moreover, it is also undesirable to store redundant or similar part of binary sequency. Therefore, only parts of the whole sample, which are substantially different from others, are stored to the database.

When saving data to remote computer, the process is not limited by the size of the memory, but the whole saving process has to be protected against undesirable penetration into the system from the outside. However, this is not the task of biometry. The main task is to choose right settings of security of both encrypted communication and physical data in local storage.

The Use of Biometrics

Power of biometrics is not in confidentiality of information used for authentization, but in uniqueness of this information. The latest biometric technologies allow automatic, quick and reliable identification of human person. Moreover, identity verification, which is based on biometry, offers significantly higher security level than tranditional methods, because it uses unique characteristics, which are constant over time and it is not possible to forge and steal them.

There is a wide spectrum of application of biometric authentication: access to working station or notebook, acces to internet network, login application, data protection, remote access to resources, transaction security and server security. Confidence in these electronic transactions has crucial importance for healthy growth of the global economy. Biometric authentication can be used independently or it can be integrated with other technologies such as smart card, encryption keys, digital signatures or classic passwords. Usage of biometry for personal verification becomes more advantegous and more precise than other current methods; for example, usage of password or PIN. The reason is that biometric features bring unique connection between event and specific person. Moreover, they can provide unique records.

Further alternative method of identification, which is closely related to biometry, is usage of EEG sensor. Current research examines usability of EEG for wide spectrum of applications such as RC model control, control movement of computer mouse cursor or development of applications based on audio – visual interactive environment.

Current Research on Authentication Using EEG Technology

Palaniappan (2008) describes biphasic method of biometric authentication, which uses EEG signals of these activities:

- Inactivity.
- Solving mathematical problems.
- Imagination of rotating object.
- Writing a letter.
- Visual counting.

Following features are calculated for each activity:

- Autoregression coefficients.
- Spectral power of the signal.
- Difference of spectral power of inter-hemispheric channels.
- Nonlinear complexity.

Whole authentication is carried out in two phases in which following two key authentication errors are eliminated:

- **FAE:** False Accept Error.
- **FRE:** False Reject Error.

Threshold values are calculated for each error type using the values of the mentioned features mentioned above. The threshold values determine the boundary between acceptance and rejection of submitted sample of data. Algorithm was tested using signals from six electrodes located according to international 10 – 20 system.

First phase decides about acceptance and rejection of scanned subject using the threshold for acceptance. In the second phase, the threshold value for rejection is used to detection of false accept or false reject of the subject.

Palaniappan's publication from 2007 presents also utilization of neural networks (Elman neural network) for classification phase. Described classification strategy was applied on 1600 raw EEG signals measured from 35 electrodes. Maximum recognition accuracy was 98,56%±1,87%.

Another publication, which presents algorithm intended for EEG biometry, show topicality of this theme. (Khalifa, 2012; Revett, 2012; Singh, 2012).

Despite the high number of described algorithms, identification of persons using EEG record is more complicated than was expected at the beginning of the research. It is caused by the fact that identification itself relies on information obtained from complex heterogeneous EEG features. These features are the result of elaborated models of inheritance, which are the reason why the whole problem of identification becomes very sensitive on its variables (time, frequency, place, sample record and algorithm). (Del Pozo-Banos, 2014)

Studies conducted to date, which deal with EEG, brain waves, biometry, person identification and verification, can be divided according to the approach to the issue to following categories:

- **REC a REO (Resting with Eyes Closed/Open):** Studies, which rely on EEG records of subjects, who are in the states of relaxation with close (REC) or open (REO). (Paranjape, 2001; Campisi, 2011; La Rocca, 2012)

- **ERP (Event Related Potential):** Obtained records always respond to subject reaction on different types of external stimulus. However, current studies realize only visual evoked potential (VEP). (Palaniappan, 2002; Palaniappan, 2004; Palaniappan, 2005; Signhal, 2007)
- **Multi-Tasking:** This category involves studies, which use EEG records obtained from intellectually consuming tasks; for example, solving mathematical problems, writing a letter or imagination of moving objects. Studies usually examine differences between waveforms of signals obtained from distinct activities. (Schalk, 2004; Palaniappan, 2005; Bao, 2009; Yang, 2012)
- **Indirect Identification:** Researches, which deal with identification of the subject-using password hidden in the thought. (Palaniappan, 2014; Yeom, 2013a; Yeom, 2013b)

Further issue is the technology of sensors, which are intended to sense brain activity. Even if this technology underwent a huge step forward, subject still has to touch the sensors. Moreover, instalation process of EEG equipment struggle with long time of preparation, which sometimes may require qualified expert. Therefore, the most of these equipment still rely on conductive gel, which is intended to reduce impedance between skull and electrode; this leads to obtain a better quality of signal. However, EEG technology can be considered as very promising security technology of the future. (Del Pozo-Banos, 2014)

RESEARCH ON BCI SYSTEM

This chapter contains description of authors' research, which, among others, revealed some issues with one of the most advanced EEG device intended for utilization in technology, but not in medicine applications.

Previous chapter summarized current knowledge of BCI systems, biometric systems and simulation of brain activity. Each topic is closely related with authors' research because it deals with the connection between biometry and BCI systems.

Due to the approach of authors' research, it was necessary to purchase equipment, which will be able to measure electrical activity of the brain also suitable for technical applications. Finally, it was chosen Emotiv EPOC neuroheadset, because it met all requirements of the research. The neuroheadset obtains EEG signal from 14 electrodes; thus, EEG record consists of 14 different channels. Distribution of electrodes on the skull corresponds to the description mentioned in the previous chapter. This device is able to communicate with computer during the technology of wireless data transmission. The basic software package allows user to view and save obtained records of brain activity. This allowed creating own database of EEG signals during the research. Further, these signal were intended for processing.

Results of performed analysis are mentioned in the further chapters. Signals of brain activity were obtained from volunteers. Activity, which was measured from each volunteer, is called idle state of mind. It means, that subject is asked to close eyes and then subject is instructed to not to think about something specific; thus, it corresponds to REC state mentioned above. During the measurement, it was also strived to eliminate undesirable sound stimuli, which could affect the shape of waveform of the final obtained EEG record. Then, these signals were subjected to correlation analysis. Moreover, response of BCI system to brain activity of facial expressions was also tested.

The research may be divided into the following phases:

1. The first acquaintance with the issue of BCI.
2. Purchase of headset measuring device and its first testing on the application provided by the manufacturer of the headset.
3. Measuring and recording of EEG signals.
4. Data parsing and processing in the Wolfram Mathematica environment.
5. Examining of correlation dependencies across all channels in the signal.
6. Searching classification parameters in the signal.
7. Purchase and compilation of robotic device and familiarization with the issue of control external system.
8. Programming and testing on the model of robot.
9. Development of own functional BCI model.

Phases 1 -3 represent the preparation to realization itself and exploration of this scientific field closely related to BCI technology. Further, phases 4 – 6 introduce fulfillment of the first aim of the study, which was signal verification and signal processing. Last phases lead to own design of BCI model described in the previous chapter.

The results of metioned phases of the research are described in the next chapters. Eventually, the research itself has two main parts. The first part deals with EEG signal processing with the purpose of utilization in biometric applications. The second part deals with development of software interface whose main purpose is to ensure real-time connection between input (headset) and external (robot) device.

SOLUTIONS AND RECOMMENDATIONS

Processing of EEG Signal

The purpose of authors' research was to prove whether EEG signal could be used in biometric systems; Due to that purpose, an analysis of EEG signal was performed. BCI technology was used for recording of measured data. Further, obtained data was subjected to correlation analysis in which similarities between individual signals of individual volunteers were investigated. Figure 4 contains results for three chosen volunteers (marked as subject 1 – subject 3). The same correlation threshold is set for all pairs of electrodes. Then it is count the number of similarities moving over the threshold. Obtained value is converted into percentage (marginal match). Values in the Figure 4 correspond to threshold value of 80%. Further, Figure 4 presents pair of signals for which the highest correlation was achieved together with specific subject and value of the correlation. Finally, the last column depicts the waveform of EEG signals. All values in the table were obtained for the length of 5000 samples (39 second). Although, each subject has the same laboratory conditions, the final results are significantly different between all subjects. Parameters may be use to biometric

Figure 4. Results of analysis performed for three chosen volunteers

Person	Marginal match [%]	Name of channels	Correlation [%]	Correlated channels
Subject 1	31.8681	{AF3, F3}	95.7985	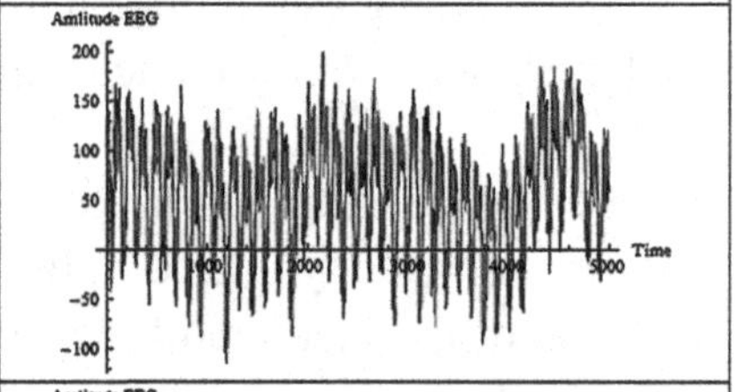
Subject 2	2.1978	{O2, P8}	81.7761	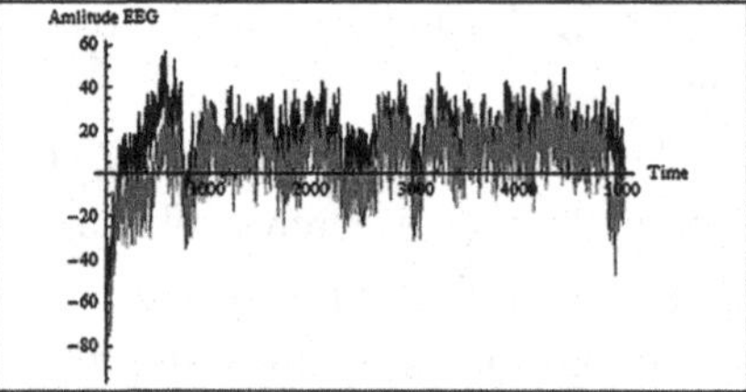
Subject 3	1.0989	{P7, O1}	87.9316	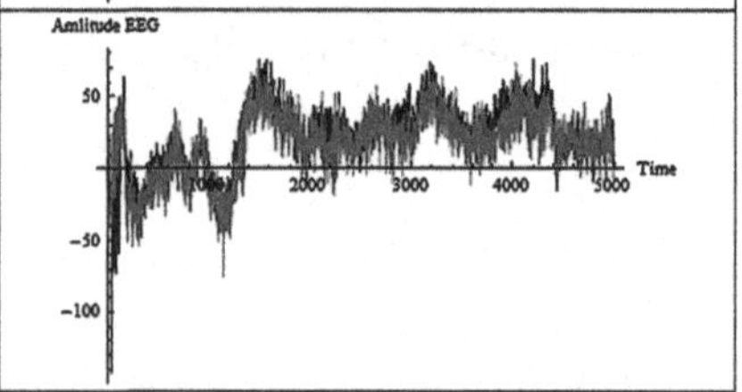

purposes, but it is necessary to perform more measurements with higher number of persons in which differences and regularities of individual statistical values could be revealed. Discovered regularities in signals of brain activity of dictinct persons would have to be proven with respect to EEG signal stacionarity.

The effect of signal length on the highest correlation value achieved between two signals was also investigated during correlation analysis. Firstly, the correlation was calculated for signal length of 1000 samples; it corresponds approximately to eight seconds of EEG record. Each additional calculation was then performed for signals, which were always about 1000 samples longer than the previous signal. Relation between signal length and value of correlation is depicted on Figure 5.

The aim of another correlation analysis was to determine how the value of mutual correlation between individual EEG signals change during the time. EEG records of calm state of mind were recorded from volunteers with a length of 25000 samples (195.3s). Again, values of mutual correlations were calculated between measured signals. This time, calculation is always performed for part of signal with the length

Figure 5. Dependency of highest correlation value on the length of the signal

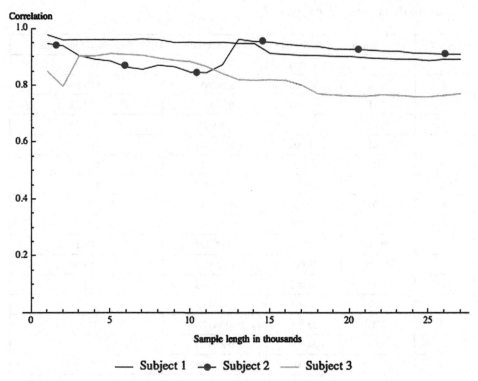

of 10000 samples (78.125s) with time offset of 1000 samples (7.8125s). An example of result of this analysis is given in Table 1 and Figure 6. Table 1 is the result of analysis for one volunteer and it presents parts of the signal for which the calculations were performed. Individual parts are bounded by initial (First sample) and end (Last Sample) sample. Further, it was searched value of the highest correlation (Max. correlation) and electrode positions (Position of electrodes) between which the correlation value was obtained. The table is supplemented by illustration of each electrode positions on the head of the subject. Highlighted positions are those, for which the value of highest correlation belongs.

Results were significantly different between individual subjects, even if all of them performed the same activity. While the first subject had the highest correlation between six different pairs of electrode during 16 partial section of the signal, the second subject always had the highest correlation between the same electrodes (O2, P8). Finally, the third subject exhibited another different behaviour. The highest correlation was found between these three pairs of electrodes: (P7, O1), (F3, P7) a (FC6, F8).

Table 1. Analysis results for subject 1

ID	First Sample	Last Sample	Max. Correlation	Position of Electrodes
1	1	10 000	0.952552	AF3 F3
2	1001	11 000	0.948659	AF3 F3
3	2001	12 000	0.950475	AF3 F3
4	3001	13 000	0.94621	AF3 F3
5	4001	14 000	0.946543	AF3 F3
6	5001	15 000	0.914729	P7 O1
7	6001	16 000	0.909592	P7 O1
8	7001	17 000	0.901304	P7 O1
9	8001	18 000	0.900297	P7 O1
10	9001	19 000	0.892232	AF3 T7
11	10 001	20 000	0.923422	AF3 F4
12	11 001	21 000	0.916445	AF3 F4
13	12 001	22 000	0.84772	AF3 F4
14	13 001	23 000	0.84772	T7 P7
15	14 001	24 000	0.839024	T7 P7
16	15 001	25 000	0.901458	T7 F8

Figure 6. Position of electrodes with the highest correlation for subject 1

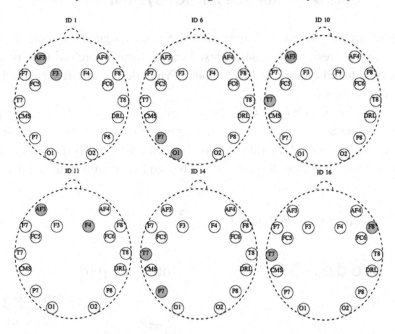

Another authors' research was aimed to eye blinking detection. This state can be recognized with the usage of universal signature database, which was created on the base of observation of similarities between brain activities of different subjects; for example, eye blinking is manifested by the similar waveform for the most people. Therefore, it was possible to create universal signature for this and many others activities such as eyebrow movement, mouth movement, eye movement idle state of mind, state of excitement, etc.) Database of these universal signatures is available within the software, which is a part of EEG equipment. The aim of testing was to prove a difficulty of realization the eye blinking, which can be recognized by the software based on the universal signature database. When the signature of eye blinking activity was used for activity detection, then the average value of reliability was 65.45%. Increase of reliability was achieved by the usage of open eye state signature. This case achieved 98% of reliability. The higher value of reliability may be caused by the fact that the open eye state is better recognizable than eye blinking state.

Results of analysis reveal possibilities of practical usage of EEG signal for person identification. Further reseach will focus on searching unique characteristics of EEG signal, which could be then used for person authentication in biometric systems.

Design of Software Interface for BCI System

The whole architecture of software interface was designed to achieve mutual compatibility between used technical resources. Scheme of architecture, proposed by authors, is based on essential BCI model. Principle of the software interface is described in Figure 7.

Parallelization was chosen due to the possibility of achieving real-time response from both (input and output) devices, thus, program functionality is divided into three individual threads. First thread is marked with the letter B (brain), because it ensures communication with the neuroheadset and it also listen to events, which

Figure 7. Architecture of BCI model

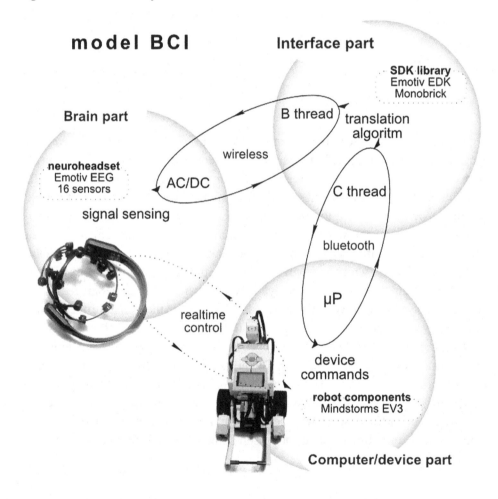

evaluates and returns discrete (for example true/false) state of brain activity. Analogously, thread C (computer or device) was implemented to monitoring the output device. Thread rutine switches control actions on output device with respect to states, which are transmitted between threads B and C. Time constants used in individual loops were chosen in hundreds of milliseconds. Firstly, signal changes were tested in neuroheadset simulator, which is able to communicate through network protocol. Later, prototype was designed a realized with the real devices; however, this prototype has to be subjected to thorough testing on all levels of its development.

Emotiv EPOC neuroheaset was chosen for measuring EEG signal. This device has many advantages, which involve solved elementary signal processing. Therefore, with its help, it is not necessary to work with raw data. The only question is the purpose of measured data utilization.

EPOC research edition offers software driver and elementary libraries for reading and processing of data obtained from the neuroheadset. Good demonstration example of library usage is initialization of connection with device (Computer Code 1).

EmoEngine itself is library, which contains settings and properties of Emotiv device. It is necessary to assign event listener, which can be used to reading specific input. Fifth row contains command, which ensures connection to the neuroheadset. It is possible to connect to the simulator with using method RemoteConnect("127.0.0.1", port_number).

Robotic construction kit Mindstroms EV3 was chosen as an output device. Variable robotic kits are quality and variable solution, which has versatile usage even for purposes of either simulation or research tests. The core of main component (called as brick) is programmable microcomputer with ARM9 processor with Linux operating system. Brick is able to receive inputs from field of electric sensors and it can be connected with common computer through USB interface, bluetooth or wireless Wi-Fi technology. Outputs are transmitted to motors, speakers or display which are part of this main component. The kit contains many passive and active parts such as girders, gears, axles, pins and other moving parts. It is possible to

Computer Code 1

```
EmoEngine engine;
engine = EmoEngine.Instance;
engine.EmoStateUpdated += new EmoEngine.EmoStateUpdatedEventHan
dler(EmoStateUpdated);
engine.Connect();
```

Computer Code 2

```
public void moveLeft() {
 speed = 30; // speed/power in percent
 brick.MotorB.Brake();
 System.Threading.Thread.Sleep(sleep);
 brick.MotorC.Brake();
 brick.MotorB.On((sbyte)-speed);
 System.Threading.Thread.Sleep(sleep);
 brick.MotorC.On(speed);
}
```

construct sophisticated robot, which is fully programmable on the level of languages such as C# a Java. (Garber, 2013)

Research of authors required assembly of robotic model and creation of programable support for flexible adding of functionalities. Finally, the control of robot itself is relatively easy, as can be seen in Computer Code 2.

This is an example of method *MoveLeft()*, which ensures the movement of robot to the left side. Source code contains commands, which handles the activity of motor component. It is necessary to add time constant (in unit of miliseconds) between sending commands to the ouput due to achieve smooth running of the process (see constant variable *sleep*).

The final application was subjected to tests in laboratory environment in which basic functionality was verified. The funcionalty involved ability of application to send commands to extern robotic device when eye-blinking acivity was recognized using EEG technology. The subject was able to decide when the robot should move and stop with help of eye blinking activity. This basic funcionality allows testing of proposed architecture of software interface with respect to reliability of communication between individual parts of developed BCI system.

FUTURE RESEARCH DIRECTIONS

Currently, authors continue with both directions of the research described above. The field of person identification using EEG signal will deal with searching of unique characteristics, which will be suitable for subject recognition. Further, research will continue with design of an algorithm, which will be able to use founded unique characteristics to recognize a finite set of subjects.

In the field of control external device using brain activity, the research will deal with extension of the software interface so that it could be used in practice applications. Application is not limited to one recognizable state (eye blinking), but on the contrary, it is possible to add many other brain activities. Everything usually depends on specific requirements of target group to which the application should serve. The aim is to develop such software interface or application, which will be possible simply modify to variety of user requirements.

CONCLUSION

The human brain is probably the most known adept to the most complex functioning system in known universe; therefore, it is natural to consider how it works and how it is possible to use its potential for ease of existence. Mentally healthy brain does not have to always interact with the surrounding world by all of its senses. Mainly a in the case of disabled person who's some of the senses may be damaged. If the body is damaged, it is possible to try to create artificial interface, which is not as perfect as natural one, but it is still suitable for filling the function of facilitation through the brain-computer-interface connection. The creation of such connection is primary aim of the whole work deal with BCI technology. Secondary and a little easier aim is to develop another interesting application intended to creative purposes. Even the beauty, art and entertainment has its place in the human life. Applications based on audio-visual interactive enviroments mainly motivate and relax from everyday reality. Another future use of complex BCI interface can be found in the field of robotics, control RC models or other external devices.

Historical facts, description of current researches and general knowledge about BCI were summarized in Introduction. Background chapter briefly summarize information about three key topics: EEG technology, BCI technology and biometry.

Current knowledge level of this scientific field was also reported at *Background* chapter. Complexity of authentication using EEG was illustrated on description of two-phase method principle. Certainly, this method is not the only available method. Currently, new approaches to solving biometric authentication based on EEG are formed. These methods usually use the principles of artificial intelligence methods, mainly neural networks. Further, approaches to verification and authentication based on character of used EEG record were summarized. Measurements of records called as REC (Resting with Eyes Closed) were performed during research of authors. Results of this research were also presented. Further, it is summarized the main aims of researches and it offers a list of performed studies dealing with this topic. The aims of authors' research were determined on the base of these studies. Direction of the research is evident from theoretical part, which describes basic principles of

BCI model. Aforementioned interface (I), which communicates with brain (B) and computer (C), is authors' own design of architecture.

Usage of EEG signal for biometric purposes is relatively new idea, which can find its application for example in genetics and clinical neurophysiology studies. EEG identification may rely on mainly the high quality and robustness. It would be more difficult to steal passwords due to the EEG based identification, because user would not be forced to perform any password revealing activities. If the password was stolen, it would be very difficult to reproduce it due to specific EEG samples unique for each person.

ACKNOWLEDGMENT

This work was supported by Grant Agency of the Czech Republic - GACR P103/15/06700S, further by financial support of Ministry of Education, Youth and Sports of the Czech Republic within the National Sustainability Programme project No. LO1303 (MSMT-7778/2014) and also by the European Regional Development Fund under the project CEBIA-Tech No. CZ.1.05/2.1.00/03.0089; and by Internal Grant Agency of Tomas Bata University under the project No. IGA/FAI/2015/063.

REFERENCES

Bao, X., Wang, J., & Hu, J. (2009) Method of Individual Identification Based on Electroencephalogram Analysis.*International Conference on New Trends in Information and Service Science*. DOI: doi:10.1109/niss.2009.44

Blankertz, B., Müller, K. R., Curio, G., Vaughan, T. M., Schalk, G., & Wolpaw, J. R. et al. (2004). The BCI competition 2003: Progress and perspectives in detection and discrimination of EEG single trials. *Biomedical Engineering. IEEE Transactions on, 51*(6), 1044–1051.

Campisi, P., Scarano, G., Babiloni, F., DeVico Fallani, F., Colonnese, S., Maiorana, E., & Forastiere, L. (2011, November). Brain waves based user recognition using the "eyes closed resting conditions" protocol. In *Information Forensics and Security (WIFS), 2011 IEEE International Workshop on* (pp. 1-6). IEEE.

Del Pozo-Banos, M., Alonso, J. B., Ticay-Rivas, J. R., & Travieso, C. M. (2014). Electroencephalogram subject identification: A review. *Expert Systems with Applications, 41*(15), 6537–6554.

Emotiv | EEG System | Electroencephalography. (2015) Available from: http://www.emotiv.com/

Esfahani, E. T., & Sundararajan, V. (2012). Classification of primitive shapes using brain–computer interfaces. *Computer Aided Design, 44*(10), 1011–1019.

Fabiani, G. E., McFarland, D. J., Wolpaw, J. R., & Pfurtscheller, G. (2004). Conversion of EEG activity into cursor movement by a brain-computer interface (BCI). *Neural Systems and Rehabilitation Engineering. IEEE Transactions on, 12*(3), 331–338.

Gao, X., Xu, D., Cheng, M., & Gao, S. (2003). A BCI-based environmental controller for the motion-disabled. *Neural Systems and Rehabilitation Engineering. IEEE Transactions on, 11*(2), 137–140.

Garber, G. (2013). *Instant LEGO Mindstorm EV3.* Packt Publishing Ltd.

Guger, C., Edlinger, G., Harkam, W., Niedermayer, I., & Pfurtscheller, G. (2003). How many people are able to operate an EEG-based brain-computer interface (BCI)? *Neural Systems and Rehabilitation Engineering. IEEE Transactions on, 11*(2), 145–147.

Guger, C., Ramoser, H., & Pfurtscheller, G. (2000). Real-time EEG analysis with subject-specific spatial patterns for a brain-computer interface (BCI). *Rehabilitation Engineering. IEEE Transactions on, 8*(4), 447–456.

Guger, C., Schlögl, A., Neuper, C., Walterspacher, D., Strein, T., & Pfurtscheller, G. (2001). Rapid prototyping of an EEG-based brain-computer interface (BCI). *Neural Systems and Rehabilitation Engineering. IEEE Transactions on, 9*(1), 49–58.

Hazrati, M. K., & Erfanian, A. (2010). An online EEG-based brain–computer interface for controlling hand grasp using an adaptive probabilistic neural network. *Medical Engineering & Physics, 32*(7), 730–739.

Homan, R. W., Herman, J., & Purdy, P. (1987). Cerebral location of international 10–20 system electrode placement. *Electroencephalography and Clinical Neurophysiology, 66*(4), 376–382.

Kaper, M., Meinicke, P., Grossekathoefer, U., Lingner, T., & Ritter, H. (2004). BCI competition 2003-data set IIb: Support vector machines for the P300 speller paradigm. *Biomedical Engineering. IEEE Transactions on, 51*(6), 1073–1076.

Khalifa, W., Salem, A., Roushdy, M., & Revett, K. (2012, May). A survey of EEG based user authentication schemes. In *Informatics and Systems (INFOS), 2012 8th International Conference on* (pp. BIO-55). IEEE.

La Rocca, D., Campisi, P., & Scarano, G. (2012, September). EEG biometrics for individual recognition in resting state with closed eyes. In *Biometrics Special Interest Group (BIOSIG), 2012 BIOSIG-Proceedings of the International Conference of the* (pp. 1-12). IEEE.

Lal, T. N., Schröder, M., Hinterberger, T., Weston, J., Bogdan, M., Birbaumer, N., & Schölkopf, B. (2004). Support vector channel selection in BCI.*Biomedical Engineering. IEEE Transactions on, 51*(6), 1003–1010.

Li, M., & Lu, B. L. (2009, September). Emotion classification based on gamma-band EEG. In *Engineering in Medicine and Biology Society, 2009. EMBC 2009. Annual International Conference of the IEEE* (pp. 1223-1226). IEEE.

Lotte, F., Congedo, M., Lécuyer, A., & Lamarche, F. (2007). A review of classification algorithms for EEG-based brain–computer interfaces. *Journal of Neural Engineering, 4.*

Oostenveld, R., & Praamstra, P. (2001). The five percent electrode system for high-resolution EEG and ERP measurements. *Clinical Neurophysiology, 112*(4), 713–719.

Palaniappan, R. (2004). Method of identifying individuals using VEP signals and neural network. *IEE Proceedings. Science Measurement and Technology, 151*(1), 16–20.

Palaniappan, R. (2005, December). Identifying individuality using mental task based brain computer interface. In *Intelligent Sensing and Information Processing, 2005. ICISIP 2005. Third International Conference on* (pp. 238-242). IEEE.

Palaniappan, R. (2008). Two-stage biometric authentication method using thought activity brain waves. *International Journal of Neural Systems, 18*(01), 59–66.

Palaniappan, R., & Mandic, D. P. (2007). EEG based biometric framework for automatic identity verification. *The Journal of VLSI Signal Processing Systems for Signal, Image, and Video Technology, 49*(2), 243–250.

Palaniappan, R., & Raveendran, P. (2002). Individual identification technique using visual evoked potential signals. *Electronics Letters, 38*(25), 1634–1635.

Palaniappan, R., & Revett, K. (2014). PIN generation using EEG: A stability study. *International Journal of Biometrics, 6*(2), 95–105.

Paranjape, R. B., Mahovsky, J., Benedicenti, L., & Koles, Z. (2001). The electroencephalogram as a biometric. In *Electrical and Computer Engineering, 2001. Canadian Conference on* (Vol. 2, pp. 1363-1366). IEEE.

Pfurtscheller, G., Neuper, C., Guger, C., Harkam, W. A. H. W., Ramoser, H., Schlogl, A., & Pregenzer, M. A. P. M. (2000). Current trends in Graz brain-computer interface (BCI) research. *IEEE Transactions on Rehabilitation Engineering, 8*(2), 216–219.

Rak, R., Matyáš, V., Říha, Z., Porada, V., Bitto, O., Daughman, J., & Šimková, H. (2008). *Biometrie a identita člověka-ve forenzních a komerčních aplikacích.* Grada Publishing, as.

Revett, K. (2012). Cognitive biometrics: A novel approach to person authentication. *International Journal of Cognitive Biometrics, 1*(1), 1–9.

Schalk, G., McFarland, D. J., Hinterberger, T., Birbaumer, N., & Wolpaw, J. R. (2004). BCI2000: A general-purpose brain-computer interface (BCI) system. *Biomedical Engineering. IEEE Transactions on, 51*(6), 1034–1043.

Singh, Y. N., Singh, S. K., & Ray, A. K. (2012). Bioelectrical signals as emerging biometrics: Issues and challenges. *ISRN Signal Processing,* 2012.

Singhal, G. K., & RamKumar, P. (2007, September). Person identification using evoked potentials and peak matching. In *Biometrics Symposium* (pp. 1-6). IEEE. doi:10.1109/BCC.2007.4430555

Wolpaw, J. R., McFarland, D. J., Vaughan, T. M., & Schalk, G. (2003). The Wadsworth Center brain-computer interface (BCI) research and development program. *Neural Systems and Rehabilitation Engineering. IEEE Transactions on, 11*(2), 1–4.

Yang, S., & Deravi, F. (2012, September). On the effectiveness of EEG signals as a source of biometric information. In *Emerging Security Technologies (EST), 2012 Third International Conference on* (pp. 49-52). IEEE. doi:10.1109/EST.2012.8

Yeom, S. K., Suk, H. I., & Lee, S. W. (2013a, February). EEG-based person authentication using face stimuli. In *Brain-Computer Interface (BCI), 2013 International Winter Workshop on* (pp. 58-61). IEEE. doi:10.1109/IWW-BCI.2013.6506630

Yeom, S. K., Suk, H. I., & Lee, S. W. (2013b). Person authentication from neural activity of face-specific visual self-representation. *Pattern Recognition, 46*(4), 1159–1169. doi:10.1016/j.patcog.2012.10.023

KEY TERMS AND DEFINITIONS

Biometric Authentication: Typy of system that relies on the unique biological characteristics of individuals to verify identity for secure access to electronic systems.

Biometric System: Technological system that uses information about a person (or other biological organism) to identify that person.

Biometry: A scientific field, which deals with scanning the physiological or behavioural characteristics of individuals.

Brain Computer Interface: Technology, which represents the connection of brain waves with the output device through some interface.

Electroencephalography: A non-invasive method of examining the electrical impulses of the brain using electrodes attached to the head and to a recording device to make an electroencephalogram.

Identification: The act of finding out who someone is or what something is.

Neural Network: An interconnected system of neurons, as in the brain or other parts of the nervous system.

Neuroheadset: An instrument which uses EEG technology to obtain signal of brain activity.

Real-Time: A data-processing system in which a computer receives constantly changing data and processes it sufficiently rapidly to be able to control the source of the data.

Chapter 8
Distribution Signals between the Transmitter and Antenna – Event B Model:
Distribution TV Signal

Ivo Lazar
Tomas Bata University in Zlin, Czech Republic

Said Krayem
Tomas Bata University in Zlin, Czech Republic

Denisa Hrušecká
Tomas Bata University in Zlin, Czech Republic

ABSTRACT

What we have solved: the possibility to receive DVB-T (Digital Video Broadcasting Terrestrial) with respect to local conditions for signal. We have deduced: variables that represent a set of so-called useful signal, i.e. the signal suitable for further processing – amplification and distribution. As a case study we have choosed few examples using Event B Method to show possibilty of solving komplex projects by this method. The resulting program can be proven to be correct as for its theoretical backgrounds. It is based on Zermelo-Fraenkel set theory with axion of choice, the concept of generalized substitution and structuring mechanismus (machine, refinement, implementation). B methods are accompanied by mathematical proofs that justify them. Abstract machine in this example connected with mathematical modelling solves an ability to receive DVB-T signal from the plurality of signals, both useful and useless for further processing.

DOI: 10.4018/978-1-5225-0565-5.ch008

INTRODUCTION

Multiplexing is apprehended as a combination of visual and audio signals that are spread through a common data channel via a device called multiplexer. The final combined data stream is then called "multiplex" (Handley, 2010).

The source data streams (PES – Packetized Elementary Stream) generated by video recorder or audio recorder are at first lead into a channel multiplex where they are united primarily with other data streams of supplementary data service into the primary multiplexer (VPS, WSS, teletext …) by means of DVB coder (Handley, 2010), (Digital Video Broadcasting, 2009).

In practise, a video recorder, audio recorder and primary multiplexer are formed by the only device called "DVB coder".

Output data stream (PS – Program Stream) (Handley, 2010) of primary multiplexer or more precisely of DVB coder is after lead into the secondary so called transport multiplex. This unites the streams of particular TV channels with the streams of supplementary service, such as e.g. EPG (electronic programme guide), intenteractive application and such, into a single stream that is called a transport stream (TS – TransportStream) (Kyuheon, 2010).

BACKGROUND

Standard receiving equipment for digital broadcasting means:

1. Revenue on fixed dish, receiver (digital TV, set-top box in conjunction with analog TV or PC) with a minimum of $30\,\mu VdB$ sensitivity (-77 dBm) connected by coaxial cable to a fixed receiving antenna (Czech Telecommunications Office, 2008).
2. The standard reception equipment for analog or digital television is also considered as a common TV antenna or cable television distribution group home, even if the receiving antenna array located outside the fed group home.

Measuring method:

- Measurement point instead of the measured reception of television signals, which are composed of one or more measuring points.
- Test kit for measuring the intensity of the electromagnetic field kit consisting of antenna, power and measuring device (spectrum analyzer).

The method used is based on empirical measurements of MERc (Modulation Error Ratio), Pre-BER (Bit Error Ratio before correction), Post-BER (Bit Error Ratio after correction), spectrum analyzer DREAMSKY TS-80 (Dreamsky, 2013).

Another method used for DVB-T is to create coverage maps by measuring the intensity of the electromagnetic field. The measuring point is determined by geographical coordinates in WGS84 system, or the address or description (DRAFT DECREE, 2008).

THE CHOICE OF AN ANTENNA FOR DVB-T RECEPTION

From the point of view of the need for remote reception of transmitters in the area of Strážnicko-Veselsko (county of Hodonín) from Austria(Vienna-Kahlenberg), Brno (Kojál), Mikulov (Děvín), Zlín (Tlustá Hora), Nové Mesto nad Váhom (Javořina) it´s necessary to use antennae with the biggest gain possible for a sufficient quality of recorded signals. With respect to this, antennae of YAGI type are a logical choice. Antennae of this type get a gain proportional to the size and number of elements (directors).

From this reason the broadband antenna of Iskra UHF-91X (Řezáč, 2010), (Wolff, 2006) with a gain of 14–16 dBi has been chosen and used. The base of YAGI antena is formed by a boom where the particular elements are placed:

- Director,
- Radiator (dipole),
- Reflector.

The antennae of this type have a directionality in the interval of 30–35 grades depending on vertical/horizontal polarization. This value is sufficient for capturing the signal from a few transmittors at the same time during the gain decrease approximately by 3 dB.

The general rule is, the bigger number of elements (directors, reflectors) is used the bigger gain we get. But this rule doesn´t apply generally in the sense of an excessive increase of elements – the excessive increase of elements would result in getting a less gain.

For example, YAGI antenna, which contains three elements with a relative gain of 5–6 dB, will increase the signal gain approximately by 2 dB when adding "a few more" elements, but with an excessive increasing of more elements we will reach the minimum increase of the signal gain (Wolff, 2006).

Figure 1. The relative diagram of the directionality intensity of the field

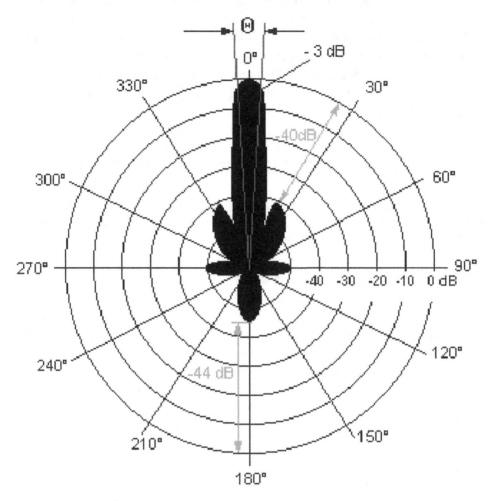

The same rule also applies in the case of the lenght of the antenna along the boom when the gain increase doesn´t compensate for the complications resulting from its further extension (Figure 1).

The ray width of directionality intensity of Θ field is the angle between two points (on the same level) in which the radiation drops to the "half capacity", that is 3 dB below the point of maximum radiation as pictured above.

DISTRIBUTION TV SIGNAL BETWEEN THE TRANSMITTER AND THE ANTENNA

The purpose of our work is to study and model the spread of DVB-T signal between the transmitter and the antenna using the Event B method and acquire new knowledge measurement.

The primary parameters of the antenna radiation pattern shown in diagrams usually depending on the azimuth (0–360 degrees) and elevation angle. Other important parameters are the beam angle, bandwidth, polarization, etc. Antenna gain is different from the amplifier gain because the antenna has no active circuitry and can therefore increase the signal strength. Antenna gain is measured in decibels, the shape of the radiated field differs from the ideal isotropic antenna (dBi unit). The ideal isotropic antenna transmits or receives evenly into (from) all directions, and of course in the real world, it can not be construct. Sometimes also compares the gain of a dipole antenna (isotropic ant.), Which can be already constructed and used as a reference.

The transmitter transmits a signal into ether with a certain frequency, modulation and power. Physical principles of electromagnetic spreading. waves in the case of digital video broadcasting (DVB-T) is the same as the analog. Reception range of the transmitting antenna (transmitter) is limited in proportion with its performance. Transmitter power is measured in ERP [W], the signal is distributed in a horizontal or vertical polarization (Procházka, 2009). On the receiving antenna signals fall with different polarizations, distant and close transmitters with different levels, quality and modulation. The receiving antenna must have sufficient earnings in [dBi] (to the isotropic radiator), directionality when profits decline by 3 dB directivity angle of 30–50°. YAGI antenna series COLOR and ISKRA need homogeneous electromagnetic. field, ie. fields, which are located in the reception location with no obstructions between the transmitter and the receiving antenna. It is always necessary to follow the rule that the antenna is the best "amplifier." Signals with a sufficient level μVdB and quality MER, Post-ber, captured by the receiving antenna ensures trouble-free TV reception from the perspective of other adjustments – merging, splitting and amplification. In practice, it is necessary to combine more leads antennas receiving signals from different directions. Each element, whether passive or active between the antenna and the TV receiver has a major impact on the quality of the signal (Figure 2).

The design of the antenna and its size affects signal reception directivity angle at the lower profits 3–5 dB can receive the signal of remote and local transmitters with different performance. The theoretical basis of the directivity angle while having no significant effect on the quality of the DVB-T except thresholds, compared

Figure 2. Minimal values of parametrers DVB-T

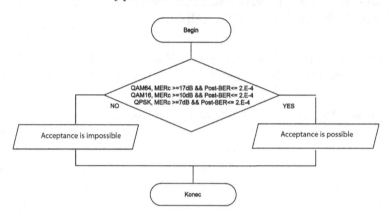

with the analog. We also found that the antennas Color, Iskra UHF91X have angled reflector, which reflects the signal from the opposite direction, in practice, measurements were found to be not quite. So in reflection acceptance in suppression (anterior-posterior ratio) as this parameter is expressed in tech. specification of the respective antenna is not in actual operation in the case of DVB-T is crucial (Řezáč, 2010).

Coverage Map gives coverage to the extent of income, but more important is to make measurements at the point of reception, because map does not reflect local conditions (antenna height above ground, hills, obstacles such. Built-up area…), should be taken into account terrain profile (Procházka, 2009).

The subject method of Event-B is an abstract mathematical modeling problem in the progressive refinement to achieve specific systems. We would like to show the possibilities of modeling DVB-T signals in this method compared to using the "B Method," which uses the method of operation.

Our example – DVB-T will address the range of signal from the transmitter in place of reception (Reception Area), which is distributed from different azimuths various transmitters in remote and local income. Physical principles of electromagnetic spreading. waves is in analog and digital broadcasts the same, but there are some differences. Signal level (its strength) in μVdB (dBm) may be in the case of digital reception of approximately 20 μVdB lower (56 versus 35 μVdB). Other parameters which indicate the quality of the signal before and after Viterbi correction Viterbi error correction and konstalece (QAM) have a significant impact on the possibility of receiving DVB-T (DRAFT DECREE, 2008).

It is always quality and μVdB, MER, Post-ber, captured by the receiving antenna ensures trouble-free TV reception from the perspective of other adjustments – merging, splitting and amplification. In practice, it is necessary to combine several leads antennas receiving signals from different directions. Each element, whether passive or active between the antenna and the TV receiver has a major impact on the quality of the signal (Sunrise Telecom, 2010).

By measuring the intake of very short wave shows that the electric field strength at the receiving location varies throughout the year and during the day. Slow fluctuations of the electric field due to the ongoing changes of meteorological conditions in the lower layers of the atmosphere. In spreading in visible distance the atmospheric refraction effects the phase relationships between the direct necessary to follow the rule that the antenna is the best "amplifier." Signals with a sufficient level of beam and the reflected beam from the ground, and thus also the resulting amplitude of the electric field. Regular changes in the strength of regular income is explained by changes in atmospheric refraction (day, night, winter, summer), irregular changes are explained by random changes in the weather (storms). When spreading beyond direct visibility is atmospheric refraction effect on the nature of bending and hence the absolute value of the electric field intensity at the reception location (Dreamsky, 2013).

In this paper we have presented a formal approach to modeling and analyzing prodcasting Band function using Event B. The abstract model of prodcasting is, done abstractly In the refinement of the abstract model, we introduced the notion of a prodcasting function.

The system development approach considered is based on Event B, which facilitates incremental development of complex systems. The work was carried out on the Rodin platform. In order to verify our broadcasting model, the initial and refinement model of prodcasting are developed by using Event-B, each model is analyzed and proved to be correct. Our experience with this case study strengthens our believe that abstraction and refinement are valuable technique for modeling complex system (Figure 3) (Hranac, 2007).

MODELLING THE PROPSAL RECEIVING SYSTEM DVB-T SIGNALS

When designing the entire system antennas for DVB-T, we must take into account each intermediate step. Design of a suitable type of antenna to receive up to the merger, amplification and split into STA sockets in the house. The slightest (even slight) change any part of the system has resulted influence on both quantitative and qualitative level of signal quality.

Mathematical model made in Event-B show us in what error values before Vterbi error correction (CBER), the error after correction (VBER) and QAM modulation error rate (MERC) will be realized income (Sunrise Telecom, 2010).

Figure 3. Conditions of accepteans DVB-T

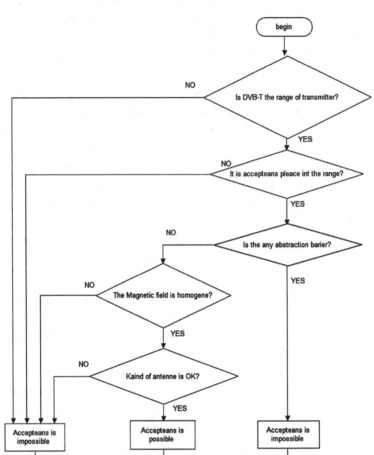

When merging the individual antennas downspouts, should must take into account the relevant channels and select whichever combiners defined for specific channels – selective band combiners (with suppression of other channels with a minimum interval of 2–3 channels) or continuous combiner (which "take" all channels) but at the cost of degrading the signal in parameter values MER, CBER and VBER due to unsuppressed very weak signals and noise and other signals propagated from different azimuths that the antenna is able to capture.

The signal that captured after the antenna combiner channel will be reinforced by continuous (line) amplifier for channels 1–60, which covers the VHF, UHF and FM. An important parameter for the selection of the antenna amplifier will be its gain and noise figure, further more, power and current consumption (DRAFT DECREE, 2008).

Due to the fact that FM is realized with an analog receiver, amplifier, selection will depend not only on the value of profits, but also on the possibility of covering the frequency range for the reception and amplification FM band – an important parameter is the size of the amplifier noise figure. Selecting a quality line amplifier is a necessary step in order to optimize the entire system DVB-T (Figure 4).

SOLUTION ABSTRACT MACHINE

The basic idea in the abstract machine is a design system for stable reception of DVB-T signal with respect to the used hardware components (antenna attenuation, combiner, amplifier, splitter), the key factor for stable income will be used quadrature amplitude modulation – the error rate for QAM 16,64 QPSK. Furthermore, the signal level [dBμV] and bit error rate after Viterbi correction (Post BER).

Abstract machine should be based on measured DVB-T parameters, based on the proposed technical solution in a subsequent mathematical description of Event-B in the progressive refinement (Figure 5).

The hardware elements have a major impact on these physical parameters (their level and error), as indicated by the measurement and comparison of the two different line amplifiers used. Line continuous amplifier was used due to amplification of all (and weak) signals throughout the UHF and FM band (Figure 6). It is a reasonable compromise in combination with the use of large YAGI antenna Iskra UHF91x big profit 14–16 dBi.

Figure 4. Solution the merger leads antennas

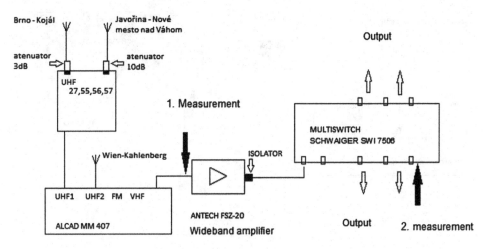

Figure 5. Solution the merger leads antennas

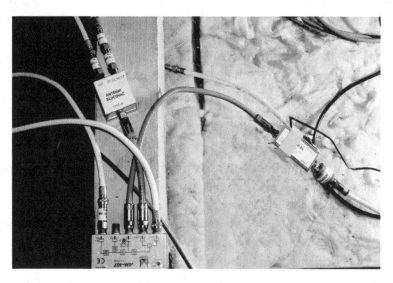

Figure 6. Schematic representation of the solution

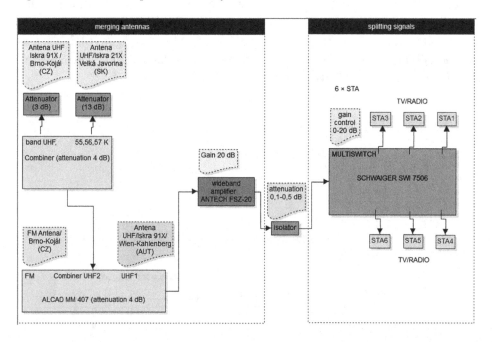

Expensive building amplifiers usually suppress weaker signals and process and amplify signals only with a sufficient level in range of transmitters. Our requirement in this solution aims to develop and strengthen the weaker signals from transmitters of different power (ERP) that are in place within the reception area.

As follows from the measurements, there is a big difference between the line amplifier – selectivity and amplification. Amplification is irrelevant in the case of DVB-T, quality plays a decisive role MER [dB]. Amplification at a high rate – more than 70 dB will be amplified noise also, which is undesirable and significantly affects the quality of the received signal. The quality of the amplifier used is affected by semiconductor elements (transistors with low noise) as well as with the design of the power supply with the possibility of crossover (after out-Coaxial) pass via a capacitor or via branching e.g. TONER with the separating capacitor.

Sold by set-top boxes and televisions now built-in DVB-T tuner signal levels are indicated as the percentage conversion [dB], as is the case with quality – that is determined by recalculating the value of the dipstick. Between DVB-T tuners there are greater or lesser difference in indication and signal quality.

Technological shift DVB-T is evident in several respects:

- In one DVB-T channels can be simultaneously streamed several television channels in Full HD quality in the respective QAM constellation.
- Signal reception in the site is not directly affected by interference from external local sources, which would be reflected "snow and ghosts" in the picture.
- Signal level plays a crucial role and minimum value measurable stable reception is approximately 16 to 20 dB lower in comparison with analog in favor of the DVB-T (56 µVdB analog versus digital 35 µVdB) ("DRAFT DECREE," 2008).
- When you use a quality splits and divorces STA is signal attenuation is within 1 dB and had no major impact on the receipt and processing of DVB-T tuner.
- **Disadvantage of Digital Reception:** Consists in the so-called. Cliff effect when exceeding the minimum required for stable measurable levels (below 35 µVdB), usually occur before error correction and after correction Procedure 1E 10^{-2}, and reception in comparison with analogue is basically impossible when the image "snowing", but the reception was tracked (DRAFT DECREE, 2008), (Czech Telecommunications Office, 2008).

PARAMETER MEASURING OF CONSTELLATION DIAGRAMS IN PARTICULAR DVB-T SIGNALS

Between analogue and digital television there is a significant qualitative difference in the sense of "purity" of the TV picture without "snow." With the transition to digital television it is true that there has been reduced some demands on the received television signal – its level, but on the other hand, the capturing and processing of the DVB-T signal, in the edge zones of the reception range of the transmitter, is without these minimum levels quite difficult, and there then appears a so – called "kostečkování" (in Czech) – the phenomenon known as the Cliff effect.

The actual signal DVB-T and its incidence according to coverage maps at the reception location does not guarantee that a particular multiplex will be detected and tuned by a DVB-T tuner. Not only the distance of the reception of the signal from the transmitter and its performance plays a key role, but also the terrain relief, whether a densely populated area with high-rise buildings, or various (hardly identifiable) interference sources, etc.

Another situation occurs when we receive signals from distant transmitters on the outskirts of potential reception, or if we receive a signal from a nearby transmitter distant only a few kilometers away from the reception site.

In the first case, we can hardly do without the large type of YAGI antenna with high gain in dBm (dBμV), and wideband amplifier and measuring the signal level in dBμV. In the second case near the transmitter it will be sufficient to have an omnidirectional antenna with a small profit, or simply a dipole.

Sold by set-top boxes and televisions now built-in DVB-T tuner signal levels are indicated as the percentage conversion [dB], as is the case with quality – that is determined by recalculating the value of the dipstick. Between DVB-T tuners there are greater or lesser difference in indication and signal quality.

FREQUENCY SPECTRUM OF DVB-T

The multiplex channel consists of a frequency of 8MHz, the multiplex is radiated by a frequency spectrum of IV and V of the television band. One multiplex (MUX) with four to six TV programs by the analog television (ATV) took four to six discrete channels of 8 MHz. For this reason, all the MUXs are operated only in IV. and V. band on channels ranging from 21 to 69, with respective frequencies of 474–858 MHz. TV bands I. to III. are not used, thus eliminating the use of large antennas (DRAFT DECREE, 2008).

The Czech Radiocommunications calculated the using of the frequency spectrum in the 474–826 MHz (21 Ch to 65 Ch), with the 61 Ch to 65 Ch being used for experimental broadcasts (DRAFT DECREE, 2008).

Transmitters of public programs MUX1 and transmitters of commercial programs MUX2, MUX3, MUX4, including MUX7 regional broadcast to 60 Ch.

LEVELS OF ANALOG AND DVB-T SIGNALS

The minimum signal level required by the system to receive DVB-T is approximately 35 dBμV at 75 Ω impedance of the antenna with a minimum signal / noise ratio 20 dB in the case of an ideal environment. In practical terms, this requirement corresponds to the equivalent of a minimum intensity of the electromagnetic field of 44 dBμV at a height of 10 m above the ground. In comparison with analog, wherein the counting of the 56 dBμV at the minimum signal / noise ratio 23 dB, the difference is about 12–20 dB higher in favor of the DVB-T.

Fewer demands on the level of DVB-T signals is achieved mainly due to the higher sensitivity and lower noise figure and high quality of TV receivers, set-top boxes.

Antenna gain of these reasons, and the only significant parameter in the covered DVB-T signal.

From the consumer's perspective there is an important difference between receiving analog and digital television, which will take effect when installing and adjusting the antenna reception quality picture and sound. For analog TV with poor reception, which was characterized by a speckling image improved by better routing and location of the antenna, increasing profit – in proportion to the noisy gradually disappeared. Each incremental, positive or negative step was reflected in the quality of picture and sound.

The expected success depended on the capture of one of the "starting signále" close reach of the respective transmitter in the intended reception. This circumstance was to facilitate the analog TV to gradually improve reception is poor in income terms to the optimum, which unfortunately did not guarantee a perfectly clear picture, but the reception was satisfactory for viewing with a slight "snow."

The principle of digital television does not switch from "no" to a good income, and vice versa – is steep. Due to weather conditions or various signal interference from multiple sources at the receiving antennas or power, even a slight change in position of the antenna, the signal strength decreases and the stable TV reception suddenly "freezes" or there begins the "Cliff effect" and gradually disappeasr – and the screen goes black. These are the socalled Cliff effect accompanying DVB-T.

MODULATION ERROR RATE (MER)

It is one of the quality parameters of the DVB-T

For 64-QAM modulation, which is used in case of Czech and Slovak MUX is the required minimum value of 22 to 24 dB, the optimal value is $\geq$ 25 dB.

16-QAM modulation correspond to values lower MER 15–19 dB, optimally $\geq$ 19 dB (Antech s.r.o., 2010).

Higher demands MER if 64-QAM is the number of bits required for transmission, wherein the transmission of one bit is needed to two states (log 0, log 1). The n bits are needed m modulation states according to the following formula:

$$m = 2^n$$

The main advantage lies in the multistate modulation bandwidth (the reserve), or vice versa, with the same bandwidth, it is possible to increase the baud rate.

Multistate modulation has the disadvantage that the signal becomes more sensitive to interference and more difficult to identify the symbol. Therefore, they are also subject to higher demands on the quality of the transmitted and received signal is required and a larger signal to noise ratio at the input of the demodulator in comparison with simpler modulation (Table 1) (FSK, PSK, etc.) (Vlajič, 2010).

In addition, modulation error rate (MER) is an important measurement of other values DVB-T signal:

- The level of signal reaching the maximum level at 40–80 dBµV antenna.
- **CBER:** Bit error rate before correction (2.0E-3) and a lover.
- **VBER:** Bit error correction ($\leq$ 2.0E-4) is closely related to CBER.
- Envelope (spectral analysis) DVB-T signals.
- Impulse response (echo) when the transmitter and signal reception occurs obstacle, such as a hill, etc.

Table 1. Parameters of particular modulations in required distance S/N

Modulation	4QAM (QPSK)	16QAM	32QAM	128QM	256QM
Number of states	4	16	32	128	256
Number of bits per state	2	4	5	7	8
Max. transmission speed [Mbit/s]	56	112	140	196	224
Real transmission speed [Mbit/s] s. Bandwith Occupancy 1,2 without FEC	47	93	117	163	187
Required distance of S/N v dB on demodulator without FEC for error rate 10E-6	13.6	20.4	23.5	26.4	28.4

In particular, the values of CBER and VBER depends stability of signal reception. From the measurements and the practical operation of DVB-T for three different STB from different manufacturers, it was found that all captured channels showed a steady income without downtime except K 46 (Sunrise Telecom, 2010).

AUSTRIA MUX

MUX1 propagated from the transmitter Kahlenberg Wien–distributed from 24 channels without any problems detected 120 km from the transmitter towards the Czech inland (Figures 7 and 8 and Figures 9 and 10). 16-QAM modulation is used, which has a "less demanding" when MERC (measurement has been empirically determined that sufficient range of 18 dB) (Procházka, 2009).

MUX2 propagated from the transmitter Kahlenberg Wien – propagated from channel 34 is no problem detected 120 km from the transmitter towards the Czech

Figure 7. The signal covering
Wien, Ch. 24.

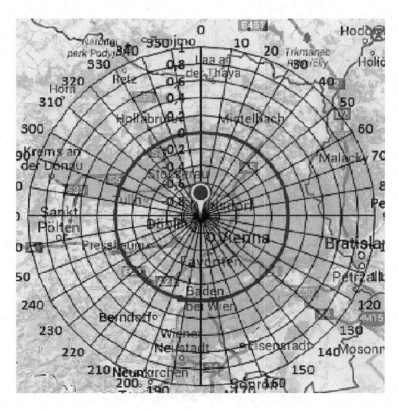

Figure 8. Constellation diagram
CBER a MERc Ch. 24.

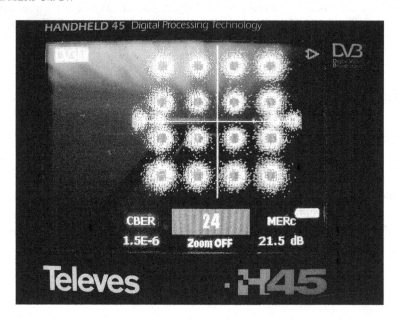

Figure 9. The signal covering
Wien, Ch. 34.

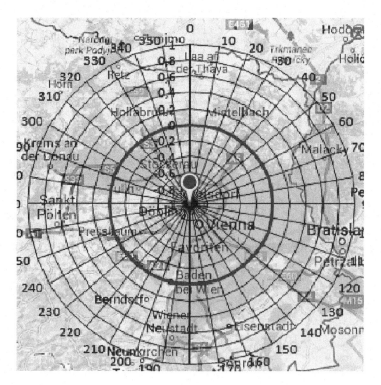

Figure 10. Constellation diagram
CBER a MERc Ch. 34.

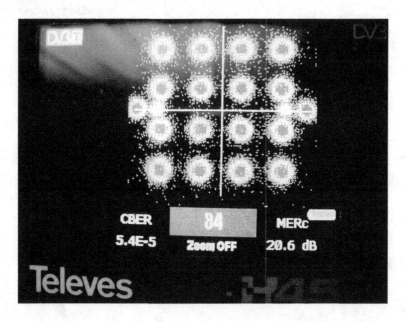

inland. As in the first MUX 16-QAM modulation is used. The signal has a "slightly" worse parameters before Viterbi error corrector and MERc, but it is good enough for remote reception at a distance of approximately 120 km from the transmitter (Procházka, 2009).

Bit error rate before correction CBER reaches values of 1.5E-6, respectively. 5.4E–fifth (Antech s.r.o., 2010). These values guarantee a stable income from even a distance of over 100 km from the transmitter.

From Velka Javorina Slovak transmitter antenna system transmitter does not transmits too much signal to Moravia and Silesia, is inhibited by approximately 25–35 dB (Figures 11). This limitation is clearly seen from the radiation patterns in the channels 55, 56 and 57 in a clear directionality toward western Slovakia.

Radiating power of individual transmitters due to the distance the signal reception falls on the very edge of the possible income (from 25 to 100 km) as the crow flies. Were therefore used large YAGI antenna with high gain (12–18 dBi).

For all Czech MUXs enough two antennas, looking toward the Brno–Kojál and Wien–Kahlenberg. On the other above antenna comes from the "other side" of the MUX Uh. Fort–Rovniny and Zlin–Thick mountains. The directors are angled toward the Hodonin–Kaplansky and town Skalica for Slovak (Slovak regional channel MUX), then Kahlenberg Wien–horizontal directivity to 37° (Figures 11 and 12).

Figure 11. The directivity of the signal from the transmitter Velká Javořina

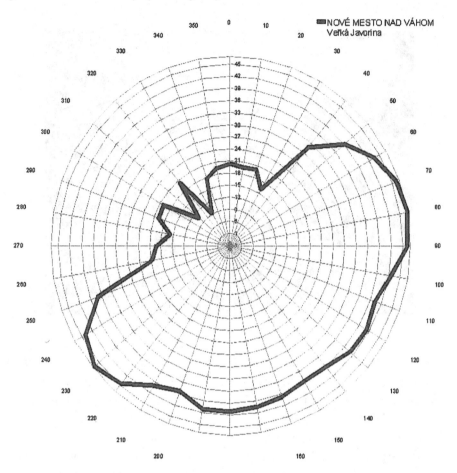

LIST OF TRANSMITTERS AND CAPTURED INDIVIDUAL CHANNELS

23: Transmitter Javořina, Nové Mesto nad Váhom, Czech coded programs MUX4, vertical polarization, Pay.

24: Transmitter Kahlenberg Vienna, Austria MUX1, horizontal polarization.

25: Transmitter Zlín – thick mountain MUX3.

29: Transmitter – Devin Mikulov, Czech MUX1, horizontal polarization.

33: Transmitter Zlín – fat hora, Czech MUX1, horizontal polarization.

34: Transmitter Kahlenberg Vienna, Austria MUX2, horizontal polarization.

Figure 12. Angle directivity antennas

It is possible to receive the signal coverage range?
It is in the reception area coverage?

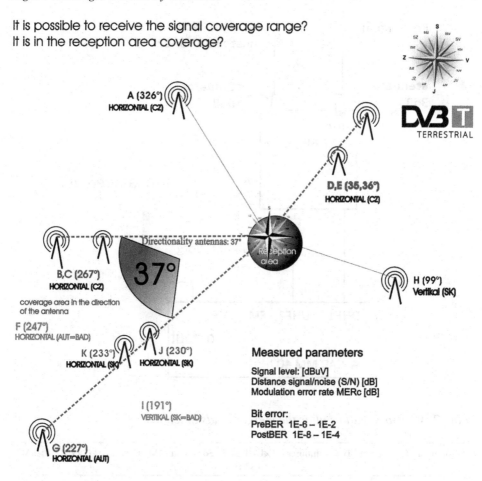

Measured parameters

Signal level: [dBuV]
Distance signal/noise (S/N) [dB]
Modulation error rate MERc [dB]

Bit error:
PreBER 1E-6 – 1E-2
PostBER 1E-8 – 1E-4

35: Sklalica transmitter (local MUX), Slovakia.
40: Transmitter Brno – Czech Kojál MUX2, horizontal polarization.
41: Transmitter Uh. Hradiště – Rovnina, Czech MUX7, horizontal polarization.
42: Transmitter Uh. Hradiště – Rovnina, Czech MUX4, horizontal polarization.
46: Transmitter Hodonín – Kaplansky, Czech MUX4, horizontal polarization.
49: Transmitter Zlín – fat hora, Czech MUX2, horizontal polarization.
55: Transmitter New Town n / weighting Javorina, Slovak MUX1, vertical polarization.
56: Transmitter New Town n / weighting Javorina, Slovak MUX2, vertical polarization.
57: Transmitter New Town n / weighting Javorina, Slovak MUX3, vertical polarization.
59: Transmitter Brno – Czech Kojál MUX3, horizontal polarization.

Figure 13. Merging the three leads two combiner

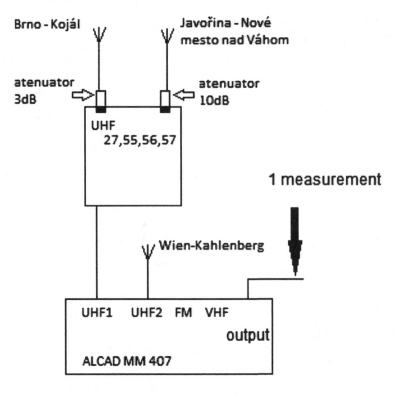

Table 2. Measured values after the merger leads antennas

Merging the Three Leads Two Combiner – 1×UHF 27,55,56,57 and MM407 ALCAD (2×UHF, 1×FM, 1×VHF)						
Channel	Modulation QAM	MERc [dB]	Level [dBµV]	Pre-BER	Post-BER	Pozn.
25	64	28	39	5,4E-5	1,0E-7	Zlín transmitter Tl. Hora (angle directivity antenna)
29	64	26	43	3,8E-5	1,0E-7	Brno Kojál transmitter (angle directivity antenna)
33	64	29	45	7,62E-5	1,0E-7	Zlín transmitter Tl. Hora (angle directivity antenna)
40	64	28	44	7,6E-6	1,0E-7	Brno Kojál transmitter (angle directivity antenna)
41	64	23	29	8,6E-4	1,0E-7	Regional transmitter Uh. Hradiště (angle directivity)
42	64	23	30	7,4E-4	1,0E-7	Regional transmitter Uh. Hradiště (angle directivity)
46	64	25	35	3,5E-4	1,0E-7	Regional transmitter hodonín (angle directivity)

continued on following page

Table 2. Continued

Merging the Three Leads Two Combiner – 1×UHF 27,55,56,57 and MM407 ALCAD (2×UHF, 1×FM, 1×VHF)						
Channel	Modulation QAM	MERc [dB]	Level [dBμV]	Pre-BER	Post-BER	Pozn.
49	64	19	31	1,41E-2	1,0E-7	Zlín transmitter Tl. Hora (angle directivity antenna)
23	64	24	30	1,53E-3	1,0E-7	New city n.Váhom Javořina – coded, vertical
57	64	29	46	2,28E-5	1,0E-7	New city n.Váhom Javořina – vertical
56	64	29	44	6,1E-5	1,0E-7	New city n.Váhom Javořina – vertical
55	64	28	42	1,51E-5	1,0E-7	New city n.Váhom Javořina – vertical
34	16	16	16	1,29E-3	1,0E-7	Wien Kahlenberg 2MUX, AUT
35	QPSK	10	11	3,5E-3	1,0E-7	Regional transmitter Skalica (SK)
48	16	5	10	1,45E-1	7,1E-3	Regional transmitter Holíč nad Moravou (SK)
24	16	22	26	1,52E-4	1,0E-7	Wien Kahlenberg 1MUX, AUT
59	64	25	37	2,47E-3	1,0E-7	Brno Koját transmitter (angle directivity antenna)

Figure 14. Gain and split signals

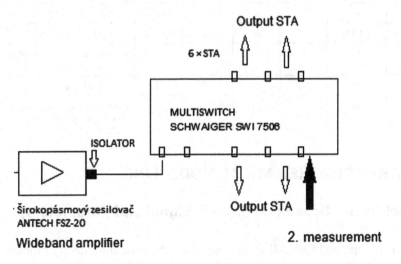

Table 3. Measured values after amplification and merger

Gain and Split – 1× Amplifier ANTECH FSZ20 and 1× Multiswitch SCHWAIGER SWI 7506						
Channel	Modulation QAM	MERc [dB]	Level [dBµV]	Pre-BER	Post-BER	Remark
25	64	28	57	1,52E-5	1,0E-7	Zlín transmitter Tl. Hora (angle directivity antenna)
29	64	27	65	1,6E-4	1,0E-7	Brno Koját transmitter (angle directivity antenna)
33	64	28	66	4,57E-5	1,0E-7	Zlín transmitter Tl. Hora (angle directivity antenna)
40	64	28	67	3,6E-5	1,0E-7	Brno Koját transmitter (angle directivity antenna)
41	64	26	51	7,62E-5	1,0E-7	Regional transmitter Uh. Hradiště (angle directivity)
42	64	25	51	1,2E-4	1,0E-7	Regional transmitter Uh. Hradiště (angle directivity)
46	64	27	54	1,5E-4	1,0E-7	Regional transmitter hodonín (angle directivity)
49	*64*	*9 - 21*	*51*	*9,14E-3*	*1,0E-7*	*Zlín transmitter Tl. Hora (angle directivity antenna)*
23	64	23	46	1,93E-3	1,0E-7	New city n.Váhom Javořina – coded, vertical
57	64	29	64	7,6E-6	1,0E-7	New city n.Váhom Javořina – vertical
56	64	29	62	3,5E-5	1,0E-7	New city n.Váhom Javořina – vertical
55	64	28	60	1,51E-5	1,0E-7	New city n.Váhom Javořina – vertical
34	16	22	38	1,52E-5	1,0E-7	Wien Kahlenberg 2MUX, AUT
35	QPSK	11	34	1,7E-3	1,0E-7	Regional transmitter (SK)
48	16	9	33	4,45E-2	1,0E-7	Regional transmitter Holíč nad Moravou (SK)
24	16	23	46	1,52E-4	1,0E-7	Wien Kahlenberg 1MUX, AUT
59	64	28	54	5,47E-4	1,0E-7	Brno Koját transmitter (angle directivity antenna)

ABSTRACT MATHEMATICAL MODELLING

Model DVB-T Broadcast (DVB-T Signal and Parameters)

The subject method Event-B is an abstract mathematical modeling problem in the progressive refinement to achieve specific systems. We would like to show the possibilities of modeling in DVB-T using this method in two ways.

Figure 15. Receiving signals in the range

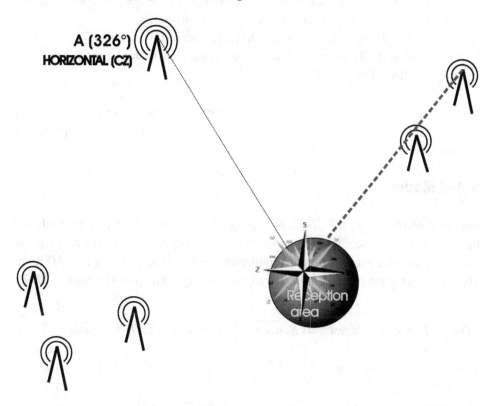

Our example – DVB-T will address the range of signal from the transmitter in place of reception (Reception Area), which is distributed from different azimuths various transmitters in remote and local income. Physical principles of electromagnetic propagation waves with analog and digital broadcasting the same, but there are some differences. Signal level (its power) in µVdB (dBm) may be in the case of digital level by approximately 20 µVdB lower (56 versus 35 µVdB). Other parameters which indicate the quality of the signal before and after Viterbi correction and constellations error (QAM) have a significant impact on the possibility to receive DVB-T (Figure 15).

- **Generally Structure Solution 1:**
  - Table requirements,
  - The definition of refirement strategy,
  - The development of initial modules refirement.

- **Generally Structure Solution 2:** The system that we are going to build will be the general structure of software and some its tools:
  - ◦ **First Tool:** Will be called EQP (Equipment) (Hranac, 2007).
  - ◦ **Second:** Requirements witch are connected system function will be called FUN.

The aim of this system will be investigation of signals acceptance and its range. The main system function is FUN_1, will examine DVB-T The acceptance of its range.

Initial Model

We are concentrating on FUN_2, that means the number of accepted signals are limited. At first phase construction we are going to ignore the quality and signals level. The distance between antenna transmitter and receiver will be ignored (Figure 16). The description of state looks like we are looking from upstairs (Hranac, 2007).

FUN_1. The System Investigats Range of the Transmitter DVB-T Signals

```
EQP-1, System is supported with a spectural analyser for DVB-T
measurment
The Result will be afile with measured parameters
EQP-2, The level of the measured signal  in µVdB (dBm)
Achieved level shoud be minimum 30 µVdB
EQP-3, Signal accepteance in µVdB (dBm)
Minimum level accepteance shoud be achieved 30 µVdB
EQP-4, Measured level MERc in dB
Achieved level shoud be minimum MERc 10 dB
EQP-5, Measured bit fault before Viterbi korektor
Achieved minimum level shoud be CBER 2.10-³
EQP-6, Measured bit fault after Viterbi correction
Achieved minimum level shoud be CBER 2.10-⁴
This system has one limitation
FUN_2, The number of signals are limited
FUN_3, Multidirection signals and any time and verious direc-
tion
```

Figure 16. Signals receiving area

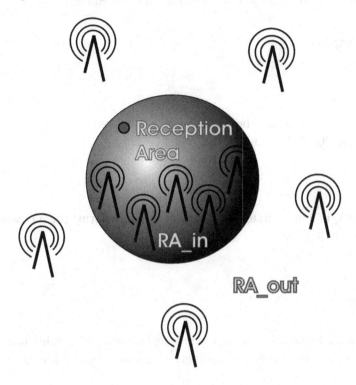

The initial model has two following events:

RA_out: The dependence signals whi arech spread by terrestrial transmitter out of the acception range.

RA_in: Realated with signals acceptence by a received antenna.

State Creation: Constants, Axioms, and Variables

Constant and Variable

Constant: $d\ axm0\_1 : d \in \mathbb{N}$

Constant d: The constant of maximum number accepted signals.

Variable: n $\begin{array}{l} inv0\_1 : n \in \mathbb{N} \\ inv0\_2 : n \leq d \end{array}$

Variable *n*: Demonstrates actual number acceptance signals.

$$FUN\_2; \exp lain \ d \leq n$$

Events

Event RA_out demonstrates broadcasting signals of transmitter, number of signals grow (Abrial, 2009). RA_out:

$$n := n - 1$$

Event RA_in demonstrates acepteans of signals entering the receptive antenna (Abrial, 2009). RA_in:

$$n := n + 1$$

Invariants

Invariants are defined as the values, which accept variables are conditioned. Invariants should all have state model. To fillfull invariants we should fullfill the following:

- Invariant shoud have initial states.
- Invariant should be kept after birth of events.

Proof: Bore-After Predicates

We can speak about each events before and after. In this case we can describe the realation between values before and after the event. We usually mark the value before the event by n and after the event n´.

Example:

$$
\begin{array}{ll}
\text{RA\_out} & \text{RA\_in} \\
n := n - 1 & n := n + 1 \\
n' = n - 1 & n' := n + 1
\end{array}
$$

Invariant Preservation

- The constant is called c.
- Axiom, which is in relation with this constant, is called A(c).
- The variable name is called v.
- Invariant, which is in relations with variable (v), is called Abstract Invariants I (c,v) (Abrial, 2009).
- After event remark v´=E (c,v) note (E – Expression – amout of expressions)

Rule, which we should proof always:

$$A(c), I(c, v) \quad I_i = (c, E(c, v)) \quad INV$$

- **Axioms:** $A(c)$
- **Invariants:** $I(c, v)$
- **Modified Invariant:** $I_i(c, E(c, v)) \quad INV$

According to our example, we have two events.

$$RA\_out \quad RA\_in$$
$$n := n - 1 \quad n := n + 1$$

Two invariants:

$$inv0\_1 : n \in \mathbb{N} \quad inv0\_2 : n \leq d$$

This means that we have four proofs – for each event we have to proof the correctness of these invariants. The four Required proofs are shown in Figure 17.

Solution 1: Optimalization of Parameters of DVB-T Signals for DVB-T Amplifier

In the first step – through the abstraction we detect whether the given set of signals there are some which may be captured by the respective antenna in DVB-T reception. There are three sets:

The first set "S" represents the set of all signals – i.e. arbitrary signals and frequency bands, including those of "useless." The second set of "D" represents a set

Figure 17. Four proofs – invariant preservation

RA_out / **inv0_1** / INV

$$d \in \mathbb{N}$$
$$n \in \mathbb{N}$$
$$n \leq d$$
$$\vdash$$
$$n + |1 \in \mathbb{N}$$

RA_out / **inv0_2** / INV

$$d \in \mathbb{N}$$
$$n \in \mathbb{N}$$
$$n \leq d$$
$$\vdash$$
$$n + 1 \leq d$$

RA_in / **inv0_1** / INV

$$d \in \mathbb{N}$$
$$n \in \mathbb{N}$$
$$n \leq d$$
$$\vdash$$
$$n - 1 \in \mathbb{N}$$

RA_in / **inv0_2** / INV

$$d \in \mathbb{N}$$
$$n \in \mathbb{N}$$
$$n \leq d$$
$$\vdash$$
$$n - 1 \leq d$$

of signals for terrestrial reception in the UHF band, in which the payload signals as appropriate for processing and useless signals from distant transmitters with insufficient level and quality.

The third set – the variable "n" is the set of signals that are received and processed as useful, i.e. they are tuned as multiplex DVB-T tuner. Machine (machine) named Reception_0 contains Reception_r0 context in which are contained two constants (the set S and D) and four axioms.

The first axiom indicates that the set of signal "S" is a subset of all positive integers N1. The second axiom indicates that the set of signals "D" in the UHF band belonging to the plurality of signals. The third axiom says that the set of all signals "S" cannot be an empty set. Finally, the fourth axiom expresses a condition where the number of signals in the UHF band sets "D" must be greater than zero (Figure 18).

Figure 18. Mathematical model of the family: Context Reception_r0, which includes four axioms

```
● Reception_r0 ⊠ | Ⓜ Reception_0
 1 context Reception_r0
 2
 3 constants S D
 4|
 5 axioms
 6    @axm1 S ⊆ ℕ1
 7    @axm2 D ∈ S
 8    @axm3 S ≠∅
 9    @axm4 D > 0
10 //S - Set all signals
11 //D - Signal unless, usefull
12
13 end
```

Abstract Machine

The abstract machine is declared variable n, which indicates the number of accepted one hand the useful signals in RA_in, partly unaccepted – useless signals from the set "D" RA_out. Invariants are a total of three and a variable "n" in the event RA_out secondly subtracted from the set of "D" all the useful signals suitable for further processing in the event RA_in added all the useful signal for amplification and tune DVB-T tuner (Figure 19).

Proving of Hypothesis

Evidence in Event-B is through entering predicates, which, however, must be validly entered. The evidence used tool Proof control, which contains fields for Manual predicate keyboard.

The first step before we enter into evidence Proof Control is necessary to switch from Event-B (Event-B perspective) Proving menu (Proving perspective). The proof trees are clicked at Project Reception / Machine / Reception_0 / Proof Obligations,

Figure 19. Mathematical model of the family – abstract machine Reception_0 which includes three invariants and two events

```
● Reception_r0    ◎ Reception_0 ⊠   ● Reception_0      ⁱ
 1 machine Reception_0 sees Reception_r0
 2
 3 variables n
 4 invariants
 5 @inv1 D ∈ S
 6 @inv2 n ∈ ℕ
 7 @inv3 D > 0
 8 events
 9    event INITIALISATION
10      then
11         @act1 n ≔ 0
12    end
13 event RA_out
14 where
15 @grd1 n < D
16      then
17      @act1 n ≔ n - 1
18    end
19 event RA_in
20 where
21 @grd1 n ≥ D
22       then
23         @act1 n ≔ n + 1
24    end
25 end
```

as illustrated in Figure 20. Then in Event-B Explorer displays a tree individual compulsory evidence to prove their actual status.

In the proof of evidence of checks there can be made trivial proof (true) directly by clicking on the icon called auto provers. Another option is to use Prover only choice hypothesis or hypotheses lasso with multiple hypotheses. Before beginning the actual evidence is necessary to deactivate the menu Project / Make Automatically select Automatically Prove otherwise would be to release individual pieces of evidence occurred automatically, and we could not interfere in the process of proving (Figure 20).

In the Proof Obligations there we can see three initializations and two invariants (RA_out, RA_in). Now we can start with the taking of evidence. The menu field Proof Control put the hypothesis to the first proof $D > 0$. The Proof Tree is proven the first invariants $D \in S$, where it is possible to prove its truth by clicking

Figure 20. Event-B explorer: proof obligations

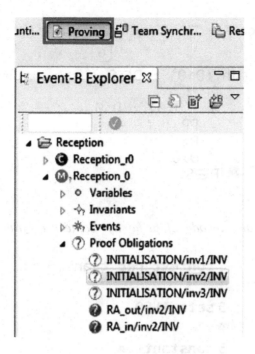

on p1 or pp, or on the green icon called auto provers. Now, however, we put first hypothesis keyboard entry and click on the red shortcut ah (add hypothesis) and insert into the hypothesis Proof Tree, where they appear. The red smiley indicates that the evidence was not released.

After adding hypotheses red button ah disables a hypothesis is added to Proof tree (Proof Tree).

Embedded hypothesis $D > 0$ is true, which indicates the character "T" (True). Trivial evidence can be done by clicking on the icon p0 (predicate Prover on selected hypotheses) proving PP: T. Add another hypothesis $D \neq 0$ and display the target Proof Tree (key G – Goal Show). Again, perform trivial proof by clicking on p0 proving PP: T (Figure 21).

In the next steps we will use the evidence p1 External prover: predicate Prover he'd lasso hypotheses and then Run auto provers (green icon). Finally, save the initialisation / INV1 / INV and red question mark icon turns green checkmark icon. This demonstrates the first invariant and in the next steps of proof will proceed in the same way.

Figure 21. Inserting a hypothesis appears in proof tree for further evidence

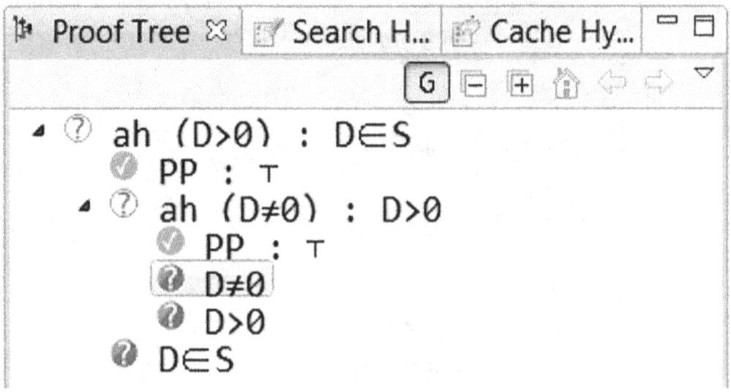

Figure 22. Mathematical model of the family: Context rec_transm_rt1

```
1 context rec_transm_rt1
2
3 sets INFO
4
5 constants n
6
7 axioms
8    @axm1 n ∈ ℕ1
9 end
```

Solution 2: Distribution TV Signal between the Transmitter and the Antenna

In the abstract MACHINE rt1 contains three variables and three invariants (Figure 23) (Antiogbé, 2011)

- ns // number of signals
- sb// send been
- rb// receiver been

First Invariant: All signals spreading ethers belonging to the set of natural numbers.
Second Invariant: Sent signals (sb) are all signals that lie in the set INFO.
Third Invariant: Received signals (rb) are all signals that are received by DVB-T
 tuner, but only a portion of the signals from the set INFO.

Figure 23. Abstract model transmitter–receiver

```
1     MACHINE
2         rt1        ›
3     SEES
4     ▯     rec_transm_rt1
5     VARIABLES
6     ▯   ns    Physical Unit:  Inferred Physical Unit:  private ›number of signals
7     ▯   sb    Physical Unit:  Inferred Physical Unit:  private ›send beam (sf)
8     ▯   rb    Physical Unit:  Inferred Physical Unit:  private ›receiver beam (rf)
9     INVARIANTS
10    ▯   inv1:   ns∈N not theorem ›
11    ▯   inv2:   sb ∈ 1..ns → INFO not theorem ›
12    ▯   inv3:   rb ∈ 1..ns ↠ INFO not theorem ›
13    EVENTS
14    ▯     INITIALISATION:    not extended ordinary external  ›
15        THEN
16    ▯     act1:   sb=ø ›
17    ▯     act2:   rb=ø ›
18    ▯     act3:   ns= 0 ›
19        END
20
21    ▯     reception:  not extended ordinary internal   ›
22        THEN
23    ▯     act1:   rb=sb ›
24        END
25
26    END
```

Initialization of the individual variables (sb), (sb) signal is set to the empty set, the total number of signals is set to zero for initialization.

In the event of "reception" are signals that were sent from the transmitter "sb", captured and adopted DVB-T tuner.

MACHINE rt1 an abstract machine that can soften in achieving further provided in terms of efficiency and the amount of transmitted and received signals in the UHF band and in it the appropriate channels. This assumption is reached MACHINE rt2 (Figure 24) (Antiogbé, 2011).

The first refinement MACHINE rt2 we have six variables and six invariants

- nch // number of channels
- sb// send beam
- rb// receiver beam
- cb// current beam to be send
- cr// current beam received
- erf// effectively of channel

Assume that the DVB-T signal is spread in the UHF band in the respective frequency in the range 470 MHz to 890 MHz with a bandwidth of 8MHz. These frequencies belong to the respective channels in the range of 21-60 (DRAFT DECREE, 2008)

Figure 24. The first refinement of an abstract model of a transmitter receiver

```
 1 machine rt2 refines rt1   sees rec_transm_rt1
 2
 3 variables nch // number of channels
 4           sb // send beam (sf)
 5           rb // receiver beam (rf)
 6           cb // current beam to be send
 7           cr // current beam received
 8           erf // effectively of channel
 9
10 invariants
11    @inv1 nch∈ℕ
12    @inv2 cb ∈1··nch+1
13    @inv3 cr ∈0··nch
14    @inv4 cr≤cb
15    @inv5 cb≤cr+1
16    @inv6 erf=(1··cr)◁sb
17
18 events
19    event INITIALISATION
20       then
21          @act1 cb≔1
22          @act2 cr≔0
23          @act3 rb≔∅
24          @act4 sb≔∅
25          @act5 erf≔∅
26          @act6 nch ≔0
27
28    end
29
30    event recep refines reception
31       where
32          @act1 cb=(nch+1)
33       then
34          @act2 rb≔erf
35    end
36 end
```

All UHF channels belong to the set of natural numbers.

Second Invariant: Signals (cb) to be transmitted from the transmitter.
Third Invariant: Only some of the received signals (cr) belongs to set INFO.
Fourth Invariant: The received signals (cr) is always less or equal to the current number (cs) propagating signals.
Fifth Invariant: Number of propagating signals (cs) is less than or equal signals received (cr).
Sixth Invariant: Effective erf received signals equal to the number of received signals (cr), which is part of the domain of sent signals (sb).

CONCLUSION

The hardware elements have a major impact physical parameters (their level and error), as indicated by the measurement and comparison of the two different line amplifiers used. Line continuous amplifier was used due to amplification of all (and weak) signals throughout the UHF and FM band. It is a reasonable compromise in combination with the use of large YAGI antenna Iskra UHF91x big profit 14-16 dBi.

Expensive building amplifiers usually suppress weaker signals and process and amplify signals only with a sufficient level in range of transmitters. Our requirement in this solution aims to develop and strengthen the weaker signals from transmitters of different power (ERP) that are in place within the reception area.

As follows from the measurements, there is a big difference between the line amplifier – selectivity and amplification. Amplification is irrelevant in the case of DVB-T, quality plays a decisive role MER [dB]. Amplification at a high rate – more than 70 µVdB will be amplified noise also, which is undesirable and significantly affects the quality of the received signal. The quality of the amplifier used is affected by semiconductor elements (transistors with low noise) as well as with the design of the power supply with the possibility of crossover (after out-Coaxial) pass via a capacitor or via branching e.g. TONER with the separating capacitor.

Technological shift DVB-T is evident in several respects:

- In one DVB-T channels can be simultaneously streamed several television channels in Full HD quality in the respective QAM constellation.
- Signal reception in the site is not directly affected by interference from external local sources, which would be reflected "snow and ghosts" in the picture
- Signal level plays a crucial role and minimum value measurable stable reception is approximately 16 to 20 dB lower in comparison with analog in favor of the DVB-T (56 µVdB analog versus digital 35 µVdB).

213

- When you use a quality splits and divorces STA is signal attenuation is within 1 dB and had no major impact on the receipt and processing of DVB-T tuner.

Disadvantage of digital reception consists in the so-called. Cliff effect when exceeding the minimum required for stable measurable levels (below 35 µVdB), usually occur before error correction and after correction procedure 1E-2, and reception in comparison with analogue is basically impossible when the image "snowing", but the reception was tracked.

In this article, we also wanted to show the capability of Event-B how to use Event-B for solution of complex projects. Abstract machine of Event-B based on measured DVB-T parameters.

Manual of taking evidence hypotheses in Event-B for any mathematical model is a very powerful sophisticated tool. Math reasoning through procuring hypotheses virtually eliminates errors in the algorithm including extremes and handle errors that may occur. The Tester is able to remove most errors in the algorithm but there is a risk that a smaller percentage of errors and checked. This method therefore aims to eliminate all errors and error conditions that may occur in the algorithm.

Integrated DVB-T tuner to detect minimal values of the parameters of MER and post -BER that will ensure a stable income. For various QAM (16, 64, QPSK) are minimum values MER for various stable income. For 16-QAM is min. value of 15 dB for 64-QAM value of 23 dB. Bit error rate Post-BER has value for all QAM modulation maximal 2.E-4 (DRAFT DECREE, 2008).

The proposed system of antennae in this solution ensures stable reception even if the value of MER 64-QAM worth 19 dB amplification before (1st measurement).

Empirically it independently of several DVB-T tuner shown that the signal has been detected and processed.

REFERENCES

Abrial, J. R. (2009). *2. Controlling Cars on a Bridge.* Retrieved 10 July 2014 from http://deploy-eprints.ecs.soton.ac.uk/112/1/sld.ch2.car.pdf

Antech, o. (2010). *The measurement signal. What requirements must comply with the meter?* (in Czech) Retrieved 22 June 2014 from http://eshop.antech.cz/mereni-signalu/

Attiogbé, J. C. (2011). *Software Construction*. Retrieved May 02, 2011 from https://www.google.cz/url?sa=t&rct=j&q=&esrc=s&source=web&cd=1& ved=0ahUKEwit4aOj58DLAhWq9HIKHfH_CwwQFggbMAA&url=http% 3A%2F%2Fpagesperso.lina.univ-nantes.fr%2Finfo%2Fperso%2Fpermanent s%2Fattiogbe%2Fmespages%2FMSFORMEL%2Fslides_intro_EventB.1x1. pdf&usg=AFQjCNGrW0U6zZ6xUs19qYLU-O8KjV7LMA&sig2=6qipL7XqW Dj1tpg6GhrNTA&bvm=bv.116636494,d.bGQ&cad=rja

Czech Telecommunications Office. (2008). *163 DECREE on the method for determining terrestrial television broadcasting signal coverage*. Retrieved April 30, 2008, from http://download.mpo.cz/get/39700/50315/582024/priloha005.pdf

Digital Video Broadcasting. (2009). *Digital Video Broadcasting (DVB); Specification for the use of Video and Audio Coding in Broadcasting Applications based on the MPEG-2 Transport Stream*. Retrieved 30 September 2009 from http://www.etsi. org/deliver/etsi_ts/101100_101199/101154/01.09.01_60/ts_101154v010901p.pdf

Draft Decree. (2008) *A method of determining the area covered by a broadcaster method determining the intensity of the electromagnetic field and the resulting derivative Population coverage television broadcasting signal (a method of determining coverage television broadcasting signal*. (in Czech). Retrieved April 30, 2008, from http://www.proglas.cz/res/data/019/002385.pdf

Dreamsky, T. S. (2013) *DREAMSKY TS-80 MultiCOMBO*. (in Czech) Retrieved 10 November, 2013, from http://www.dreamsky.cz/dreamsky-ts-80-combo.html

Handley, M. (2010). *10: System Streams*. Retrieved 2 May 2013 from http://www0. cs.ucl.ac.uk/teaching/GZ05/10-system-streams.pdf

Hranac, R. (2007). *CISCO Systems. BER and MER Fundamentals*. Retrieved 10 May 2013 from http://www.scribd.com/doc/231656951/Ron-Hranac-Presentation-BER-MER-Fun#scribd

Kyuheon, K. (2010). *MPEG-2 ES/PES/TS/PSI*. Retrieved 4 October 2010 from http://cmm.khu.ac.kr/korean/files/02.mpeg2ts1_es_pes_ps_ts_psi.pdf

Procházka, J. (2009). *Interactive map of transmitters*. Retrieved 1 November 2009, from http://www.mapavysilacu.cz/mapcoverage.html

Řezáč, P. (2010). *Are you watching digitally? Part 3. Antennas for the remote reception DVB-T*. (in Czech) Retrieved 4 April 2010, from http://www.itest.cz/old/ videofoto/digitalni-vysilani-3.htm

Sunrise Telecom. (2010). *Measuring and Qualifying the Dosis Upstream Path.* Retrieved 5 May 2010, from http://www.gcscte.org/presentations/2010/Tom%20 64QAM%20SCTE1.pdf

Vlajič, N. (2010). *Analog Transmission Analog Transmission of Digital Data: of Digital Data: ASK, FSK, PSK, QAM.* Retrieved 22 April 2010, from http://www.eecs. yorku.ca/course_archive/2010-11/F/3213/CSE3213_07_ShiftKeying_F2010.pdf

Wolff, Ch. (2006). *Radar Basic. Horizontal patterns.* Retrieved 3 June 2006, from http://www.radartutorial.eu/06.antennas/Half-wave%20Antenna.en.html

Wolff, Ch. (2006). *Radar Basic. Yagi Antenna.* Retrieved 10 June 2007 from http:// www.radartutorial.eu/06.antennas/Yagi%20Antenna.en.html

KEY TERM AND DEFINITIONS

Event: Each abstract event can be refined by one or more concrete events in the Event-B method. An event has the following elements: name, parameters, guards, witnesses, actions.

Invariant: The full invariant of the machine consists of both type abstract and concrete invariants. The invariants are accumulated during refinements.

Machine: A machine describes the dynamic behavior of a model by means of variables whose values are changed by events.

Multiplexing Equipment: Multiplexing is the simultaneous transmission of a number of intelligible signals (messages) in either or both directions using only a single carrier. You may use two methods of multiplexing. These are TIME-DIVISION and FREQUENCY-DIVISION.

Receiver Equipment: An DVB-T receiver processes amplitude-modulated signals received by its antenna. It delivers an output, a reproduction of the signal that originally modulated the carrier at the transmitter.

Reception: Reception occurs when a transmitted electromagnetic wave passes through the receiver antenna and andinduces a voltage in the antenna.

Refinement: Refinement can be used to subsequently add complexity to the model – this is called superposition refinement.

Transmitter: In electronics and telecommunications a transmitter or radio transmitter is an electronic device which, with the aid of an antenna, produces radio waves. The transmitter itself generates a radio frequency alternating current, which is applied to the antenna.

UHF Amplifier: UHF wideband amplifier (Ultra High Frequency amplifier) has usually gain of 10 to 20 dB in the 400 – 850 MHz domain frequency so it can be used where the tv signal is weak.

YAGI Antenna: Antenna structure consisting of a dipole emitter, reflector and system directors proposed in r. 1926, Japanese scientists H. Yagi and S. Uda. For its simple design, easy reproducibility and good electrical properties with Yagi antennas have become the most widely used in the VHF and UHF band.

Related of References

To continue our tradition of advancing information science and technology research, we have compiled a list of recommended IGI Global readings. These references will provide additional information and guidance to further enrich your knowledge and assist you with your own research and future publications.

Aalmink, J., von der Dovenmühle, T., & Gómez, J. M. (2013). Enterprise tomography: Maintenance and root-cause-analysis of federated erp in enterprise clouds. In P. Ordóñez de Pablos, H. Nigro, R. Tennyson, S. Gonzalez Cisaro, & W. Karwowski (Eds.), *Advancing information management through semantic web concepts and ontologies* (pp. 133–153). Hershey, PA: Information Science Reference; doi:10.4018/978-1-4666-2494-8.ch007

Abu, S. T., & Tsuji, M. (2011). The development of ICT for envisioning cloud computing and innovation in South Asia.[IJIDE]. *International Journal of Innovation in the Digital Economy*, 2(1), 61–72. doi:10.4018/jide.2011010105

Abu, S. T., & Tsuji, M. (2012). The development of ICT for envisioning cloud computing and innovation in South Asia. In *Grid and cloud computing: Concepts, methodologies, tools and applications* (pp. 453–465). Hershey, PA: Information Science Reference; doi:10.4018/978-1-4666-0879-5.ch207

Abu, S. T., & Tsuji, M. (2013). The development of ICT for envisioning cloud computing and innovation in South Asia. In I. Oncioiu (Ed.), *Business innovation, development, and advancement in the digital economy* (pp. 35–47). Hershey, PA: Business Science Reference; doi:10.4018/978-1-4666-2934-9.ch003

Adams, R. (2013). The emergence of cloud storage and the need for a new digital forensic process model. In K. Ruan (Ed.), *Cybercrime and cloud forensics: Applications for investigation processes* (pp. 79–104). Hershey, PA: Information Science Reference; doi:10.4018/978-1-4666-2662-1.ch004

Related of References

Adeyeye, M. (2013). Provisioning converged applications and services via the cloud. In D. Kanellopoulos (Ed.), *Intelligent multimedia technologies for networking applications: Techniques and tools* (pp. 248–269). Hershey, PA: Information Science Reference; doi:10.4018/978-1-4666-2833-5.ch010

Aggarwal, A. (2013). A systems approach to cloud computing services. In A. Bento & A. Aggarwal (Eds.), *Cloud computing service and deployment models: Layers and management* (pp. 124–136). Hershey, PA: Business Science Reference; doi:10.4018/978-1-4666-2187-9.ch006

Ahmed, K., Hussain, A., & Gregory, M. A. (2013). An efficient, robust, and secure SSO architecture for cloud computing implemented in a service oriented architecture. In X. Yang & L. Liu (Eds.), *Principles, methodologies, and service-oriented approaches for cloud computing* (pp. 259–282). Hershey, PA: Business Science Reference; doi:10.4018/978-1-4666-2854-0.ch011

Ahuja, S. P., & Mani, S. (2013). Empirical performance analysis of HPC benchmarks across variations in cloud computing.[IJCAC]. *International Journal of Cloud Applications and Computing, 3*(1), 13–26. doi:10.4018/ijcac.2013010102

Ahuja, S. P., & Rolli, A. C. (2011). Survey of the state-of-the-art of cloud computing.[IJCAC]. *International Journal of Cloud Applications and Computing, 1*(4), 34–43. doi:10.4018/ijcac.2011100103

Ahuja, S. P., & Rolli, A. C. (2013). Survey of the state-of-the-art of cloud computing. In S. Aljawarneh (Ed.), *Cloud computing advancements in design, implementation, and technologies* (pp. 252–262). Hershey, PA: Information Science Reference; doi:10.4018/978-1-4666-1879-4.ch018

Ahuja, S. P., & Sridharan, S. (2012). Performance evaluation of hypervisors for cloud computing.[IJCAC]. *International Journal of Cloud Applications and Computing, 2*(3), 26–67. doi:10.4018/ijcac.2012070102

Akyuz, G. A., & Rehan, M. (2013). A generic, cloud-based representation for supply chains (SC's).[IJCAC]. *International Journal of Cloud Applications and Computing, 3*(2), 12–20. doi:10.4018/ijcac.2013040102

Al-Aqrabi, H., & Liu, L. (2013). IT security and governance compliant service oriented computing in cloud computing environments. In X. Yang & L. Liu (Eds.), *Principles, methodologies, and service-oriented approaches for cloud computing* (pp. 143–163). Hershey, PA: Business Science Reference; doi:10.4018/978-1-4666-2854-0.ch006

Al-Zoube, M., & Wyne, M. F. (2012). Building integrated e-learning environment using cloud services and social networking sites. In Q. Jin (Ed.), *Intelligent learning systems and advancements in computer-aided instruction: Emerging studies* (pp. 214–233). Hershey, PA: Information Science Reference; doi:10.4018/978-1-61350-483-3.ch013

Alam, N., & Karmakar, R. (2014). Cloud computing and its application to information centre. In S. Dhamdhere (Ed.), *Cloud computing and virtualization technologies in libraries* (pp. 63–76). Hershey, PA: Information Science Reference; doi:10.4018/978-1-4666-4631-5.ch004

Alhaj, A., Aljawarneh, S., Masadeh, S., & Abu-Taieh, E. (2013). A secure data transmission mechanism for cloud outsourced data.[IJCAC]. *International Journal of Cloud Applications and Computing, 3*(1), 34–43. doi:10.4018/ijcac.2013010104

Alharbi, S. T. (2012). Users' acceptance of cloud computing in Saudi Arabia: An extension of technology acceptance model.[IJCAC]. *International Journal of Cloud Applications and Computing, 2*(2), 1–11. doi:10.4018/ijcac.2012040101

Ali, S. S., & Khan, M. N. (2013). ICT infrastructure framework for microfinance institutions and banks in Pakistan: An optimized approach.[IJOM]. *International Journal of Online Marketing, 3*(2), 75–86. doi:10.4018/ijom.2013040105

Aljawarneh, S. (2011). Cloud security engineering: Avoiding security threats the right way.[IJCAC]. *International Journal of Cloud Applications and Computing, 1*(2), 64–70. doi:10.4018/ijcac.2011040105

Aljawarneh, S. (2013). Cloud security engineering: Avoiding security threats the right way. In S. Aljawarneh (Ed.), *Cloud computing advancements in design, implementation, and technologies* (pp. 147–153). Hershey, PA: Information Science Reference; doi:10.4018/978-1-4666-1879-4.ch010

Alshattnawi, S. (2013). Utilizing cloud computing in developing a mobile location-aware tourist guide system.[IJAPUC]. *International Journal of Advanced Pervasive and Ubiquitous Computing, 5*(2), 9–18. doi:10.4018/japuc.2013040102

Alsmadi, I. (2013). Software development methodologies for cloud computing. In K. Buragga & N. Zaman (Eds.), *Software development techniques for constructive information systems design* (pp. 110–117). Hershey, PA: Information Science Reference; doi:10.4018/978-1-4666-3679-8.ch006

Anand, V. (2013). Survivable mapping of virtual networks onto a shared substrate network. In X. Yang & L. Liu (Eds.), *Principles, methodologies, and service-oriented approaches for cloud computing* (pp. 325–343). Hershey, PA: Business Science Reference; doi:10.4018/978-1-4666-2854-0.ch014

Antonova, A. (2013). Green, sustainable, or clean: What type of IT/IS technologies will we need in the future? In P. Ordóñez de Pablos (Ed.), *Green technologies and business practices: An IT approach* (pp. 151–162). Hershey, PA: Information Science Reference; doi:10.4018/978-1-4666-1972-2.ch008

Ardissono, L., Bosio, G., Goy, A., Petrone, G., Segnan, M., & Torretta, F. (2011). Collaboration support for activity management in a personal cloud environment. [IJDST]. *International Journal of Distributed Systems and Technologies*, 2(4), 30–43. doi:10.4018/jdst.2011100103

Ardissono, L., Bosio, G., Goy, A., Petrone, G., Segnan, M., & Torretta, F. (2013). Collaboration support for activity management in a personal cloud environment. In N. Bessis (Ed.), *Development of distributed systems from design to application and maintenance* (pp. 199–212). Hershey, PA: Information Science Reference; doi:10.4018/978-1-4666-2647-8.ch012

Argiolas, M., Atzori, M., Dessì, N., & Pes, B. (2012). Dataspaces enhancing decision support systems in clouds.[IJWP]. *International Journal of Web Portals*, 4(2), 35–55. doi:10.4018/jwp.2012040103

Arinze, B., & Anandarajan, M. (2012). Factors that determine the adoption of cloud computing: A global perspective. In M. Tavana (Ed.), *Enterprise Information Systems and Advancing Business Solutions: Emerging Models* (pp. 210–223). Hershey, PA: Business Science Reference; doi:10.4018/978-1-4666-1761-2.ch012

Arinze, B., & Sylla, C. (2012). Conducting research in the cloud. In L. Chao (Ed.), *Cloud computing for teaching and learning: Strategies for design and implementation* (pp. 50–63). Hershey, PA: Information Science Reference; doi:10.4018/978-1-4666-0957-0.ch004

Arshad, J., Townend, P., & Xu, J. (2011). An abstract model for integrated intrusion detection and severity analysis for clouds.[IJCAC]. *International Journal of Cloud Applications and Computing*, 1(1), 1–16. doi:10.4018/ijcac.2011010101

Arshad, J., Townend, P., & Xu, J. (2013). An abstract model for integrated intrusion detection and severity analysis for clouds. In S. Aljawarneh (Ed.), *Cloud computing advancements in design, implementation, and technologies* (pp. 1–17). Hershey, PA: Information Science Reference; doi:10.4018/978-1-4666-1879-4.ch001

Arshad, J., Townend, P., Xu, J., & Jie, W. (2012). Cloud computing security: Opportunities and pitfalls.[IJGHPC]. *International Journal of Grid and High Performance Computing*, 4(1), 52–66. doi:10.4018/jghpc.2012010104

Baars, T., & Spruit, M. (2012). Designing a secure cloud architecture: The SeCA model.[IJISP]. *International Journal of Information Security and Privacy*, 6(1), 14–32. doi:10.4018/jisp.2012010102

Bai, X., Gao, J. Z., & Tsai, W. (2013). Cloud scalability measurement and testing. In S. Tilley & T. Parveen (Eds.), *Software testing in the cloud: Perspectives on an emerging discipline* (pp. 356–381). Hershey, PA: Information Science Reference; doi:10.4018/978-1-4666-2536-5.ch017

Baldini, G., & Stirparo, P. (2014). A cognitive access framework for security and privacy protection in mobile cloud computing. In J. Rodrigues, K. Lin, & J. Lloret (Eds.), *Mobile networks and cloud computing convergence for progressive services and applications* (pp. 92–117). Hershey, PA: Information Science Reference; doi:10.4018/978-1-4666-4781-7.ch006

Balduf, S., Balke, T., & Eymann, T. (2012). Cultural differences in managing cloud computing service level agreements. In *Grid and cloud computing: Concepts, methodologies, tools and applications* (pp. 1237–1263). Hershey, PA: Information Science Reference; doi:10.4018/978-1-4666-0879-5.ch512

Banerjee, S., Sing, T. Y., Chowdhury, A. R., & Anwar, H. (2013). Motivations to adopt green ICT: A tale of two organizations.[IJGC]. *International Journal of Green Computing*, 4(2), 1–11. doi:10.4018/jgc.2013070101

Barreto, J., Di Sanzo, P., Palmieri, R., & Romano, P. (2013). Cloud-TM: An elastic, self-tuning transactional store for the cloud. In D. Kyriazis, A. Voulodimos, S. Gogouvitis, & T. Varvarigou (Eds.), *Data intensive storage services for cloud environments* (pp. 192–224). Hershey, PA: Business Science Reference; doi:10.4018/978-1-4666-3934-8.ch013

Belalem, G., & Limam, S. (2011). Fault tolerant architecture to cloud computing using adaptive checkpoint.[IJCAC]. *International Journal of Cloud Applications and Computing*, 1(4), 60–69. doi:10.4018/ijcac.2011100105

Belalem, G., & Limam, S. (2013). Fault tolerant architecture to cloud computing using adaptive checkpoint. In S. Aljawarneh (Ed.), *Cloud computing advancements in design, implementation, and technologies* (pp. 280–289). Hershey, PA: Information Science Reference; doi:10.4018/978-1-4666-1879-4.ch020

Ben Belgacem, M., Abdennadher, N., & Niinimaki, M. (2012). Virtual EZ grid: A volunteer computing infrastructure for scientific medical applications.[IJHCR]. *International Journal of Handheld Computing Research*, *3*(1), 74–85. doi:10.4018/jhcr.2012010105

Bhatt, S., Chaudhary, S., & Bhise, M. (2013). Migration of data between cloud and non-cloud datastores. In A. Ionita, M. Litoiu, & G. Lewis (Eds.), *Migrating legacy applications: Challenges in service oriented architecture and cloud computing environments* (pp. 206–225). Hershey, PA: Information Science Reference; doi:10.4018/978-1-4666-2488-7.ch009

Biancofiore, G., & Leone, S. (2014). Google apps as a cloud computing solution in Italian municipalities: Technological features and implications. In S. Leone (Ed.), *Synergic integration of formal and informal e-learning environments for adult lifelong learners* (pp. 244–274). Hershey, PA: Information Science Reference; doi:10.4018/978-1-4666-4655-1.ch012

Bibi, S., Katsaros, D., & Bozanis, P. (2012). How to choose the right cloud. In *Grid and cloud computing: Concepts, methodologies, tools and applications* (pp. 1530–1552). Hershey, PA: Information Science Reference; doi:10.4018/978-1-4666-0879-5.ch701

Bibi, S., Katsaros, D., & Bozanis, P. (2012). How to choose the right cloud. In X. Liu & Y. Li (Eds.), *Advanced design approaches to emerging software systems: Principles, methodologies and tools* (pp. 219–240). Hershey, PA: Information Science Reference; doi:10.4018/978-1-60960-735-7.ch010

Bitam, S., Batouche, M., & Talbi, E. (2012). A bees life algorithm for cloud computing services selection. In S. Ali, N. Abbadeni, & M. Batouche (Eds.), *Multidisciplinary computational intelligence techniques: Applications in business, engineering, and medicine* (pp. 31–46). Hershey, PA: Information Science Reference; doi:10.4018/978-1-4666-1830-5.ch003

Bittencourt, L. F., Madeira, E. R., & da Fonseca, N. L. (2014). Communication aspects of resource management in hybrid clouds. In H. Mouftah & B. Kantarci (Eds.), *Communication infrastructures for cloud computing* (pp. 409–433). Hershey, PA: Information Science Reference; doi:10.4018/978-1-4666-4522-6.ch018

Bonelli, L., Giudicianni, L., Immediata, A., & Luzzi, A. (2013). Compliance in the cloud. In D. Kyriazis, A. Voulodimos, S. Gogouvitis, & T. Varvarigou (Eds.), *Data intensive storage services for cloud environments* (pp. 109–131). Hershey, PA: Business Science Reference; doi:10.4018/978-1-4666-3934-8.ch008

Boniface, M., Nasser, B., Surridge, M., & Oliveros, E. (2012). Securing real-time interactive applications in federated clouds. In *Grid and cloud computing: Concepts, methodologies, tools and applications* (pp. 1822–1835). Hershey, PA: Information Science Reference; doi:10.4018/978-1-4666-0879-5.ch806

Boukhobza, J. (2013). Flashing in the cloud: Shedding some light on NAND flash memory storage systems. In D. Kyriazis, A. Voulodimos, S. Gogouvitis, & T. Varvarigou (Eds.), *Data intensive storage services for cloud environments* (pp. 241–266). Hershey, PA: Business Science Reference; doi:10.4018/978-1-4666-3934-8.ch015

Bracci, F., Corradi, A., & Foschini, L. (2014). Cloud standards: Security and interoperability issues. In H. Mouftah & B. Kantarci (Eds.), *Communication infrastructures for cloud computing* (pp. 465–495). Hershey, PA: Information Science Reference; doi:10.4018/978-1-4666-4522-6.ch020

Brown, A. W. (2013). Experiences with cloud technology to realize software testing factories. In S. Tilley & T. Parveen (Eds.), *Software testing in the cloud: Perspectives on an emerging discipline* (pp. 1–27). Hershey, PA: Information Science Reference; doi:10.4018/978-1-4666-2536-5.ch001

Calcavecchia, N. M., Celesti, A., & Di Nitto, E. (2012). Understanding decentralized and dynamic brokerage in federated cloud environments. In M. Villari, I. Brandic, & F. Tusa (Eds.), *Achieving federated and self-manageable cloud infrastructures: Theory and practice* (pp. 36–56). Hershey, PA: Business Science Reference; doi:10.4018/978-1-4666-1631-8.ch003

Calero, J. M., König, B., & Kirschnick, J. (2012). Cross-layer monitoring in cloud computing. In H. Rashvand & Y. Kavian (Eds.), *Using cross-layer techniques for communication systems* (pp. 328–348). Hershey, PA: Information Science Reference; doi:10.4018/978-1-4666-0960-0.ch014

Cardellini, V., Casalicchio, E., & Silvestri, L. (2012). Service level provisioning for cloud-based applications service level provisioning for cloud-based applications. In A. Pathan, M. Pathan, & H. Lee (Eds.), *Advancements in distributed computing and internet technologies: Trends and issues* (pp. 363–385). Hershey, PA: Information Science Publishing; doi:10.4018/978-1-61350-110-8.ch017

Cardellini, V., Casalicchio, E., & Silvestri, L. (2012). Service level provisioning for cloud-based applications service level provisioning for cloud-based applications. In *Grid and cloud computing: Concepts, methodologies, tools and applications* (pp. 1479–1500). Hershey, PA: Information Science Reference; doi:10.4018/978-1-4666-0879-5.ch611

Carlin, S., & Curran, K. (2013). Cloud computing security. In K. Curran (Ed.), *Pervasive and ubiquitous technology innovations for ambient intelligence environments* (pp. 12–17). Hershey, PA: Information Science Reference; doi:10.4018/978-1-4666-2041-4.ch002

Carlton, G. H., & Zhou, H. (2011). A survey of cloud computing challenges from a digital forensics perspective.[IJITN]. *International Journal of Interdisciplinary Telecommunications and Networking, 3*(4), 1–16. doi:10.4018/jitn.2011100101

Carlton, G. H., & Zhou, H. (2012). A survey of cloud computing challenges from a digital forensics perspective. In *Grid and cloud computing: Concepts, methodologies, tools and applications* (pp. 1221–1236). Hershey, PA: Information Science Reference; doi:10.4018/978-1-4666-0879-5.ch511

Carlton, G. H., & Zhou, H. (2013). A survey of cloud computing challenges from a digital forensics perspective. In M. Bartolacci & S. Powell (Eds.), *Advancements and innovations in wireless communications and network technologies* (pp. 213–228). Hershey, PA: Information Science Reference; doi:10.4018/978-1-4666-2154-1.ch016

Carpen-Amarie, A., Costan, A., Leordeanu, C., Basescu, C., & Antoniu, G. (2012). Towards a generic security framework for cloud data management environments. [IJDST]. *International Journal of Distributed Systems and Technologies, 3*(1), 17–34. doi:10.4018/jdst.2012010102

Casola, V., Cuomo, A., Villano, U., & Rak, M. (2012). Access control in federated clouds: The cloudgrid case study. In M. Villari, I. Brandic, & F. Tusa (Eds.), *Achieving Federated and Self-Manageable Cloud Infrastructures: Theory and Practice* (pp. 395–417). Hershey, PA: Business Science Reference; doi:10.4018/978-1-4666-1631-8.ch020

Casola, V., Cuomo, A., Villano, U., & Rak, M. (2013). Access control in federated clouds: The cloudgrid case study. In *IT policy and ethics: Concepts, methodologies, tools, and applications* (pp. 148–169). Hershey, PA: Information Science Reference; doi:10.4018/978-1-4666-2919-6.ch008

Celesti, A., Tusa, F., & Villari, M. (2012). Toward cloud federation: Concepts and challenges. In M. Villari, I. Brandic, & F. Tusa (Eds.), *Achieving federated and self-manageable cloud infrastructures: Theory and practice* (pp. 1–17). Hershey, PA: Business Science Reference; doi:10.4018/978-1-4666-1631-8.ch001

Chaka, C. (2013). Virtualization and cloud computing: Business models in the virtual cloud. In A. Loo (Ed.), *Distributed computing innovations for business, engineering, and science* (pp. 176–190). Hershey, PA: Information Science Reference; doi:10.4018/978-1-4666-2533-4.ch009

Chang, J. (2011). A framework for analysing the impact of cloud computing on local government in the UK.[IJCAC]. *International Journal of Cloud Applications and Computing, 1*(4), 25–33. doi:10.4018/ijcac.2011100102

Chang, J. (2013). A framework for analysing the impact of cloud computing on local government in the UK. In S. Aljawarneh (Ed.), *Cloud computing advancements in design, implementation, and technologies* (pp. 243–251). Hershey, PA: Information Science Reference; doi:10.4018/978-1-4666-1879-4.ch017

Chang, J., & Johnston, M. (2012). Cloud computing in local government: From the perspective of four London borough councils.[IJCAC]. *International Journal of Cloud Applications and Computing, 2*(4), 1–15. doi:10.4018/ijcac.2012100101

Chang, K., & Wang, K. (2012). Efficient support of streaming videos through patching proxies in the cloud.[IJGHPC]. *International Journal of Grid and High Performance Computing, 4*(4), 22–36. doi:10.4018/jghpc.2012100102

Chang, R., Liao, C., & Liu, C. (2013). Choosing clouds for an enterprise: Modeling and evaluation.[IJEEI]. *International Journal of E-Entrepreneurship and Innovation, 4*(2), 38–53. doi:10.4018/ijeei.2013040103

Chang, V., De Roure, D., Wills, G., & Walters, R. J. (2011). Case studies and organisational sustainability modelling presented by cloud computing business framework.[IJWSR]. *International Journal of Web Services Research, 8*(3), 26–53. doi:10.4018/jwsr.2011070102

Chang, V., Li, C., De Roure, D., Wills, G., Walters, R. J., & Chee, C. (2011). The financial clouds review.[IJCAC]. *International Journal of Cloud Applications and Computing, 1*(2), 41–63. doi:10.4018/ijcac.2011040104

Chang, V., Li, C., De Roure, D., Wills, G., Walters, R. J., & Chee, C. (2013). The financial clouds review. In S. Aljawarneh (Ed.), *Cloud computing advancements in design, implementation, and technologies* (pp. 125–146). Hershey, PA: Information Science Reference; doi:10.4018/978-1-4666-1879-4.ch009

Chang, V., Walters, R. J., & Wills, G. (2012). Business integration as a service. [IJCAC]. *International Journal of Cloud Applications and Computing, 2*(1), 16–40. doi:10.4018/ijcac.2012010102

Chang, V., & Wills, G. (2013). A University of Greenwich case study of cloud computing: Education as a service. In D. Graham, I. Manikas, & D. Folinas (Eds.), *E-logistics and e-supply chain management: Applications for evolving business* (pp. 232–253). Hershey, PA: Business Science Reference; doi:10.4018/978-1-4666-3914-0.ch013

Chang, V., Wills, G., Walters, R. J., & Currie, W. (2012). Towards a structured cloud ROI: The University of Southampton cost-saving and user satisfaction case studies. In W. Hu & N. Kaabouch (Eds.), *Sustainable ICTs and management systems for green computing* (pp. 179–200). Hershey, PA: Information Science Reference; doi:10.4018/978-1-4666-1839-8.ch008

Chang, Y., Lee, Y., Juang, T., & Yen, J. (2013). Cost evaluation on building and operating cloud platform.[IJGHPC]. *International Journal of Grid and High Performance Computing, 5*(2), 43–53. doi:10.4018/jghpc.2013040103

Chao, L. (2012). Cloud computing solution for internet based teaching and learning. In L. Chao (Ed.), *Cloud computing for teaching and learning: Strategies for design and implementation* (pp. 210–235). Hershey, PA: Information Science Reference; doi:10.4018/978-1-4666-0957-0.ch015

Chao, L. (2012). Overview of cloud computing and its application in e-learning. In L. Chao (Ed.), *Cloud computing for teaching and learning: Strategies for design and implementation* (pp. 1–16). Hershey, PA: Information Science Reference; doi:10.4018/978-1-4666-0957-0.ch001

Chauhan, S., Raman, A., & Singh, N. (2013). A comparative cost analysis of on premises IT infrastructure and cloud-based email services in an Indian business school.[IJCAC]. *International Journal of Cloud Applications and Computing, 3*(2), 21–34. doi:10.4018/ijcac.2013040103

Chen, C., Chao, H., Wu, T., Fan, C., Chen, J., Chen, Y., & Hsu, J. (2011). IoT-IMS communication platform for future internet.[IJARAS]. *International Journal of Adaptive, Resilient and Autonomic Systems, 2*(4), 74–94. doi:10.4018/jaras.2011100105

Chen, C., Chao, H., Wu, T., Fan, C., Chen, J., Chen, Y., & Hsu, J. (2013). IoT-IMS communication platform for future internet. In V. De Florio (Ed.), *Innovations and approaches for resilient and adaptive systems* (pp. 68–86). Hershey, PA: Information Science Reference; doi:10.4018/978-1-4666-2056-8.ch004

Chen, C. C. (2013). Cloud computing in case-based pedagogy: An information systems success perspective.[IJDTIS]. *International Journal of Dependable and Trustworthy Information Systems, 2*(3), 1–16. doi:10.4018/jdtis.2011070101

Cheney, A. W., Riedl, R. E., Sanders, R., & Tashner, J. H. (2012). The new company water cooler: Use of 3D virtual immersive worlds to promote networking and professional learning in organizations. In Organizational learning and knowledge: Concepts, methodologies, tools and applications (pp. 2848-2861). Hershey, PA: Business Science Reference. doi:10.4018/978-1-60960-783-8.ch801

Chiang, C., & Yu, S. (2013). Cloud-enabled software testing based on program understanding. In S. Tilley & T. Parveen (Eds.), *Software testing in the cloud: Perspectives on an emerging discipline* (pp. 54–67). Hershey, PA: Information Science Reference; doi:10.4018/978-1-4666-2536-5.ch003

Chou, Y., & Oetting, J. (2011). Risk assessment for cloud-based IT systems. [IJGHPC]. *International Journal of Grid and High Performance Computing*, 3(2), 1–13. doi:10.4018/jghpc.2011040101

Chou, Y., & Oetting, J. (2012). Risk assessment for cloud-based IT systems. In *Grid and cloud computing: Concepts, methodologies, tools and applications* (pp. 272–285). Hershey, PA: Information Science Reference; doi:10.4018/978-1-4666-0879-5.ch113

Chou, Y., & Oetting, J. (2013). Risk assessment for cloud-based IT systems. In E. Udoh (Ed.), *Applications and developments in grid, cloud, and high performance computing* (pp. 1–14). Hershey, PA: Information Science Reference; doi:10.4018/978-1-4666-2065-0.ch001

Cohen, F. (2013). Challenges to digital forensic evidence in the cloud. In K. Ruan (Ed.), *Cybercrime and cloud forensics: Applications for investigation processes* (pp. 59–78). Hershey, PA: Information Science Reference; doi:10.4018/978-1-4666-2662-1.ch003

Cossu, R., Di Giulio, C., Brito, F., & Petcu, D. (2013). Cloud computing for earth observation. In D. Kyriazis, A. Voulodimos, S. Gogouvitis, & T. Varvarigou (Eds.), *Data intensive storage services for cloud environments* (pp. 166–191). Hershey, PA: Business Science Reference; doi:10.4018/978-1-4666-3934-8.ch012

Costa, J. E., & Rodrigues, J. J. (2014). Mobile cloud computing: Technologies, services, and applications. In J. Rodrigues, K. Lin, & J. Lloret (Eds.), *Mobile networks and cloud computing convergence for progressive services and applications* (pp. 1–17). Hershey, PA: Information Science Reference; doi:10.4018/978-1-4666-4781-7.ch001

Creaner, G., & Pahl, C. (2013). Flexible coordination techniques for dynamic cloud service collaboration. In G. Ortiz & J. Cubo (Eds.), *Adaptive web services for modular and reusable software development: Tactics and solutions* (pp. 239–252). Hershey, PA: Information Science Reference; doi:10.4018/978-1-4666-2089-6.ch009

Crosbie, M. (2013). Hack the cloud: Ethical hacking and cloud forensics. In K. Ruan (Ed.), *Cybercrime and cloud forensics: Applications for investigation processes* (pp. 42–58). Hershey, PA: Information Science Reference; doi:10.4018/978-1-4666-2662-1.ch002

Curran, K., Carlin, S., & Adams, M. (2012). Security issues in cloud computing. In L. Chao (Ed.), *Cloud computing for teaching and learning: Strategies for design and implementation* (pp. 200–208). Hershey, PA: Information Science Reference; doi:10.4018/978-1-4666-0957-0.ch014

Dahbur, K., & Mohammad, B. (2011). Toward understanding the challenges and countermeasures in computer anti-forensics.[IJCAC]. *International Journal of Cloud Applications and Computing, 1*(3), 22–35. doi:10.4018/ijcac.2011070103

Dahbur, K., Mohammad, B., & Tarakji, A. B. (2011). Security issues in cloud computing: A survey of risks, threats and vulnerabilities.[IJCAC]. *International Journal of Cloud Applications and Computing, 1*(3), 1–11. doi:10.4018/ijcac.2011070101

Dahbur, K., Mohammad, B., & Tarakji, A. B. (2012). Security issues in cloud computing: A survey of risks, threats and vulnerabilities. In *Grid and cloud computing: Concepts, methodologies, tools and applications* (pp. 1644–1655). Hershey, PA: Information Science Reference; doi:10.4018/978-1-4666-0879-5.ch707

Dahbur, K., Mohammad, B., & Tarakji, A. B. (2013). Security issues in cloud computing: A survey of risks, threats and vulnerabilities. In S. Aljawarneh (Ed.), *Cloud computing advancements in design, implementation, and technologies* (pp. 154–165). Hershey, PA: Information Science Reference; doi:10.4018/978-1-4666-1879-4.ch011

Daim, T., Britton, M., Subramanian, G., Brenden, R., & Intarode, N. (2012). Adopting and integrating cloud computing. In E. Eyob & E. Tetteh (Eds.), *Customer-oriented global supply chains: Concepts for effective management* (pp. 175–197). Hershey, PA: Information Science Reference; doi:10.4018/978-1-4666-0246-5.ch011

Davis, M., & Sedsman, A. (2012). Grey areas: The legal dimensions of cloud computing. In C. Li & A. Ho (Eds.), *Crime prevention technologies and applications for advancing criminal investigation* (pp. 263–273). Hershey, PA: Information Science Reference; doi:10.4018/978-1-4666-1758-2.ch017

De Coster, R., & Albesher, A. (2013). The development of mobile service applications for consumers and intelligent networks. In I. Lee (Ed.), *Mobile services industries, technologies, and applications in the global economy* (pp. 273–289). Hershey, PA: Information Science Reference; doi:10.4018/978-1-4666-1981-4.ch017

De Filippi, P. (2014). Ubiquitous computing in the cloud: User empowerment vs. user obsequity. In J. Pelet & P. Papadopoulou (Eds.), *User behavior in ubiquitous online environments* (pp. 44–63). Hershey, PA: Information Science Reference; doi:10.4018/978-1-4666-4566-0.ch003

De Silva, S. (2013). Key legal issues with cloud computing: A UK law perspective. In A. Bento & A. Aggarwal (Eds.), *Cloud computing service and deployment models: Layers and management* (pp. 242–256). Hershey, PA: Business Science Reference; doi:10.4018/978-1-4666-2187-9.ch013

Deed, C., & Cragg, P. (2013). Business impacts of cloud computing. In A. Bento & A. Aggarwal (Eds.), *Cloud computing service and deployment models: Layers and management* (pp. 274–288). Hershey, PA: Business Science Reference; doi:10.4018/978-1-4666-2187-9.ch015

Deng, M., Petkovic, M., Nalin, M., & Baroni, I. (2013). Home healthcare in cloud computing. In M. Cruz-Cunha, I. Miranda, & P. Gonçalves (Eds.), *Handbook of research on ICTs and management systems for improving efficiency in healthcare and social care* (pp. 614–634). Hershey, PA: Medical Information Science Reference; doi:10.4018/978-1-4666-3990-4.ch032

Desai, A. M., & Mock, K. (2013). Security in cloud computing. In A. Bento & A. Aggarwal (Eds.), *Cloud computing service and deployment models: Layers and management* (pp. 208–221). Hershey, PA: Business Science Reference; doi:10.4018/978-1-4666-2187-9.ch011

Deshpande, R. M., Patle, B. V., & Bhoskar, R. D. (2014). Planning and implementation of cloud computing in NIT's in India: Special reference to VNIT. In S. Dhamdhere (Ed.), *Cloud computing and virtualization technologies in libraries* (pp. 90–106). Hershey, PA: Information Science Reference; doi:10.4018/978-1-4666-4631-5.ch006

Dhamdhere, S. N., & Lihitkar, R. (2014). The university cloud library model and the role of the cloud librarian. In S. Dhamdhere (Ed.), *Cloud computing and virtualization technologies in libraries* (pp. 150–161). Hershey, PA: Information Science Reference; doi:10.4018/978-1-4666-4631-5.ch009

Di Martino, S., Ferrucci, F., Maggio, V., & Sarro, F. (2013). Towards migrating genetic algorithms for test data generation to the cloud. In S. Tilley & T. Parveen (Eds.), *Software testing in the cloud: Perspectives on an emerging discipline* (pp. 113–135). Hershey, PA: Information Science Reference; doi:10.4018/978-1-4666-2536-5.ch006

Di Sano, M., Di Stefano, A., Morana, G., & Zito, D. (2013). FSaaS: Configuring policies for managing shared files among cooperating, distributed applications.[IJWP]. *International Journal of Web Portals*, 5(1), 1–14. doi:10.4018/jwp.2013010101

Dippl, S., Jaeger, M. C., Luhn, A., Shulman-Peleg, A., & Vernik, G. (2013). Towards federation and interoperability of cloud storage systems. In D. Kyriazis, A. Voulodimos, S. Gogouvitis, & T. Varvarigou (Eds.), *Data intensive storage services for cloud environments* (pp. 60–71). Hershey, PA: Business Science Reference; doi:10.4018/978-1-4666-3934-8.ch005

Distefano, S., & Puliafito, A. (2012). The cloud@home volunteer and interoperable cloud through the future internet. In M. Villari, I. Brandic, & F. Tusa (Eds.), *Achieving federated and self-manageable cloud infrastructures: Theory and practice* (pp. 79–96). Hershey, PA: Business Science Reference; doi:10.4018/978-1-4666-1631-8.ch005

Djoleto, W. (2013). Cloud computing and ecommerce or ebusiness: "The now it way" – An overview. In *Electronic commerce and organizational leadership: perspectives and methodologies* (pp. 239–254). Hershey, PA: Business Science Reference; doi:10.4018/978-1-4666-2982-0.ch010

Dollmann, T. J., Loos, P., Fellmann, M., Thomas, O., Hoheisel, A., Katranuschkov, P., & Scherer, R. (2011). Design and usage of a process-centric collaboration methodology for virtual organizations in hybrid environments.[IJIIT]. *International Journal of Intelligent Information Technologies*, 7(1), 45–64. doi:10.4018/jiit.2011010104

Dollmann, T. J., Loos, P., Fellmann, M., Thomas, O., Hoheisel, A., Katranuschkov, P., & Scherer, R. (2013). Design and usage of a process-centric collaboration methodology for virtual organizations in hybrid environments. In V. Sugumaran (Ed.), *Organizational efficiency through intelligent information technologies* (pp. 45–64). Hershey, PA: Information Science Reference; doi:10.4018/978-1-4666-2047-6.ch004

Dreher, P., & Vouk, M. (2012). Utilizing open source cloud computing environments to provide cost effective support for university education and research. In L. Chao (Ed.), *Cloud computing for teaching and learning: Strategies for design and implementation* (pp. 32–49). Hershey, PA: Information Science Reference; doi:10.4018/978-1-4666-0957-0.ch003

Drum, D., Becker, D., & Fish, M. (2013). Technology adoption in troubled times: A cloud computing case study.[JCIT]. *Journal of Cases on Information Technology*, 15(2), 57–71. doi:10.4018/jcit.2013040104

Dunaway, D. M. (2013). Creating virtual collaborative learning experiences for aspiring teachers. In R. Hartshorne, T. Heafner, & T. Petty (Eds.), *Teacher education programs and online learning tools: Innovations in teacher preparation* (pp. 167–180). Hershey, PA: Information Science Reference; doi:10.4018/978-1-4666-1906-7.ch009

Dykstra, J. (2013). Seizing electronic evidence from cloud computing environ-ments. In K. Ruan (Ed.), *Cybercrime and cloud forensics: Applications for inves-tigation processes* (pp. 156–185). Hershey, PA: Information Science Reference; doi:10.4018/978-1-4666-2662-1.ch007

El-Refaey, M., & Rimal, B. P. (2012). Grid, SOA and cloud computing: On-demand computing models. In *Grid and cloud computing: Concepts, methodologies, tools and applications* (pp. 12–51). Hershey, PA: Information Science Reference; doi:10.4018/978-1-4666-0879-5.ch102

El-Refaey, M., & Rimal, B. P. (2012). Grid, SOA and cloud computing: On-demand computing models. In N. Preve (Ed.), *Computational and data grids: Principles, applications and design* (pp. 45–85). Hershey, PA: Information Science Reference; doi:10.4018/978-1-61350-113-9.ch003

Elnaffar, S., Maamar, Z., & Sheng, Q. Z. (2013). When clouds start socializing: The sky model.[IJEBR]. *International Journal of E-Business Research*, *9*(2), 1–7. doi:10.4018/jebr.2013040101

Elwood, S., & Keengwe, J. (2012). Microbursts: A design format for mobile cloud computing.[IJICTE]. *International Journal of Information and Communication Technology Education*, *8*(2), 102–110. doi:10.4018/jicte.2012040109

Emeakaroha, V. C., Netto, M. A., Calheiros, R. N., & De Rose, C. A. (2012). Achiev-ing flexible SLA and resource management in clouds. In M. Villari, I. Brandic, & F. Tusa (Eds.), *Achieving federated and self-manageable cloud infrastructures: Theory and practice* (pp. 266–287). Hershey, PA: Business Science Reference; doi:10.4018/978-1-4666-1631-8.ch014

Etro, F. (2013). The economics of cloud computing. In A. Bento & A. Aggarwal (Eds.), *Cloud computing service and deployment models: Layers and management* (pp. 296–309). Hershey, PA: Business Science Reference; doi:10.4018/978-1-4666-2187-9.ch017

Ezugwu, A. E., Buhari, S. M., & Junaidu, S. B. (2013). Virtual machine allocation in cloud computing environment.[IJCAC]. *International Journal of Cloud Applica-tions and Computing*, *3*(2), 47–60. doi:10.4018/ijcac.2013040105

Fauzi, A. H., & Taylor, H. (2013). Secure community trust stores for peer-to-peer e-commerce applications using cloud services.[IJEEI]. *International Journal of E-Entrepreneurship and Innovation*, *4*(1), 1–15. doi:10.4018/jeei.2013010101

Ferguson-Boucher, K., & Endicott-Popovsky, B. (2013). Forensic readiness in the cloud (FRC): Integrating records management and digital forensics. In K. Ruan (Ed.), *Cybercrime and cloud forensics: Applications for investigation processes* (pp. 105–128). Hershey, PA: Information Science Reference; doi:10.4018/978-1-4666-2662-1.ch005

Ferraro de Souza, R., Westphall, C. B., dos Santos, D. R., & Westphall, C. M. (2013). A review of PACS on cloud for archiving secure medical images.[IJPHIM]. *International Journal of Privacy and Health Information Management, 1*(1), 53–62. doi:10.4018/ijphim.2013010104

Firdhous, M., Hassan, S., & Ghazali, O. (2013). Statistically enhanced multi-dimensional trust computing mechanism for cloud computing.[IJMCMC]. *International Journal of Mobile Computing and Multimedia Communications, 5*(2), 1–17. doi:10.4018/jmcmc.2013040101

Formisano, C., Bonelli, L., Balraj, K. R., & Shulman-Peleg, A. (2013). Cloud access control mechanisms. In D. Kyriazis, A. Voulodimos, S. Gogouvitis, & T. Varvarigou (Eds.), *Data intensive storage services for cloud environments* (pp. 94–108). Hershey, PA: Business Science Reference; doi:10.4018/978-1-4666-3934-8.ch007

Frank, H., & Mesentean, S. (2012). Efficient communication interfaces for distributed energy resources. In E. Udoh (Ed.), *Evolving developments in grid and cloud computing: Advancing research* (pp. 185–196). Hershey, PA: Information Science Reference; doi:10.4018/978-1-4666-0056-0.ch013

Gallina, B., & Guelfi, N. (2012). Reusing transaction models for dependable cloud computing. In H. Yang & X. Liu (Eds.), *Software reuse in the emerging cloud computing era* (pp. 248–277). Hershey, PA: Information Science Reference; doi:10.4018/978-1-4666-0897-9.ch011

Garofalo, D. A. (2013). Empires of the future: Libraries, technology, and the academic environment. In E. Iglesias (Ed.), *Robots in academic libraries: Advancements in library automation* (pp. 180–206). Hershey, PA: Information Science Reference; doi:10.4018/978-1-4666-3938-6.ch010

Gebremeskel, G. B., He, Z., & Jing, X. (2013). Semantic integrating for intelligent cloud data mining platform and cloud based business intelligence for optimization of mobile social networks. In V. Bhatnagar (Ed.), *Data mining in dynamic social networks and fuzzy systems* (pp. 173–211). Hershey, PA: Information Science Reference; doi:10.4018/978-1-4666-4213-3.ch009

Gentleman, W. M. (2013). Using the cloud for testing NOT adjunct to development. In S. Tilley & T. Parveen (Eds.), *Software testing in the cloud: Perspectives on an emerging discipline* (pp. 216–230). Hershey, PA: Information Science Reference; doi:10.4018/978-1-4666-2536-5.ch010

Ghafoor, K. Z., Mohammed, M. A., Abu Bakar, K., Sadiq, A. S., & Lloret, J. (2014). Vehicular cloud computing: Trends and challenges. In J. Rodrigues, K. Lin, & J. Lloret (Eds.), *Mobile networks and cloud computing convergence for progressive services and applications* (pp. 262–274). Hershey, PA: Information Science Reference; doi:10.4018/978-1-4666-4781-7.ch014

Giannakaki, M. (2012). The "right to be forgotten" in the era of social media and cloud computing. In C. Akrivopoulou & N. Garipidis (Eds.), *Human rights and risks in the digital era: Globalization and the effects of information technologies* (pp. 10–24). Hershey, PA: Information Science Reference; doi:10.4018/978-1-4666-0891-7.ch002

Gillam, L., Li, B., & O'Loughlin, J. (2012). Teaching clouds: Lessons taught and lessons learnt. In L. Chao (Ed.), *Cloud computing for teaching and learning: Strategies for design and implementation* (pp. 82–94). Hershey, PA: Information Science Reference; doi:10.4018/978-1-4666-0957-0.ch006

Gonsowski, D. (2013). Compliance in the cloud and the implications on electronic discovery. In K. Ruan (Ed.), *Cybercrime and cloud forensics: Applications for investigation processes* (pp. 230–250). Hershey, PA: Information Science Reference; doi:10.4018/978-1-4666-2662-1.ch009

Gonzalez-Sanchez, J., Conley, Q., Chavez-Echeagaray, M., & Atkinson, R. K. (2012). Supporting the assembly process by leveraging augmented reality, cloud computing, and mobile devices.[IJCBPL]. *International Journal of Cyber Behavior, Psychology and Learning, 2*(3), 86–102. doi:10.4018/ijcbpl.2012070107

Gopinath, R., & Geetha, B. (2013). An e-learning system based on secure data storage services in cloud computing.[IJITWE]. *International Journal of Information Technology and Web Engineering, 8*(2), 1–17. doi:10.4018/jitwe.2013040101

Gossin, P. C., & LaBrie, R. C. (2013). Data center waste management. In P. Ordóñez de Pablos (Ed.), *Green technologies and business practices: An IT approach* (pp. 226–235). Hershey, PA: Information Science Reference; doi:10.4018/978-1-4666-1972-2.ch014

Goswami, V., Patra, S. S., & Mund, G. B. (2012). Performance analysis of cloud computing centers for bulk services.[IJCAC]. *International Journal of Cloud Applications and Computing, 2*(4), 53–65. doi:10.4018/ijcac.2012100104

Goswami, V., & Sahoo, C. N. (2013). Optimal resource usage in multi-cloud computing environment.[IJCAC]. *International Journal of Cloud Applications and Computing, 3*(1), 44–57. doi:10.4018/ijcac.2013010105

Gräuler, M., Teuteberg, F., Mahmoud, T., & Gómez, J. M. (2013). Requirements prioritization and design considerations for the next generation of corporate environmental management information systems: A foundation for innovation.[IJITSA]. *International Journal of Information Technologies and Systems Approach, 6*(1), 98–116. doi:10.4018/jitsa.2013010106

Grieve, G. P., & Heston, K. (2012). Finding liquid salvation: Using the cardean ethnographic method to document second life residents and religious cloud communities. In N. Zagalo, L. Morgado, & A. Boa-Ventura (Eds.), *Virtual worlds and metaverse platforms: New communication and identity paradigms* (pp. 288–305). Hershey, PA: Information Science Reference; doi:10.4018/978-1-60960-854-5.ch019

Grispos, G., Storer, T., & Glisson, W. B. (2012). Calm before the storm: The challenges of cloud computing in digital forensics.[IJDCF]. *International Journal of Digital Crime and Forensics, 4*(2), 28–48. doi:10.4018/jdcf.2012040103

Grispos, G., Storer, T., & Glisson, W. B. (2013). Calm before the storm: The challenges of cloud computing in digital forensics. In C. Li (Ed.), *Emerging digital forensics applications for crime detection, prevention, and security* (pp. 211–233). Hershey, PA: Information Science Reference; doi:10.4018/978-1-4666-4006-1.ch015

Guster, D., & Lee, O. F. (2011). Enhancing the disaster recovery plan through virtualization.[JITR]. *Journal of Information Technology Research, 4*(4), 18–40. doi:10.4018/jitr.2011100102

Hanawa, T., & Sato, M. (2013). D-Cloud: Software testing environment for dependable distributed systems using cloud computing technology. In S. Tilley & T. Parveen (Eds.), *Software testing in the cloud: Perspectives on an emerging discipline* (pp. 340–355). Hershey, PA: Information Science Reference; doi:10.4018/978-1-4666-2536-5.ch016

Hardy, J., Liu, L., Lei, C., & Li, J. (2013). Internet-based virtual computing infrastructure for cloud computing. In X. Yang & L. Liu (Eds.), *Principles, methodologies, and service-oriented approaches for cloud computing* (pp. 371–389). Hershey, PA: Business Science Reference; doi:10.4018/978-1-4666-2854-0.ch016

Hashizume, K., Yoshioka, N., & Fernandez, E. B. (2013). Three misuse patterns for cloud computing. In D. Rosado, D. Mellado, E. Fernandez-Medina, & M. Piattini (Eds.), *Security engineering for cloud computing: Approaches and tools* (pp. 36–53). Hershey, PA: Information Science Reference; doi:10.4018/978-1-4666-2125-1.ch003

Hassan, Q. F., Riad, A. M., & Hassan, A. E. (2012). Understanding cloud computing. In H. Yang & X. Liu (Eds.), *Software reuse in the emerging cloud computing era* (pp. 204–227). Hershey, PA: Information Science Reference; doi:10.4018/978-1-4666-0897-9.ch009

Hasselmeyer, P., Katsaros, G., Koller, B., & Wieder, P. (2012). Cloud monitoring. In M. Villari, I. Brandic, & F. Tusa (Eds.), *Achieving federated and self-manageable cloud infrastructures: Theory and practice* (pp. 97–116). Hershey, PA: Business Science Reference; doi:10.4018/978-1-4666-1631-8.ch006

Hertzler, B. T., Frost, E., Bressler, G. H., & Goehring, C. (2011). Experience report: Using a cloud computing environment during Haiti and Exercise24.[IJISCRAM]. *International Journal of Information Systems for Crisis Response and Management*, *3*(1), 50–64. doi:10.4018/jiscrm.2011010104

Hertzler, B. T., Frost, E., Bressler, G. H., & Goehring, C. (2013). Experience report: Using a cloud computing environment during Haiti and Exercise24. In M. Jennex (Ed.), *Using social and information technologies for disaster and crisis management* (pp. 52–66). Hershey, PA: Information Science Reference; doi:10.4018/978-1-4666-2788-8.ch004

Ho, R. (2013). Cloud computing and enterprise migration strategies. In A. Loo (Ed.), *Distributed computing innovations for business, engineering, and science* (pp. 156–175). Hershey, PA: Information Science Reference; doi:10.4018/978-1-4666-2533-4.ch008

Hobona, G., Jackson, M., & Anand, S. (2012). Implementing geospatial web services for cloud computing. In *Grid and cloud computing: Concepts, methodologies, tools and applications* (pp. 615–636). Hershey, PA: Information Science Reference; doi:10.4018/978-1-4666-0879-5.ch305

Hochstein, L., Schott, B., & Graybill, R. B. (2011). Computational engineering in the cloud: Benefits and challenges.[JOEUC]. *Journal of Organizational and End User Computing*, *23*(4), 31–50. doi:10.4018/joeuc.2011100103

Hochstein, L., Schott, B., & Graybill, R. B. (2013). Computational engineering in the cloud: Benefits and challenges. In A. Dwivedi & S. Clarke (Eds.), *Innovative strategies and approaches for end-user computing advancements* (pp. 314–332). Hershey, PA: Information Science Reference; doi:10.4018/978-1-4666-2059-9.ch017

Honarvar, A. R. (2013). Developing an elastic cloud computing application through multi-agent systems.[IJCAC]. *International Journal of Cloud Applications and Computing*, *3*(1), 58–64. doi:10.4018/ijcac.2013010106

Hossain, S. (2013). Cloud computing terms, definitions, and taxonomy. In A. Bento & A. Aggarwal (Eds.), *Cloud computing service and deployment models: Layers and management* (pp. 1–25). Hershey, PA: Business Science Reference; doi:10.4018/978-1-4666-2187-9.ch001

Hudzia, B., Sinclair, J., & Lindner, M. (2013). Deploying and running enterprise grade applications in a federated cloud. In *Supply chain management: Concepts, methodologies, tools, and applications* (pp. 1350–1370). Hershey, PA: Business Science Reference; doi:10.4018/978-1-4666-2625-6.ch080

Hung, S., Shieh, J., & Lee, C. (2011). Migrating android applications to the cloud. [IJGHPC]. *International Journal of Grid and High Performance Computing*, *3*(2), 14–28. doi:10.4018/jghpc.2011040102

Hung, S., Shieh, J., & Lee, C. (2013). Migrating android applications to the cloud. In E. Udoh (Ed.), *Applications and developments in grid, cloud, and high performance computing* (pp. 307–322). Hershey, PA: Information Science Reference; doi:10.4018/978-1-4666-2065-0.ch020

Islam, S., Mouratidis, H., & Weippl, E. R. (2013). A goal-driven risk management approach to support security and privacy analysis of cloud-based system. In D. Rosado, D. Mellado, E. Fernandez-Medina, & M. Piattini (Eds.), *Security engineering for cloud computing: Approaches and tools* (pp. 97–122). Hershey, PA: Information Science Reference; doi:10.4018/978-1-4666-2125-1.ch006

Itani, W., Kayssi, A., & Chehab, A. (2013). Hardware-based security for ensuring data privacy in the cloud. In D. Rosado, D. Mellado, E. Fernandez-Medina, & M. Piattini (Eds.), *Security engineering for cloud computing: Approaches and tools* (pp. 147–170). Hershey, PA: Information Science Reference; doi:10.4018/978-1-4666-2125-1.ch008

Jackson, A., & Weiland, M. (2013). Cloud computing for scientific simulation and high performance computing. In X. Yang & L. Liu (Eds.), *Principles, methodologies, and service-oriented approaches for cloud computing* (pp. 51–70). Hershey, PA: Business Science Reference; doi:10.4018/978-1-4666-2854-0.ch003

Jaeger, M. C., & Hohenstein, U. (2013). Content centric storage and current storage systems. In D. Kyriazis, A. Voulodimos, S. Gogouvitis, & T. Varvarigou (Eds.), *Data intensive storage services for cloud environments* (pp. 27–46). Hershey, PA: Business Science Reference; doi:10.4018/978-1-4666-3934-8.ch003

James, J. I., Shosha, A. F., & Gladyshev, P. (2013). Digital forensic investigation and cloud computing. In K. Ruan (Ed.), *Cybercrime and cloud forensics: Applications for investigation processes* (pp. 1–41). Hershey, PA: Information Science Reference; doi:10.4018/978-1-4666-2662-1.ch001

Jena, R. K. (2013). Green computing to green business. In P. Ordóñez de Pablos (Ed.), *Green technologies and business practices: An IT approach* (pp. 138–150). Hershey, PA: Information Science Reference; doi:10.4018/978-1-4666-1972-2.ch007

Jeyarani, R., & Nagaveni, N. (2012). A heuristic meta scheduler for optimal resource utilization and improved QoS in cloud computing environment.[IJCAC]. *International Journal of Cloud Applications and Computing*, 2(1), 41–52. doi:10.4018/ijcac.2012010103

Jeyarani, R., Nagaveni, N., & Ram, R. V. (2011). Self adaptive particle swarm optimization for efficient virtual machine provisioning in cloud.[IJIIT]. *International Journal of Intelligent Information Technologies*, 7(2), 25–44. doi:10.4018/jiit.2011040102

Jeyarani, R., Nagaveni, N., & Ram, R. V. (2013). Self adaptive particle swarm optimization for efficient virtual machine provisioning in cloud. In V. Sugumaran (Ed.), *Organizational efficiency through intelligent information technologies* (pp. 88–107). Hershey, PA: Information Science Reference; doi:10.4018/978-1-4666-2047-6.ch006

Jeyarani, R., Nagaveni, N., Sadasivam, S. K., & Rajarathinam, V. R. (2011). Power aware meta scheduler for adaptive VM provisioning in IaaS cloud.[IJCAC]. *International Journal of Cloud Applications and Computing*, 1(3), 36–51. doi:10.4018/ijcac.2011070104

Jeyarani, R., Nagaveni, N., Sadasivam, S. K., & Rajarathinam, V. R. (2013). Power aware meta scheduler for adaptive VM provisioning in IaaS cloud. In S. Aljawarneh (Ed.), *Cloud computing advancements in design, implementation, and technologies* (pp. 190–204). Hershey, PA: Information Science Reference; doi:10.4018/978-1-4666-1879-4.ch014

Jiang, J., Huang, X., Wu, Y., & Yang, G. (2013). Campus cloud storage and preservation: From distributed file system to data sharing service. In X. Yang & L. Liu (Eds.), *Principles, methodologies, and service-oriented approaches for cloud computing* (pp. 284–301). Hershey, PA: Business Science Reference; doi:10.4018/978-1-4666-2854-0.ch012

Jing, S. (2012). The application exploration of cloud computing in information technology teaching.[IJAPUC]. *International Journal of Advanced Pervasive and Ubiquitous Computing*, 4(4), 23–27. doi:10.4018/japuc.2012100104

Related of References

Johansson, D., & Wiberg, M. (2012). Conceptually advancing "application mobility" towards design: Applying a concept-driven approach to the design of mobile IT for home care service groups.[IJACI]. *International Journal of Ambient Computing and Intelligence*, *4*(3), 20–32. doi:10.4018/jaci.2012070102

Jorda, J., & M'zoughi, A. (2013). Securing cloud storage. In D. Rosado, D. Mellado, E. Fernandez-Medina, & M. Piattini (Eds.), *Security engineering for cloud computing: Approaches and tools* (pp. 171–190). Hershey, PA: Information Science Reference; doi:10.4018/978-1-4666-2125-1.ch009

Juiz, C., & Alexander de Pous, V. (2014). Cloud computing: IT governance, legal, and public policy aspects. In I. Portela & F. Almeida (Eds.), *Organizational, legal, and technological dimensions of information system administration* (pp. 139–166). Hershey, PA: Information Science Reference; doi:10.4018/978-1-4666-4526-4.ch009

Kaisler, S. H., Money, W., & Cohen, S. J. (2013). Cloud computing: A decision framework for small businesses. In A. Bento & A. Aggarwal (Eds.), *Cloud computing service and deployment models: Layers and management* (pp. 151–172). Hershey, PA: Business Science Reference; doi:10.4018/978-1-4666-2187-9.ch008

Kanamori, Y., & Yen, M. Y. (2013). Cloud computing security and risk management. In A. Bento & A. Aggarwal (Eds.), *Cloud computing service and deployment models: Layers and management* (pp. 222–240). Hershey, PA: Business Science Reference; doi:10.4018/978-1-4666-2187-9.ch012

Karadsheh, L., & Alhawari, S. (2011). Applying security policies in small business utilizing cloud computing technologies.[IJCAC]. *International Journal of Cloud Applications and Computing*, *1*(2), 29–40. doi:10.4018/ijcac.2011040103

Karadsheh, L., & Alhawari, S. (2013). Applying security policies in small business utilizing cloud computing technologies. In S. Aljawarneh (Ed.), *Cloud computing advancements in design, implementation, and technologies* (pp. 112–124). Hershey, PA: Information Science Reference; doi:10.4018/978-1-4666-1879-4.ch008

Kaupins, G. (2012). Laws associated with mobile computing in the cloud.[IJWNBT]. *International Journal of Wireless Networks and Broadband Technologies*, *2*(3), 1–9. doi:10.4018/ijwnbt.2012070101

Kemp, M. L., Robb, S., & Deans, P. C. (2013). The legal implications of cloud computing. In A. Bento & A. Aggarwal (Eds.), *Cloud computing service and deployment models: Layers and management* (pp. 257–272). Hershey, PA: Business Science Reference; doi:10.4018/978-1-4666-2187-9.ch014

Khan, N., Ahmad, N., Herawan, T., & Inayat, Z. (2012). Cloud computing: Locally sub-clouds instead of globally one cloud.[IJCAC]. *International Journal of Cloud Applications and Computing, 2*(3), 68–85. doi:10.4018/ijcac.2012070103

Khan, N., Noraziah, A., Ismail, E. I., Deris, M. M., & Herawan, T. (2012). Cloud computing: Analysis of various platforms.[IJEEI]. *International Journal of E-Entrepreneurship and Innovation, 3*(2), 51–59. doi:10.4018/jeei.2012040104

Khansa, L., Forcade, J., Nambari, G., Parasuraman, S., & Cox, P. (2012). Proposing an intelligent cloud-based electronic health record system.[IJBDCN]. *International Journal of Business Data Communications and Networking, 8*(3), 57–71. doi:10.4018/jbdcn.2012070104

Kierkegaard, S. (2012). Not every cloud brings rain: Legal risks on the horizon. In M. Gupta, J. Walp, & R. Sharman (Eds.), *Strategic and practical approaches for information security governance: Technologies and applied solutions* (pp. 181–194). Hershey, PA: Information Science Reference; doi:10.4018/978-1-4666-0197-0.ch011

Kifayat, K., Shamsa, T. B., Mackay, M., Merabti, M., & Shi, Q. (2013). Real time risk management in cloud computation. In D. Rosado, D. Mellado, E. Fernandez-Medina, & M. Piattini (Eds.), *Security engineering for cloud computing: Approaches and tools* (pp. 123–145). Hershey, PA: Information Science Reference; doi:10.4018/978-1-4666-2125-1.ch007

King, T. M., Ganti, A. S., & Froslie, D. (2013). Towards improving the testability of cloud application services. In S. Tilley & T. Parveen (Eds.), *Software testing in the cloud: Perspectives on an emerging discipline* (pp. 322–339). Hershey, PA: Information Science Reference; doi:10.4018/978-1-4666-2536-5.ch015

Kipp, A., Schneider, R., & Schubert, L. (2013). Encapsulation of complex HPC services. In C. Rückemann (Ed.), *Integrated information and computing systems for natural, spatial, and social sciences* (pp. 153–176). Hershey, PA: Information Science Reference; doi:10.4018/978-1-4666-2190-9.ch008

Kldiashvili, E. (2012). The cloud computing as the tool for implementation of virtual organization technology for ehealth.[JITR]. *Journal of Information Technology Research, 5*(1), 18–34. doi:10.4018/jitr.2012010102

Kldiashvili, E. (2013). Implementation of telecytology in georgia for quality assurance programs.[JITR]. *Journal of Information Technology Research, 6*(2), 24–45. doi:10.4018/jitr.2013040102

Kosmatov, N. (2013). Concolic test generation and the cloud: deployment and verification perspectives. In S. Tilley & T. Parveen (Eds.), *Software testing in the cloud: Perspectives on an emerging discipline* (pp. 231–251). Hershey, PA: Information Science Reference; doi:10.4018/978-1-4666-2536-5.ch011

Kotamarti, R. M., Thornton, M. A., & Dunham, M. H. (2012). Quantum computing approach for alignment-free sequence search and classification. In S. Ali, N. Abbadeni, & M. Batouche (Eds.), *Multidisciplinary computational intelligence techniques: Applications in business, engineering, and medicine* (pp. 279–300). Hershey, PA: Information Science Reference; doi:10.4018/978-1-4666-1830-5.ch017

Kremmydas, D., Petsakos, A., & Rozakis, S. (2012). Parametric optimization of linear and non-linear models via parallel computing to enhance web-spatial DSS interactivity.[IJDSST]. *International Journal of Decision Support System Technology*, *4*(1), 14–29. doi:10.4018/jdsst.2012010102

Krishnadas, N., & Pillai, R. R. (2013). Cloud computing diagnosis: A comprehensive study. In X. Yang & L. Liu (Eds.), *Principles, methodologies, and service-oriented approaches for cloud computing* (pp. 1–18). Hershey, PA: Business Science Reference; doi:10.4018/978-1-4666-2854-0.ch001

Kübert, R., & Katsaros, G. (2011). Using free software for elastic web hosting on a private cloud.[IJCAC]. *International Journal of Cloud Applications and Computing*, *1*(2), 14–28. doi:10.4018/ijcac.2011040102

Kübert, R., & Katsaros, G. (2013). Using free software for elastic web hosting on a private cloud. In S. Aljawarneh (Ed.), *Cloud computing advancements in design, implementation, and technologies* (pp. 97–111). Hershey, PA: Information Science Reference; doi:10.4018/978-1-4666-1879-4.ch007

Kumar, P. S., Ashok, M. S., & Subramanian, R. (2012). A publicly verifiable dynamic secret sharing protocol for secure and dependable data storage in cloud computing. [IJCAC]. *International Journal of Cloud Applications and Computing*, *2*(3), 1–25. doi:10.4018/ijcac.2012070101

Lasluisa, S., Rodero, I., & Parashar, M. (2013). Software design for passing sarbanes-oxley in cloud computing. In C. Rückemann (Ed.), *Integrated information and computing systems for natural, spatial, and social sciences* (pp. 27–42). Hershey, PA: Information Science Reference; doi:10.4018/978-1-4666-2190-9.ch002

Lasluisa, S., Rodero, I., & Parashar, M. (2014). Software design for passing sarbanes-oxley in cloud computing. In *Software design and development: Concepts, methodologies, tools, and applications* (pp. 1659–1674). Hershey, PA: Information Science Reference; doi:10.4018/978-1-4666-4301-7.ch080

Lee, W. N. (2013). An economic analysis of cloud: "Software as a service" (saas) computing and "virtual desktop infrastructure" (VDI) models. In A. Bento & A. Aggarwal (Eds.), *Cloud computing service and deployment models: Layers and management* (pp. 289–295). Hershey, PA: Business Science Reference; doi:10.4018/978-1-4666-2187-9.ch016

Levine, K., & White, B. A. (2011). A crisis at hafford furniture: Cloud computing case study.[JCIT]. *Journal of Cases on Information Technology, 13*(1), 57–71. doi:10.4018/jcit.2011010104

Levine, K., & White, B. A. (2013). A crisis at Hafford furniture: Cloud computing case study. In M. Khosrow-Pour (Ed.), *Cases on emerging information technology research and applications* (pp. 70–87). Hershey, PA: Information Science Reference; doi:10.4018/978-1-4666-3619-4.ch004

Li, J., Meng, L., Zhu, Z., Li, X., Huai, J., & Liu, L. (2013). CloudRank: A cloud service ranking method based on both user feedback and service testing. In X. Yang & L. Liu (Eds.), *Principles, methodologies, and service-oriented approaches for cloud computing* (pp. 230–258). Hershey, PA: Business Science Reference; doi:10.4018/978-1-4666-2854-0.ch010

Liang, T., Lu, F., & Chiu, J. (2012). A hybrid resource reservation method for workflows in clouds.[IJGHPC]. *International Journal of Grid and High Performance Computing, 4*(4), 1–21. doi:10.4018/jghpc.2012100101

Lorenz, M., Rath-Wiggins, L., Runde, W., Messina, A., Sunna, P., Dimino, G., & Borgotallo, R. et al. (2013). Media convergence and cloud technologies: Smart storage, better workflows. In D. Kyriazis, A. Voulodimos, S. Gogouvitis, & T. Varvarigou (Eds.), *Data intensive storage services for cloud environments* (pp. 132–144). Hershey, PA: Business Science Reference; doi:10.4018/978-1-4666-3934-8.ch009

M., S. G., & G., S. K. (2012). An enterprise mashup integration service framework for clouds. *International Journal of Cloud Applications and Computing (IJCAC), 2*(2), 31-40. doi:10.4018/ijcac.2012040103

Maharana, S. K., P., G. P., & Bhati, A. (2012). A study of cloud computing for retinal image processing through MATLAB.[IJCAC]. *International Journal of Cloud Applications and Computing, 2*(2), 59–69. doi:10.4018/ijcac.2012040106

Maharana, S. K., Mali, P. B., Prabhakar, G. J. S., & Kumar, V. (2011). Cloud computing applied for numerical study of thermal characteristics of SIP.[IJCAC]. *International Journal of Cloud Applications and Computing, 1*(3), 12–21. doi:10.4018/ijcac.2011070102

Maharana, S. K., Mali, P. B., Prabhakar, G. J. S., & Kumar, V. (2013). Cloud computing applied for numerical study of thermal characteristics of SIP. In S. Aljawarneh (Ed.), *Cloud computing advancements in design, implementation, and technologies* (pp. 166–175). Hershey, PA: Information Science Reference; doi:10.4018/978-1-4666-1879-4.ch012

Maharana, S. K., Prabhakar, P. G., & Bhati, A. (2013). A study of cloud computing for retinal image processing through MATLAB. In *Image processing: Concepts, methodologies, tools, and applications* (pp. 101–111). Hershey, PA: Information Science Reference; doi:10.4018/978-1-4666-3994-2.ch006

Mahesh, S., Landry, B. J., Sridhar, T., & Walsh, K. R. (2011). A decision table for the cloud computing decision in small business.[IRMJ]. *Information Resources Management Journal, 24*(3), 9–25. doi:10.4018/irmj.2011070102

Mahesh, S., Landry, B. J., Sridhar, T., & Walsh, K. R. (2013). A decision table for the cloud computing decision in small business. In M. Khosrow-Pour (Ed.), *Managing information resources and technology: Emerging Applications and theories* (pp. 159–176). Hershey, PA: Information Science Reference; doi:10.4018/978-1-4666-3616-3.ch012

Marquezan, C. C., Metzger, A., Pohl, K., Engen, V., Boniface, M., Phillips, S. C., & Zlatev, Z. (2013). Adaptive future internet applications: Opportunities and challenges for adaptive web services technology. In G. Ortiz & J. Cubo (Eds.), *Adaptive web services for modular and reusable software development: Tactics and solutions* (pp. 333–353). Hershey, PA: Information Science Reference; doi:10.4018/978-1-4666-2089-6.ch014

Marshall, P. J. (2012). Cloud computing: Next generation education. In L. Chao (Ed.), *Cloud computing for teaching and learning: Strategies for design and implementation* (pp. 180–185). Hershey, PA: Information Science Reference; doi:10.4018/978-1-4666-0957-0.ch012

Martinez-Ortiz, A. (2012). Open cloud technologies. In L. Vaquero, J. Cáceres, & J. Hierro (Eds.), *Open source cloud computing systems: Practices and paradigms* (pp. 1–17). Hershey, PA: Information Science Reference; doi:10.4018/978-1-4666-0098-0.ch001

Massonet, P., Michot, A., Naqvi, S., Villari, M., & Latanicki, J. (2013). Securing the external interfaces of a federated infrastructure cloud. In *IT policy and ethics: Concepts, methodologies, tools, and applications* (pp. 1876–1903). Hershey, PA: Information Science Reference; doi:10.4018/978-1-4666-2919-6.ch082

Mavrogeorgi, N., Gogouvitis, S. V., Voulodimos, A., & Alexandrou, V. (2013). SLA management in storage clouds. In D. Kyriazis, A. Voulodimos, S. Gogouvitis, & T. Varvarigou (Eds.), *Data intensive storage services for cloud environments* (pp. 72–93). Hershey, PA: Business Science Reference; doi:10.4018/978-1-4666-3934-8.ch006

Mehta, H. K. (2013). Cloud selection for e-business a parameter based solution. In K. Tarnay, S. Imre, & L. Xu (Eds.), *Research and development in e-business through service-oriented solutions* (pp. 199–207). Hershey, PA: Business Science Reference; doi:10.4018/978-1-4666-4181-5.ch009

Mehta, H. K., & Gupta, E. (2013). Economy based resource allocation in IaaS cloud. [IJCAC]. *International Journal of Cloud Applications and Computing*, *3*(2), 1–11. doi:10.4018/ijcac.2013040101

Miah, S. J. (2012). Cloud-based intelligent DSS design for emergency professionals. In S. Ali, N. Abbadeni, & M. Batouche (Eds.), *Multidisciplinary computational intelligence techniques: Applications in business, engineering, and medicine* (pp. 47–60). Hershey, PA: Information Science Reference; doi:10.4018/978-1-4666-1830-5.ch004

Miah, S. J. (2013). Cloud-based intelligent DSS design for emergency professionals. In *Data mining: Concepts, methodologies, tools, and applications* (pp. 991–1003). Hershey, PA: Information Science Reference; doi:10.4018/978-1-4666-2455-9.ch050

Mikkilineni, R. (2012). Architectural resiliency in distributed computing.[IJGHPC]. *International Journal of Grid and High Performance Computing*, *4*(4), 37–51. doi:10.4018/jghpc.2012100103

Millham, R. (2012). Software asset re-use: Migration of data-intensive legacy system to the cloud computing paradigm. In H. Yang & X. Liu (Eds.), *Software reuse in the emerging cloud computing era* (pp. 1–27). Hershey, PA: Information Science Reference; doi:10.4018/978-1-4666-0897-9.ch001

Mircea, M. (2011). Building the agile enterprise with service-oriented architecture, business process management and decision management.[IJEEI]. *International Journal of E-Entrepreneurship and Innovation*, *2*(4), 32–48. doi:10.4018/jeei.2011100103

Modares, H., Lloret, J., Moravejosharieh, A., & Salleh, R. (2014). Security in mobile cloud computing. In J. Rodrigues, K. Lin, & J. Lloret (Eds.), *Mobile networks and cloud computing convergence for progressive services and applications* (pp. 79–91). Hershey, PA: Information Science Reference; doi:10.4018/978-1-4666-4781-7.ch005

Related of References

Moedjiono, S., & Mas'at, A. (2012). Cloud computing implementation strategy for information dissemination on meteorology, climatology, air quality, and geophysics (MKKuG).[JITR]. *Journal of Information Technology Research, 5*(3), 71–84. doi:10.4018/jitr.2012070104

Moiny, J. (2012). Cloud based social network sites: Under whose control? In A. Dudley, J. Braman, & G. Vincenti (Eds.), *Investigating cyber law and cyber ethics: Issues, impacts and practices* (pp. 147–219). Hershey, PA: Information Science Reference; doi:10.4018/978-1-61350-132-0.ch009

Moreno, I. S., & Xu, J. (2011). Energy-efficiency in cloud computing environments: Towards energy savings without performance degradation.[IJCAC]. *International Journal of Cloud Applications and Computing, 1*(1), 17–33. doi:10.4018/ijcac.2011010102

Moreno, I. S., & Xu, J. (2013). Energy-efficiency in cloud computing environments: Towards energy savings without performance degradation. In S. Aljawarneh (Ed.), *Cloud computing advancements in design, implementation, and technologies* (pp. 18–36). Hershey, PA: Information Science Reference; doi:10.4018/978-1-4666-1879-4.ch002

Muñoz, A., Maña, A., & González, J. (2013). Dynamic security properties monitoring architecture for cloud computing. In D. Rosado, D. Mellado, E. Fernandez-Medina, & M. Piattini (Eds.), *Security engineering for cloud computing: Approaches and tools* (pp. 1–18). Hershey, PA: Information Science Reference; doi:10.4018/978-1-4666-2125-1.ch001

Mvelase, P., Dlodlo, N., Williams, Q., & Adigun, M. O. (2011). Custom-made cloud enterprise architecture for small medium and micro enterprises.[IJCAC]. *International Journal of Cloud Applications and Computing, 1*(3), 52–63. doi:10.4018/ijcac.2011070105

Mvelase, P., Dlodlo, N., Williams, Q., & Adigun, M. O. (2012). Custom-made cloud enterprise architecture for small medium and micro enterprises. In *Grid and cloud computing: Concepts, methodologies, tools and applications* (pp. 589–601). Hershey, PA: Information Science Reference; doi:10.4018/978-1-4666-0879-5.ch303

Mvelase, P., Dlodlo, N., Williams, Q., & Adigun, M. O. (2013). Custom-made cloud enterprise architecture for small medium and micro enterprises. In S. Aljawarneh (Ed.), *Cloud computing advancements in design, implementation, and technologies* (pp. 205–217). Hershey, PA: Information Science Reference; doi:10.4018/978-1-4666-1879-4.ch015

Naeem, M. A., Dobbie, G., & Weber, G. (2014). Big data management in the context of real-time data warehousing. In W. Hu & N. Kaabouch (Eds.), *Big data management, technologies, and applications* (pp. 150–176). Hershey, PA: Information Science Reference; doi:10.4018/978-1-4666-4699-5.ch007

Ofosu, W. K., & Saliah-Hassane, H. (2013). Cloud computing in the education environment for developing nations.[IJITN]. *International Journal of Interdisciplinary Telecommunications and Networking*, 5(3), 54–62. doi:10.4018/jitn.2013070106

Oliveros, E., Cucinotta, T., Phillips, S. C., Yang, X., Middleton, S., & Voith, T. (2012). Monitoring and metering in the cloud. In D. Kyriazis, T. Varvarigou, & K. Konstanteli (Eds.), *Achieving real-time in distributed computing: From grids to clouds* (pp. 94–114). Hershey, PA: Information Science Reference; doi:10.4018/978-1-60960-827-9.ch006

Orton, I., Alva, A., & Endicott-Popovsky, B. (2013). Legal process and requirements for cloud forensic investigations. In K. Ruan (Ed.), *Cybercrime and cloud forensics: Applications for investigation processes* (pp. 186–229). Hershey, PA: Information Science Reference; doi:10.4018/978-1-4666-2662-1.ch008

Pakhira, A., & Andras, P. (2013). Leveraging the cloud for large-scale software testing – A case study: Google Chrome on Amazon. In S. Tilley & T. Parveen (Eds.), *Software testing in the cloud: Perspectives on an emerging discipline* (pp. 252–279). Hershey, PA: Information Science Reference; doi:10.4018/978-1-4666-2536-5.ch012

Pal, K., & Karakostas, B. (2013). The use of cloud computing in shipping logistics. In D. Graham, I. Manikas, & D. Folinas (Eds.), *E-logistics and e-supply chain management: Applications for evolving business* (pp. 104–124). Hershey, PA: Business Science Reference; doi:10.4018/978-1-4666-3914-0.ch006

Pal, S. (2013). Cloud computing: Security concerns and issues. In A. Bento & A. Aggarwal (Eds.), *Cloud computing service and deployment models: Layers and management* (pp. 191–207). Hershey, PA: Business Science Reference; doi:10.4018/978-1-4666-2187-9.ch010

Pal, S. (2013). Storage security and technical challenges of cloud computing. In D. Kyriazis, A. Voulodimos, S. Gogouvitis, & T. Varvarigou (Eds.), *Data intensive storage services for cloud environments* (pp. 225–240). Hershey, PA: Business Science Reference; doi:10.4018/978-1-4666-3934-8.ch014

Palanivel, K., & Kuppuswami, S. (2014). A cloud-oriented reference architecture to digital library systems. In S. Dhamdhere (Ed.), *Cloud computing and virtualization technologies in libraries* (pp. 230–254). Hershey, PA: Information Science Reference; doi:10.4018/978-1-4666-4631-5.ch014

Paletta, M. (2012). Intelligent clouds: By means of using multi-agent systems environments. In L. Chao (Ed.), *Cloud computing for teaching and learning: Strategies for design and implementation* (pp. 254–279). Hershey, PA: Information Science Reference; doi:10.4018/978-1-4666-0957-0.ch017

Pallot, M., Le Marc, C., Richir, S., Schmidt, C., & Mathieu, J. (2012). Innovation gaming: An immersive experience environment enabling co-creation. In M. Cruz-Cunha (Ed.), *Handbook of research on serious games as educational, business and research tools* (pp. 1–24). Hershey, PA: Information Science Reference; doi:10.4018/978-1-4666-0149-9.ch001

Pankowska, M. (2011). Information technology resources virtualization for sustainable development.[IJAL]. *International Journal of Applied Logistics, 2*(2), 35–48. doi:10.4018/jal.2011040103

Pankowska, M. (2013). Information technology resources virtualization for sustainable development. In Z. Luo (Ed.), *Technological solutions for modern logistics and supply chain management* (pp. 248–262). Hershey, PA: Business Science Reference; doi:10.4018/978-1-4666-2773-4.ch016

Parappallil, J. J., Zarvic, N., & Thomas, O. (2012). A context and content reflection on business-IT alignment research.[IJITBAG]. *International Journal of IT/Business Alignment and Governance, 3*(2), 21–37. doi:10.4018/jitbag.2012070102

Parashar, V., Vishwakarma, M. L., & Parashar, R. (2014). A new framework for building academic library through cloud computing. In S. Dhamdhere (Ed.), *Cloud computing and virtualization technologies in libraries* (pp. 107–123). Hershey, PA: Information Science Reference; doi:10.4018/978-1-4666-4631-5.ch007

Pendyala, V. S., & Holliday, J. (2012). Cloud as a computer. In X. Liu & Y. Li (Eds.), *Advanced design approaches to emerging software systems: Principles, methodologies and tools* (pp. 241–249). Hershey, PA: Information Science Reference; doi:10.4018/978-1-60960-735-7.ch011

Petruch, K., Tamm, G., & Stantchev, V. (2012). Deriving in-depth knowledge from IT-performance data simulations.[IJKSR]. *International Journal of Knowledge Society Research, 3*(2), 13–29. doi:10.4018/jksr.2012040102

Philipson, G. (2011). A framework for green computing.[IJGC]. *International Journal of Green Computing, 2*(1), 12–26. doi:10.4018/jgc.2011010102

Philipson, G. (2013). A framework for green computing. In K. Ganesh & S. Anbuu-dayasankar (Eds.), *International and interdisciplinary studies in green computing* (pp. 12–26). Hershey, PA: Information Science Reference; doi:10.4018/978-1-4666-2646-1.ch002

Phythian, M. (2013). The 'cloud' of unknowing – What a government cloud may and may not offer: A practitioner perspective.[IJT]. *International Journal of Technoethics, 4*(1), 1–10. doi:10.4018/jte.2013010101

Pym, D., & Sadler, M. (2012). Information stewardship in cloud computing. In *Grid and cloud computing: Concepts, methodologies, tools and applications* (pp. 185–202). Hershey, PA: Information Science Reference; doi:10.4018/978-1-4666-0879-5.ch109

Pym, D., & Sadler, M. (2012). Information stewardship in cloud computing. In S. Galup (Ed.), *Technological applications and advancements in service science, management, and engineering* (pp. 52–69). Hershey, PA: Business Science Reference; doi:10.4018/978-1-4666-1583-0.ch004

Qiu, J., Ekanayake, J., Gunarathne, T., Choi, J. Y., Bae, S., & Ruan, Y. … Tang, H. (2013). Data intensive computing for bioinformatics. In Bioinformatics: Concepts, methodologies, tools, and applications (pp. 287-321). Hershey, PA: Medical Information Science Reference. doi:10.4018/978-1-4666-3604-0.ch016

Rabaey, M. (2012). A public economics approach to enabling enterprise architecture with the government cloud in Belgium. In P. Saha (Ed.), *Enterprise architecture for connected e-government: Practices and innovations* (pp. 467–493). Hershey, PA: Information Science Reference; doi:10.4018/978-1-4666-1824-4.ch020

Rabaey, M. (2013). A complex adaptive system thinking approach of government e-procurement in a cloud computing environment. In P. Ordóñez de Pablos, J. Lovelle, J. Gayo, & R. Tennyson (Eds.), *E-procurement management for successful electronic government systems* (pp. 193–219). Hershey, PA: Information Science Reference; doi:10.4018/978-1-4666-2119-0.ch013

Rabaey, M. (2013). Holistic investment framework for cloud computing: A management-philosophical approach based on complex adaptive systems. In A. Bento & A. Aggarwal (Eds.), *Cloud computing service and deployment models: Layers and management* (pp. 94–122). Hershey, PA: Business Science Reference; doi:10.4018/978-1-4666-2187-9.ch005

Related of References

Rak, M., Ficco, M., Luna, J., Ghani, H., Suri, N., Panica, S., & Petcu, D. (2012). Security issues in cloud federations. In M. Villari, I. Brandic, & F. Tusa (Eds.), *Achieving federated and self-manageable cloud infrastructures: Theory and practice* (pp. 176–194). Hershey, PA: Business Science Reference; doi:10.4018/978-1-4666-1631-8.ch010

Ramanathan, R. (2013). Extending service-driven architectural approaches to the cloud. In R. Ramanathan & K. Raja (Eds.), *Service-driven approaches to architecture and enterprise integration* (pp. 334–359). Hershey, PA: Information Science Reference; doi:10.4018/978-1-4666-4193-8.ch013

Ramírez, M., Gutiérrez, A., Monguet, J. M., & Muñoz, C. (2012). An internet cost model, assignment of costs based on actual network use.[IJWP]. *International Journal of Web Portals*, 4(4), 19–34. doi:10.4018/jwp.2012100102

Rashid, A., Wang, W. Y., & Tan, F. B. (2013). Value co-creation in cloud services. In A. Lin, J. Foster, & P. Scifleet (Eds.), *Consumer information systems and relationship management: Design, implementation, and use* (pp. 74–91). Hershey, PA: Business Science Reference; doi:10.4018/978-1-4666-4082-5.ch005

Ratten, V. (2012). Cloud computing services: Theoretical foundations of ethical and entrepreneurial adoption behaviour.[IJCAC]. *International Journal of Cloud Applications and Computing*, 2(2), 48–58. doi:10.4018/ijcac.2012040105

Ratten, V. (2013). Exploring behaviors and perceptions affecting the adoption of cloud computing.[IJIDE]. *International Journal of Innovation in the Digital Economy*, 4(3), 51–68. doi:10.4018/jide.2013070104

Ravi, V. (2012). Cloud computing paradigm for indian education sector.[IJCAC]. *International Journal of Cloud Applications and Computing*, 2(2), 41–47. doi:10.4018/ijcac.2012040104

Rawat, A., Kapoor, P., & Sushil, R. (2014). Application of cloud computing in library information service sector. In S. Dhamdhere (Ed.), *Cloud computing and virtualization technologies in libraries* (pp. 77–89). Hershey, PA: Information Science Reference; doi:10.4018/978-1-4666-4631-5.ch005

Reich, C., Hübner, S., & Kuijs, H. (2012). Cloud computing for on-demand virtual desktops and labs. In L. Chao (Ed.), *Cloud computing for teaching and learning: strategies for design and implementation* (pp. 111–125). Hershey, PA: Information Science Reference; doi:10.4018/978-1-4666-0957-0.ch008

Rice, R. W. (2013). Testing in the cloud: Balancing the value and risks of cloud computing. In S. Tilley & T. Parveen (Eds.), *Software testing in the cloud: Perspectives on an emerging discipline* (pp. 404–416). Hershey, PA: Information Science Reference; doi:10.4018/978-1-4666-2536-5.ch019

Ruan, K. (2013). Designing a forensic-enabling cloud ecosystem. In K. Ruan (Ed.), *Cybercrime and cloud forensics: Applications for investigation processes* (pp. 331–344). Hershey, PA: Information Science Reference; doi:10.4018/978-1-4666-2662-1.ch014

Sabetzadeh, F., & Tsui, E. (2011). Delivering knowledge services in the cloud. [IJKSS]. *International Journal of Knowledge and Systems Science, 2*(4), 14–20. doi:10.4018/jkss.2011100102

Sabetzadeh, F., & Tsui, E. (2013). Delivering knowledge services in the cloud. In G. Yang (Ed.), *Multidisciplinary studies in knowledge and systems science* (pp. 247–254). Hershey, PA: Information Science Reference; doi:10.4018/978-1-4666-3998-0.ch017

Saedi, A., & Iahad, N. A. (2013). Future research on cloud computing adoption by small and medium-sized enterprises: A critical analysis of relevant theories.[IJAN-TTI]. *International Journal of Actor-Network Theory and Technological Innovation, 5*(2), 1–16. doi:10.4018/jantti.2013040101

Saha, D., & Sridhar, V. (2011). Emerging areas of research in business data communications.[IJBDCN]. *International Journal of Business Data Communications and Networking, 7*(4), 52–59. doi:10.4018/ijbdcn.2011100104

Saha, D., & Sridhar, V. (2013). Platform on platform (PoP) model for meta-networking: A new paradigm for networks of the future.[IJBDCN]. *International Journal of Business Data Communications and Networking, 9*(1), 1–10. doi:10.4018/jbdcn.2013010101

Sahlin, J. P. (2013). Cloud computing: Past, present, and future. In X. Yang & L. Liu (Eds.), *Principles, methodologies, and service-oriented approaches for cloud computing* (pp. 19–50). Hershey, PA: Business Science Reference; doi:10.4018/978-1-4666-2854-0.ch002

Salama, M., & Shawish, A. (2012). Libraries: From the classical to cloud-based era. [IJDLS]. *International Journal of Digital Library Systems, 3*(3), 14–32. doi:10.4018/jdls.2012070102

Related of References

Sánchez, C. M., Molina, D., Vozmediano, R. M., Montero, R. S., & Llorente, I. M. (2012). On the use of the hybrid cloud computing paradigm. In M. Villari, I. Brandic, & F. Tusa (Eds.), *Achieving federated and self-manageable cloud infrastructures: Theory and practice* (pp. 196–218). Hershey, PA: Business Science Reference; doi:10.4018/978-1-4666-1631-8.ch011

Sasikala, P. (2011). Architectural strategies for green cloud computing: Environments, infrastructure and resources.[IJCAC]. *International Journal of Cloud Applications and Computing, 1*(4), 1–24. doi:10.4018/ijcac.2011100101

Sasikala, P. (2011). Cloud computing in higher education: Opportunities and issues. [IJCAC]. *International Journal of Cloud Applications and Computing, 1*(2), 1–13. doi:10.4018/ijcac.2011040101

Sasikala, P. (2011). Cloud computing towards technological convergence.[IJCAC]. *International Journal of Cloud Applications and Computing, 1*(4), 44–59. doi:10.4018/ijcac.2011100104

Sasikala, P. (2012). Cloud computing and e-governance: Advances, opportunities and challenges.[IJCAC]. *International Journal of Cloud Applications and Computing, 2*(4), 32–52. doi:10.4018/ijcac.2012100103

Sasikala, P. (2012). Cloud computing in higher education: Opportunities and issues. In *Grid and cloud computing: Concepts, methodologies, tools and applications* (pp. 1672–1685). Hershey, PA: Information Science Reference; doi:10.4018/978-1-4666-0879-5.ch709

Sasikala, P. (2012). Cloud computing towards technological convergence. In *Grid and cloud computing: Concepts, methodologies, tools and applications* (pp. 1576–1592). Hershey, PA: Information Science Reference; doi:10.4018/978-1-4666-0879-5.ch703

Sasikala, P. (2013). Architectural strategies for green cloud computing: Environments, infrastructure and resources. In S. Aljawarneh (Ed.), *Cloud computing advancements in design, implementation, and technologies* (pp. 218–242). Hershey, PA: Information Science Reference; doi:10.4018/978-1-4666-1879-4.ch016

Sasikala, P. (2013). Cloud computing in higher education: Opportunities and issues. In S. Aljawarneh (Ed.), *Cloud computing advancements in design, implementation, and technologies* (pp. 83–96). Hershey, PA: Information Science Reference; doi:10.4018/978-1-4666-1879-4.ch006

Sasikala, P. (2013). Cloud computing towards technological convergence. In S. Aljawarneh (Ed.), *Cloud computing advancements in design, implementation, and technologies* (pp. 263–279). Hershey, PA: Information Science Reference; doi:10.4018/978-1-4666-1879-4.ch019

Sasikala, P. (2013). New media cloud computing: Opportunities and challenges. [IJCAC]. *International Journal of Cloud Applications and Computing, 3*(2), 61–72. doi:10.4018/ijcac.2013040106

Schrödl, H., & Wind, S. (2013). Requirements engineering for cloud application development. In A. Bento & A. Aggarwal (Eds.), *Cloud computing service and deployment models: Layers and management* (pp. 137–150). Hershey, PA: Business Science Reference; doi:10.4018/978-1-4666-2187-9.ch007

Sclater, N. (2012). Legal and contractual issues of cloud computing for educational institutions. In L. Chao (Ed.), *Cloud computing for teaching and learning: Strategies for design and implementation* (pp. 186–199). Hershey, PA: Information Science Reference; doi:10.4018/978-1-4666-0957-0.ch013

Sen, J. (2014). Security and privacy issues in cloud computing. In A. Ruiz-Martinez, R. Marin-Lopez, & F. Pereniguez-Garcia (Eds.), *Architectures and protocols for secure information technology infrastructures* (pp. 1–45). Hershey, PA: Information Science Reference; doi:10.4018/978-1-4666-4514-1.ch001

Shah, B. (2013). Cloud environment controls assessment framework. In *IT policy and ethics: Concepts, methodologies, tools, and applications* (pp. 1822–1847). Hershey, PA: Information Science Reference; doi:10.4018/978-1-4666-2919-6.ch080

Shah, B. (2013). Cloud environment controls assessment framework. In S. Tilley & T. Parveen (Eds.), *Software testing in the cloud: Perspectives on an emerging discipline* (pp. 28–53). Hershey, PA: Information Science Reference; doi:10.4018/978-1-4666-2536-5.ch002

Shang, X., Zhang, R., & Chen, Y. (2012). Internet of things (IoT) service architecture and its application in e-commerce.[JECO]. *Journal of Electronic Commerce in Organizations, 10*(3), 44–55. doi:10.4018/jeco.2012070104

Shankararaman, V., & Kit, L. E. (2013). Integrating the cloud scenarios and solutions. In A. Bento & A. Aggarwal (Eds.), *Cloud computing service and deployment models: Layers and management* (pp. 173–189). Hershey, PA: Business Science Reference; doi:10.4018/978-1-4666-2187-9.ch009

Sharma, A., & Maurer, F. (2013). A roadmap for software engineering for the cloud: Results of a systematic review. In X. Wang, N. Ali, I. Ramos, & R. Vidgen (Eds.), *Agile and lean service-oriented development: Foundations, theory, and practice* (pp. 48–63). Hershey, PA: Information Science Reference; doi:10.4018/978-1-4666-2503-7.ch003

Sharma, A., & Maurer, F. (2014). A roadmap for software engineering for the cloud: Results of a systematic review. In *Software design and development: Concepts, methodologies, tools, and applications* (pp. 1–16). Hershey, PA: Information Science Reference; doi:10.4018/978-1-4666-4301-7.ch001

Sharma, S. C., & Bagoria, H. (2014). Libraries and cloud computing models: A changing paradigm. In S. Dhamdhere (Ed.), *Cloud computing and virtualization technologies in libraries* (pp. 124–149). Hershey, PA: Information Science Reference; doi:10.4018/978-1-4666-4631-5.ch008

Shawish, A., & Salama, M. (2013). Cloud computing in academia, governments, and industry. In X. Yang & L. Liu (Eds.), *Principles, methodologies, and service-oriented approaches for cloud computing* (pp. 71–114). Hershey, PA: Business Science Reference; doi:10.4018/978-1-4666-2854-0.ch004

Shebanow, A., Perez, R., & Howard, C. (2012). The effect of firewall testing types on cloud security policies.[IJSITA]. *International Journal of Strategic Information Technology and Applications*, *3*(3), 60–68. doi:10.4018/jsita.2012070105

Sheikhalishahi, M., Devare, M., Grandinetti, L., & Incutti, M. C. (2012). A complementary approach to grid and cloud distributed computing paradigms. In *Grid and cloud computing: Concepts, methodologies, tools and applications* (pp. 1929–1942). Hershey, PA: Information Science Reference; doi:10.4018/978-1-4666-0879-5.ch811

Sheikhalishahi, M., Devare, M., Grandinetti, L., & Incutti, M. C. (2012). A complementary approach to grid and cloud distributed computing paradigms. In N. Preve (Ed.), *Computational and data grids: Principles, applications and design* (pp. 31–44). Hershey, PA: Information Science Reference; doi:10.4018/978-1-61350-113-9.ch002

Shen, Y., Li, Y., Wu, L., Liu, S., & Wen, Q. (2014). Cloud computing overview. In Y. Shen, Y. Li, L. Wu, S. Liu, & Q. Wen (Eds.), *Enabling the new era of cloud computing: Data security, transfer, and management* (pp. 1–24). Hershey, PA: Information Science Reference; doi:10.4018/978-1-4666-4801-2.ch001

Shen, Y., Li, Y., Wu, L., Liu, S., & Wen, Q. (2014). Main components of cloud computing. In Y. Shen, Y. Li, L. Wu, S. Liu, & Q. Wen (Eds.), *Enabling the new era of cloud computing: Data security, transfer, and management* (pp. 25–50). Hershey, PA: Information Science Reference; doi:10.4018/978-1-4666-4801-2.ch002

Shen, Y., Yang, J., & Keskin, T. (2014). Impact of cultural differences on the cloud computing ecosystems in the USA and China. In Y. Shen, Y. Li, L. Wu, S. Liu, & Q. Wen (Eds.), *Enabling the new era of cloud computing: Data security, transfer, and management* (pp. 269–283). Hershey, PA: Information Science Reference; doi:10.4018/978-1-4666-4801-2.ch014

Shetty, S., & Rawat, D. B. (2013). Cloud computing based cognitive radio networking. In N. Meghanathan & Y. Reddy (Eds.), *Cognitive radio technology applications for wireless and mobile ad hoc networks* (pp. 153–164). Hershey, PA: Information Science Reference; doi:10.4018/978-1-4666-4221-8.ch008

Shi, Z., & Beard, C. (2014). QoS in the mobile cloud computing environment. In J. Rodrigues, K. Lin, & J. Lloret (Eds.), *Mobile networks and cloud computing convergence for progressive services and applications* (pp. 200–217). Hershey, PA: Information Science Reference; doi:10.4018/978-1-4666-4781-7.ch011

Shuster, L. (2013). Enterprise integration: Challenges and solution architecture. In R. Ramanathan & K. Raja (Eds.), *Service-driven approaches to architecture and enterprise integration* (pp. 43–66). Hershey, PA: Information Science Reference; doi:10.4018/978-1-4666-4193-8.ch002

Siahos, Y., Papanagiotou, I., Georgopoulos, A., Tsamis, F., & Papaioannou, I. (2012). An architecture paradigm for providing cloud services in school labs based on open source software to enhance ICT in education.[IJCEE]. *International Journal of Cyber Ethics in Education, 2*(1), 44–57. doi:10.4018/ijcee.2012010105

Simon, E., & Estublier, J. (2013). Model driven integration of heterogeneous software artifacts in service oriented computing. In A. Ionita, M. Litoiu, & G. Lewis (Eds.), *Migrating legacy applications: Challenges in service oriented architecture and cloud computing environments* (pp. 332–360). Hershey, PA: Information Science Reference; doi:10.4018/978-1-4666-2488-7.ch014

Singh, J., & Kumar, V. (2013). Compliance and regulatory standards for cloud computing. In R. Khurana & R. Aggarwal (Eds.), *Interdisciplinary perspectives on business convergence, computing, and legality* (pp. 54–64). Hershey, PA: Business Science Reference; doi:10.4018/978-1-4666-4209-6.ch006

Singh, V. V. (2012). Software development using service syndication based on API handshake approach between cloud-based and SOA-based reusable services. In H. Yang & X. Liu (Eds.), *Software reuse in the emerging cloud computing era* (pp. 136–157). Hershey, PA: Information Science Reference; doi:10.4018/978-1-4666-0897-9.ch006

Smeitink, M., & Spruit, M. (2013). Maturity for sustainability in IT: Introducing the MITS.[IJITSA]. *International Journal of Information Technologies and Systems Approach*, *6*(1), 39–56. doi:10.4018/jitsa.2013010103

Smith, P. A., & Cockburn, T. (2013). Socio-digital technologies. In *Dynamic leadership models for global business: Enhancing digitally connected environments* (pp. 142–168). Hershey, PA: Business Science Reference; doi:10.4018/978-1-4666-2836-6.ch006

Sneed, H. M. (2013). Testing web services in the cloud. In S. Tilley & T. Parveen (Eds.), *Software testing in the cloud: Perspectives on an emerging discipline* (pp. 136–173). Hershey, PA: Information Science Reference; doi:10.4018/978-1-4666-2536-5.ch007

Solomon, B., Ionescu, D., Gadea, C., & Litoiu, M. (2013). Geographically distributed cloud-based collaborative application. In A. Ionita, M. Litoiu, & G. Lewis (Eds.), *Migrating legacy applications: Challenges in service oriented architecture and cloud computing environments* (pp. 248–274). Hershey, PA: Information Science Reference; doi:10.4018/978-1-4666-2488-7.ch011

Song, W., & Xiao, Z. (2013). An infrastructure-as-a-service cloud: On-demand resource provisioning. In X. Yang & L. Liu (Eds.), *Principles, methodologies, and service-oriented approaches for cloud computing* (pp. 302–324). Hershey, PA: Business Science Reference; doi:10.4018/978-1-4666-2854-0.ch013

Sood, S. K. (2013). A value based dynamic resource provisioning model in cloud. [IJCAC]. *International Journal of Cloud Applications and Computing*, *3*(1), 1–12. doi:10.4018/ijcac.2013010101

Sotiriadis, S., Bessis, N., & Antonopoulos, N. (2012). Exploring inter-cloud load balancing by utilizing historical service submission records.[IJDST]. *International Journal of Distributed Systems and Technologies*, *3*(3), 72–81. doi:10.4018/jdst.2012070106

Soyata, T., Ba, H., Heinzelman, W., Kwon, M., & Shi, J. (2014). Accelerating mobile-cloud computing: A survey. In H. Mouftah & B. Kantarci (Eds.), *Communication infrastructures for cloud computing* (pp. 175–197). Hershey, PA: Information Science Reference; doi:10.4018/978-1-4666-4522-6.ch008

Spyridopoulos, T., & Katos, V. (2011). Requirements for a forensically ready cloud storage service.[IJDCF]. *International Journal of Digital Crime and Forensics*, *3*(3), 19–36. doi:10.4018/jdcf.2011070102

Spyridopoulos, T., & Katos, V. (2013). Data recovery strategies for cloud environments. In K. Ruan (Ed.), *Cybercrime and cloud forensics: Applications for investigation processes* (pp. 251–265). Hershey, PA: Information Science Reference; doi:10.4018/978-1-4666-2662-1.ch010

Srinivasa, K. G., S., H. R., H., M. K., & Venkatesh, N. (2012). MeghaOS: A framework for scalable, interoperable cloud based operating system.[IJCAC]. *International Journal of Cloud Applications and Computing*, 2(1), 53–70. doi:10.4018/ijcac.2012010104

Stantchev, V., & Stantcheva, L. (2012). Extending traditional IT-governance knowledge towards SOA and cloud governance.[IJKSR]. *International Journal of Knowledge Society Research*, 3(2), 30–43. doi:10.4018/jksr.2012040103

Stantchev, V., & Tamm, G. (2012). Reducing information asymmetry in cloud marketplaces.[IJHCITP]. *International Journal of Human Capital and Information Technology Professionals*, 3(4), 1–10. doi:10.4018/jhcitp.2012100101

Steinbuß, S., & Weißenberg, N. (2013). Service design and process design for the logistics mall cloud. In X. Yang & L. Liu (Eds.), *Principles, methodologies, and service-oriented approaches for cloud computing* (pp. 186–206). Hershey, PA: Business Science Reference; doi:10.4018/978-1-4666-2854-0.ch008

Stender, J., Berlin, M., & Reinefeld, A. (2013). XtreemFS: A file system for the cloud. In D. Kyriazis, A. Voulodimos, S. Gogouvitis, & T. Varvarigou (Eds.), *Data intensive storage services for cloud environments* (pp. 267–285). Hershey, PA: Business Science Reference; doi:10.4018/978-1-4666-3934-8.ch016

Sticklen, D. J., & Issa, T. (2011). An initial examination of free and proprietary software-selection in organizations.[IJWP]. *International Journal of Web Portals*, 3(4), 27–43. doi:10.4018/jwp.2011100103

Sun, Y., White, J., Gray, J., & Gokhale, A. (2012). Model-driven automated error recovery in cloud computing. In *Grid and cloud computing: Concepts, methodologies, tools and applications* (pp. 680–700). Hershey, PA: Information Science Reference; doi:10.4018/978-1-4666-0879-5.ch308

Sun, Z., Yang, Y., Zhou, Y., & Cruickshank, H. (2014). Agent-based resource management for mobile cloud. In J. Rodrigues, K. Lin, & J. Lloret (Eds.), *Mobile networks and cloud computing convergence for progressive services and applications* (pp. 118–134). Hershey, PA: Information Science Reference; doi:10.4018/978-1-4666-4781-7.ch007

Sutherland, S. (2013). Convergence of interoperability of cloud computing, service oriented architecture and enterprise architecture.[IJEEI]. *International Journal of E-Entrepreneurship and Innovation, 4*(1), 43–51. doi:10.4018/jeei.2013010104

Takabi, H., & Joshi, J. B. (2013). Policy management in cloud: Challenges and approaches. In D. Rosado, D. Mellado, E. Fernandez-Medina, & M. Piattini (Eds.), *Security engineering for cloud computing: Approaches and tools* (pp. 191–211). Hershey, PA: Information Science Reference; doi:10.4018/978-1-4666-2125-1.ch010

Takabi, H., & Joshi, J. B. (2013). Policy management in cloud: Challenges and approaches. In *IT policy and ethics: Concepts, methodologies, tools, and applications* (pp. 814–834). Hershey, PA: Information Science Reference; doi:10.4018/978-1-4666-2919-6.ch037

Takabi, H., Joshi, J. B., & Ahn, G. (2013). Security and privacy in cloud computing: Towards a comprehensive framework. In X. Yang & L. Liu (Eds.), *Principles, methodologies, and service-oriented approaches for cloud computing* (pp. 164–184). Hershey, PA: Business Science Reference; doi:10.4018/978-1-4666-2854-0.ch007

Takabi, H., Zargar, S. T., & Joshi, J. B. (2014). Mobile cloud computing and its security and privacy challenges. In D. Rawat, B. Bista, & G. Yan (Eds.), *Security, privacy, trust, and resource management in mobile and wireless communications* (pp. 384–407). Hershey, PA: Information Science Reference; doi:10.4018/978-1-4666-4691-9.ch016

Teixeira, C., Pinto, J. S., Ferreira, F., Oliveira, A., Teixeira, A., & Pereira, C. (2013). Cloud computing enhanced service development architecture for the living usability lab. In R. Martinho, R. Rijo, M. Cruz-Cunha, & J. Varajão (Eds.), *Information systems and technologies for enhancing health and social care* (pp. 33–53). Hershey, PA: Medical Information Science Reference; doi:10.4018/978-1-4666-3667-5.ch003

Thimm, H. (2012). Cloud-based collaborative decision making: Design considerations and architecture of the GRUPO-MOD system.[IJDSST]. *International Journal of Decision Support System Technology, 4*(4), 39–59. doi:10.4018/jdsst.2012100103

Thomas, P. (2012). Harnessing the potential of cloud computing to transform higher education. In L. Chao (Ed.), *Cloud computing for teaching and learning: Strategies for design and implementation* (pp. 147–158). Hershey, PA: Information Science Reference; doi:10.4018/978-1-4666-0957-0.ch010

T.M. K., & Gopalakrishnan, S. (2014). Green economic and secure libraries on cloud. In S. Dhamdhere (Ed.), Cloud computing and virtualization technologies in libraries (pp. 297-315). Hershey, PA: Information Science Reference. doi:10.4018/978-1-4666-4631-5.ch017

Toka, A., Aivazidou, E., Antoniou, A., & Arvanitopoulos-Darginis, K. (2013). Cloud computing in supply chain management: An overview. In D. Graham, I. Manikas, & D. Folinas (Eds.), *E-logistics and e-supply chain management: Applications for evolving business* (pp. 218–231). Hershey, PA: Business Science Reference; doi:10.4018/978-1-4666-3914-0.ch012

Torrealba, S. M., Morales, P. M., Campos, J. M., & Meza, S. M. (2013). A software tool to support risks analysis about what should or should not go to the cloud. In D. Rosado, D. Mellado, E. Fernandez-Medina, & M. Piattini (Eds.), *Security engineering for cloud computing: Approaches and tools* (pp. 72–96). Hershey, PA: Information Science Reference; doi:10.4018/978-1-4666-2125-1.ch005

Trivedi, M., & Suthar, V. (2013). Cloud computing: A feasible platform for ICT enabled health science libraries in India.[IJUDH]. *International Journal of User-Driven Healthcare, 3*(2), 69–77. doi:10.4018/ijudh.2013040108

Truong, H., Pham, T., Thoai, N., & Dustdar, S. (2012). Cloud computing for education and research in developing countries. In L. Chao (Ed.), *Cloud computing for teaching and learning: Strategies for design and implementation* (pp. 64–80). Hershey, PA: Information Science Reference; doi:10.4018/978-1-4666-0957-0.ch005

Tsirmpas, C., Giokas, K., Iliopoulou, D., & Koutsouris, D. (2012). Magnetic resonance imaging and magnetic resonance spectroscopy cloud computing framework. [IJRQEH]. *International Journal of Reliable and Quality E-Healthcare, 1*(4), 1–12. doi:10.4018/ijrqeh.2012100101

Turner, H., White, J., Reed, J., Galindo, J., Porter, A., Marathe, M., & Gokhale, A. et al. (2013). Building a cloud-based mobile application testbed. In *IT policy and ethics: Concepts, methodologies, tools, and applications* (pp. 879–899). Hershey, PA: Information Science Reference; doi:10.4018/978-1-4666-2919-6.ch040

Turner, H., White, J., Reed, J., Galindo, J., Porter, A., Marathe, M., & Gokhale, A. et al. (2013). Building a cloud-based mobile application testbed. In S. Tilley & T. Parveen (Eds.), *Software testing in the cloud: Perspectives on an emerging discipline* (pp. 382–403). Hershey, PA: Information Science Reference; doi:10.4018/978-1-4666-2536-5.ch018

Tusa, F., Paone, M., & Villari, M. (2012). CLEVER: A cloud middleware beyond the federation. In M. Villari, I. Brandic, & F. Tusa (Eds.), *Achieving federated and self-manageable cloud infrastructures: Theory and practice* (pp. 219–241). Hershey, PA: Business Science Reference; doi:10.4018/978-1-4666-1631-8.ch012

Udoh, E. (2012). Technology acceptance model applied to the adoption of grid and cloud technology.[IJGHPC]. *International Journal of Grid and High Performance Computing, 4*(1), 1–20. doi:10.4018/jghpc.2012010101

Vannoy, S. A. (2011). A structured content analytic assessment of business services advertisements in the cloud-based web services marketplace.[IJDTIS]. *International Journal of Dependable and Trustworthy Information Systems, 2*(1), 18–49. doi:10.4018/jdtis.2011010102

Vaquero, L. M., Cáceres, J., & Morán, D. (2011). The challenge of service level scalability for the cloud.[IJCAC]. *International Journal of Cloud Applications and Computing, 1*(1), 34–44. doi:10.4018/ijcac.2011010103

Vaquero, L. M., Cáceres, J., & Morán, D. (2013). The challenge of service level scalability for the cloud. In S. Aljawarneh (Ed.), *Cloud computing advancements in design, implementation, and technologies* (pp. 37–48). Hershey, PA: Information Science Reference; doi:10.4018/978-1-4666-1879-4.ch003

Venkatraman, R., Venkatraman, S., & Asaithambi, S. P. (2013). A practical cloud services implementation framework for e-businesses. In K. Tarnay, S. Imre, & L. Xu (Eds.), *Research and development in e-business through service-oriented solutions* (pp. 167–198). Hershey, PA: Business Science Reference; doi:10.4018/978-1-4666-4181-5.ch008

Venkatraman, S. (2013). Software engineering research gaps in the cloud.[JITR]. *Journal of Information Technology Research, 6*(1), 1–19. doi:10.4018/jitr.2013010101

Vijaykumar, S., Rajkarthick, K. S., & Priya, J. (2012). Innovative business opportunities and smart business management techniques from green cloud TPS.[IJABIM]. *International Journal of Asian Business and Information Management, 3*(4), 62–72. doi:10.4018/jabim.2012100107

Wang, C., Lam, K. T., & Kui Ma, R. K. (2012). A computation migration approach to elasticity of cloud computing. In J. Abawajy, M. Pathan, M. Rahman, A. Pathan, & M. Deris (Eds.), *Network and traffic engineering in emerging distributed computing applications* (pp. 145–178). Hershey, PA: Information Science Reference; doi:10.4018/978-1-4666-1888-6.ch007

Wang, D., & Wu, J. (2014). Carrier-grade distributed cloud computing: Demands, challenges, designs, and future perspectives. In H. Mouftah & B. Kantarci (Eds.), *Communication infrastructures for cloud computing* (pp. 264–281). Hershey, PA: Information Science Reference; doi:10.4018/978-1-4666-4522-6.ch012

Wang, H., & Philips, D. (2012). Implement virtual programming lab with cloud computing for web-based distance education. In L. Chao (Ed.), *Cloud computing for teaching and learning: Strategies for design and implementation* (pp. 95–110). Hershey, PA: Information Science Reference; doi:10.4018/978-1-4666-0957-0.ch007

Warneke, D. (2013). Ad-hoc parallel data processing on pay-as-you-go clouds with nephele. In A. Loo (Ed.), *Distributed computing innovations for business, engineering, and science* (pp. 191–218). Hershey, PA: Information Science Reference; doi:10.4018/978-1-4666-2533-4.ch010

Wei, Y., & Blake, M. B. (2013). Adaptive web services monitoring in cloud environments.[IJWP]. *International Journal of Web Portals*, 5(1), 15–27. doi:10.4018/jwp.2013010102

White, S. C., Sedigh, S., & Hurson, A. R. (2013). Security concepts for cloud computing. In X. Yang & L. Liu (Eds.), *Principles, methodologies, and service-oriented approaches for cloud computing* (pp. 116–142). Hershey, PA: Business Science Reference; doi:10.4018/978-1-4666-2854-0.ch005

Williams, A. J. (2013). The role of emerging technologies in developing and sustaining diverse suppliers in competitive markets. In *Enterprise resource planning: Concepts, methodologies, tools, and applications* (pp. 1550–1560). Hershey, PA: Business Science Reference; doi:10.4018/978-1-4666-4153-2.ch082

Williams, A. J. (2013). The role of emerging technologies in developing and sustaining diverse suppliers in competitive markets. In J. Lewis, A. Green, & D. Surry (Eds.), *Technology as a tool for diversity leadership: Implementation and future implications* (pp. 95–105). Hershey, PA: Information Science Reference; doi:10.4018/978-1-4666-2668-3.ch007

Wilson, L., Goh, T. T., & Wang, W. Y. (2012). Big data management challenges in a meteorological organisation.[IJEA]. *International Journal of E-Adoption*, 4(2), 1–14. doi:10.4018/jea.2012040101

Wu, R., Ahn, G., & Hu, H. (2012). Towards HIPAA-compliant healthcare systems in cloud computing.[IJCMAM]. *International Journal of Computational Models and Algorithms in Medicine*, 3(2), 1–22. doi:10.4018/jcmam.2012040101

Xiao, J., Wang, M., Wang, L., & Zhu, X. (2013). Design and implementation of C-iLearning: A cloud-based intelligent learning system.[IJDET]. *International Journal of Distance Education Technologies*, 11(3), 79–97. doi:10.4018/jdet.2013070106

Related of References

Xing, R., Wang, Z., & Peterson, R. L. (2011). Redefining the information technology in the 21st century.[IJSITA]. *International Journal of Strategic Information Technology and Applications*, *2*(1), 1–10. doi:10.4018/jsita.2011010101

Xu, L., Huang, D., Tsai, W., & Atkinson, R. K. (2012). V-lab: A mobile, cloud-based virtual laboratory platform for hands-on networking courses.[IJCBPL]. *International Journal of Cyber Behavior, Psychology and Learning*, *2*(3), 73–85. doi:10.4018/ijcbpl.2012070106

Xu, Y., & Mao, S. (2014). Mobile cloud media: State of the art and outlook. In J. Rodrigues, K. Lin, & J. Lloret (Eds.), *Mobile networks and cloud computing convergence for progressive services and applications* (pp. 18–38). Hershey, PA: Information Science Reference; doi:10.4018/978-1-4666-4781-7.ch002

Xu, Z., Yan, B., & Zou, Y. (2013). Beyond hadoop: Recent directions in data computing for internet services. In S. Aljawarneh (Ed.), *Cloud computing advancements in design, implementation, and technologies* (pp. 49–66). Hershey, PA: Information Science Reference; doi:10.4018/978-1-4666-1879-4.ch004

Yan, Z. (2014). Trust management in mobile cloud computing. In *Trust management in mobile environments: Autonomic and usable models* (pp. 54–93). Hershey, PA: Information Science Reference; doi:10.4018/978-1-4666-4765-7.ch004

Yang, D. X. (2012). QoS-oriented service computing: Bringing SOA into cloud environment. In X. Liu & Y. Li (Eds.), *Advanced design approaches to emerging software systems: Principles, methodologies and tools* (pp. 274–296). Hershey, PA: Information Science Reference; doi:10.4018/978-1-60960-735-7.ch013

Yang, H., Huff, S. L., & Tate, M. (2013). Managing the cloud for information systems agility. In A. Bento & A. Aggarwal (Eds.), *Cloud computing service and deployment models: Layers and management* (pp. 70–93). Hershey, PA: Business Science Reference; doi:10.4018/978-1-4666-2187-9.ch004

Yang, M., Kuo, C., & Yeh, Y. (2011). Dynamic rightsizing with quality-controlled algorithms in virtualization environments.[IJGHPC]. *International Journal of Grid and High Performance Computing*, *3*(2), 29–43. doi:10.4018/jghpc.2011040103

Yang, X. (2012). QoS-oriented service computing: Bringing SOA into cloud environment. In *Grid and cloud computing: Concepts, methodologies, tools and applications* (pp. 1621–1643). Hershey, PA: Information Science Reference; doi:10.4018/978-1-4666-0879-5.ch706

Yang, Y., Chen, J., & Hu, H. (2012). The convergence between cloud computing and cable TV.[IJTD]. *International Journal of Technology Diffusion*, *3*(2), 1–11. doi:10.4018/jtd.2012040101

Yassein, M. O., Khamayseh, Y. M., & Hatamleh, A. M. (2013). Intelligent randomize round robin for cloud computing.[IJCAC]. *International Journal of Cloud Applications and Computing*, *3*(1), 27–33. doi:10.4018/ijcac.2013010103

Yau, S. S., An, H. G., & Buduru, A. B. (2012). An approach to data confidentiality protection in cloud environments.[IJWSR]. *International Journal of Web Services Research*, *9*(3), 67–83. doi:10.4018/jwsr.2012070104

Yu, W. D., Adiga, A. S., Rao, S., & Panakkel, M. J. (2012). A SOA based system development methodology for cloud computing environment: Using uhealthcare as practice.[IJEHMC]. *International Journal of E-Health and Medical Communications*, *3*(4), 42–63. doi:10.4018/jehmc.2012100104

Yu, W. D., & Bhagwat, R. (2011). Modeling emergency and telemedicine heath support system: A service oriented architecture approach using cloud computing. [IJEHMC]. *International Journal of E-Health and Medical Communications*, *2*(3), 63–88. doi:10.4018/jehmc.2011070104

Yu, W. D., & Bhagwat, R. (2013). Modeling emergency and telemedicine health support system: A service oriented architecture approach using cloud computing. In J. Rodrigues (Ed.), *Digital advances in medicine, e-health, and communication technologies* (pp. 187–213). Hershey, PA: Medical Information Science Reference; doi:10.4018/978-1-4666-2794-9.ch011

Yuan, D., Lewandowski, C., & Zhong, J. (2012). Developing a private cloud based IP telephony laboratory and curriculum. In L. Chao (Ed.), *Cloud computing for teaching and learning: Strategies for design and implementation* (pp. 126–145). Hershey, PA: Information Science Reference; doi:10.4018/978-1-4666-0957-0.ch009

Yuvaraj, M. (2014). Cloud libraries: Issues and challenges. In S. Dhamdhere (Ed.), *Cloud computing and virtualization technologies in libraries* (pp. 316–338). Hershey, PA: Information Science Reference; doi:10.4018/978-1-4666-4631-5.ch018

Zaman, M., Simmers, C. A., & Anandarajan, M. (2013). Using an ethical framework to examine linkages between "going green" in research practices and information and communication technologies. In B. Medlin (Ed.), *Integrations of technology utilization and social dynamics in organizations* (pp. 243–262). Hershey, PA: Information Science Reference; doi:10.4018/978-1-4666-1948-7.ch015

Related of References

Zapata, B. C., & Alemán, J. L. (2013). Security risks in cloud computing: An analysis of the main vulnerabilities. In D. Rosado, D. Mellado, E. Fernandez-Medina, & M. Piattini (Eds.), *Security engineering for cloud computing: Approaches and tools* (pp. 55–71). Hershey, PA: Information Science Reference; doi:10.4018/978-1-4666-2125-1.ch004

Zapata, B. C., & Alemán, J. L. (2014). Security risks in cloud computing: An analysis of the main vulnerabilities. In *Software design and development: Concepts, methodologies, tools, and applications* (pp. 936–952). Hershey, PA: Information Science Reference; doi:10.4018/978-1-4666-4301-7.ch045

Zardari, S., Faniyi, F., & Bahsoon, R. (2013). Using obstacles for systematically modeling, analysing, and mitigating risks in cloud adoption. In I. Mistrik, A. Tang, R. Bahsoon, & J. Stafford (Eds.), *Aligning enterprise, system, and software architectures* (pp. 275–296). Hershey, PA: Business Science Reference; doi:10.4018/978-1-4666-2199-2.ch014

Zech, P., Kalb, P., Felderer, M., & Breu, R. (2013). Threatening the cloud: Securing services and data by continuous, model-driven negative security testing. In S. Tilley & T. Parveen (Eds.), *Software testing in the cloud: Perspectives on an emerging discipline* (pp. 280–304). Hershey, PA: Information Science Reference; doi:10.4018/978-1-4666-2536-5.ch013

Zhang, F., Cao, J., Cai, H., & Wu, C. (2011). Provisioning virtual resources adaptively in elastic compute cloud platforms.[IJWSR]. *International Journal of Web Services Research*, *8*(3), 54–69. doi:10.4018/jwsr.2011070103

Zhang, G., Li, C., Xue, S., Liu, Y., Zhang, Y., & Xing, C. (2012). A new electronic commerce architecture in the cloud.[JECO]. *Journal of Electronic Commerce in Organizations*, *10*(4), 42–56. doi:10.4018/jeco.2012100104

Zhang, J., Yao, J., Chen, S., & Levy, D. (2011). Facilitating biodefense research with mobile-cloud computing.[IJSSOE]. *International Journal of Systems and Service-Oriented Engineering*, *2*(3), 18–31. doi:10.4018/jssoe.2011070102

Zhang, J., Yao, J., Chen, S., & Levy, D. (2013). Facilitating biodefense research with mobile-cloud computing. In D. Chiu (Ed.), *Mobile and web innovations in systems and service-oriented engineering* (pp. 318–332). Hershey, PA: Information Science Reference; doi:10.4018/978-1-4666-2470-2.ch017

Zheng, S., Chen, F., Yang, H., & Li, J. (2013). An approach to evolving legacy software system into cloud computing environment. In X. Yang & L. Liu (Eds.), *Principles, methodologies, and service-oriented approaches for cloud computing* (pp. 207–229). Hershey, PA: Business Science Reference; doi:10.4018/978-1-4666-2854-0.ch009

Zhou, J., Athukorala, K., Gilman, E., Riekki, J., & Ylianttila, M. (2012). Cloud architecture for dynamic service composition.[IJGHPC]. *International Journal of Grid and High Performance Computing*, *4*(2), 17–31. doi:10.4018/jghpc.2012040102

Compilation of References

Abdleazeem, S., & El-Sherif, E. (2008). Arabic handwritten digit recognition. *Int. J. Doc. Anal. Recognit.*, *11*(3), 127–141. doi:10.1007/s10032-008-0073-5

Abrial, J. R. (2009). *2. Controlling Cars on a Bridge.* Retrieved 10 July 2014 from http://deploy-eprints.ecs.soton.ac.uk/112/1/sld.ch2.car.pdf

Álvaro, F., Sánchez, J. A., & Benedí, J. M. (2014). Recognition of on-line handwritten mathematical expressions using 2D stochastic context-free grammars and hidden Markov models. *Pattern Recognition Letters*, *35*(1), 58–67. doi:10.1016/j.patrec.2012.09.023

Anand, S., Chin, W. N., & Khoo, S. C. (2001). Chart Patterns on Price History.*Proc. of ACM SIGPLAN Int. Conf. on Functional Programming.*

Anastassiou, G. A. (2011). Multivariate sigmoidal neural network approximation. *Neural Networks*, *24*(4), 378–386. doi:10.1016/j.neunet.2011.01.003 PMID:21310590

Anderson, T. W. (1971). *The Statistical Analysis of Time Series.* New York: John Wiley & Sons.

Antech, o. (2010). *The measurement signal. What requirements must comply with the meter?* (in Czech) Retrieved 22 June 2014 from http://eshop.antech.cz/mereni-signalu/

Atsalakis, G. S., Dimitrakakis, E. M., & Zopounidis, C. D. (2011). Elliott Wave Theory and neuro-fuzzy systems, in stock market prediction: The WASP system. *Expert Systems with Applications*, *38*(8), 9196–9206. doi:10.1016/j.eswa.2011.01.068

Attiogbé, J. C. (2011). *Software Construction.* Retrieved May 02, 2011 from https://www.google.cz/url?sa=t&rct=j&q=&esrc=s&source=web&cd=1&ved=0ahUKEwit4aOj58DLAhWq9HIKHfH_CwwQFggbMAA&url=http%3A%2F%2Fpagesperso.lina.univ-nantes.fr%2Finfo%2Fperso%2Fpermanents%2Fattiogbe%2Fmespages%2FMSFORMEL%2Fslides_intro_EventB.1x1.pdf&usg=AFQjCNGrW0U6zZ6xUs19qYLU-O8KjV7LMA&sig2=6qipL7XqWDj1tpg6GhrNTA&bvm=bv.116636494,d.bGQ&cad=rja

Awokuse, T., & Ilvento, T. (2004). *Module 6: Introduction to Time Series Forecasting.* Retrieved December 31, 2015, from http://www.udel.edu/FREC/ilvento/BUAD820/MOD604.pdf

Aymen, M., Abdelaziz, A., Halim, S., & Maaref, H. (2011). Hidden Markov Models for automatic speech recognition. *Communications, Computing and Control Applications (CCCA), 2011 International Conference on* (pp. 1-6). IEEE.

Bai, J., & Wang, P. (2011). Conditional Markov chain and its application in economic time series analysis. *Journal of Applied Econometrics*, *26*(5), 715–734. doi:10.1002/jae.1140

Bao, X., Wang, J., & Hu, J. (2009) Method of Individual Identification Based on Electroencephalogram Analysis.*International Conference on New Trends in Information and Service Science.* Doi:10.1109/niss.2009.44

Barro, R. J. (1987). *Macroeconomics* (2nd ed.). New York: John Wiley & Sons.

Baum, E. B., & Haussler, D. (1989). What size net gives valid generalization? *Neural Computation*, *1*(1), 151–160. doi:10.1162/neco.1989.1.1.151

Baum, L. E., & Petrie, T. (1966). Statistical Inference for Probabilistic Functions of Finite State Markov Chains. *Annals of Mathematical Statistics*, *37*(6), 1554–1563. doi:10.1214/aoms/1177699147

Beneš, V. (1993). *Bankovní a finanční slovník*. Prague: Svoboda - Libertas. (in Czech)

Bishop, C. M. (2005). *Neural Networks for Pattern Recognition*. New York: Oxford University Press.

Bishop, C. M. (2006). *Pattern Recognition and Machine Learning (Information Science and Statistics)*. New York: Springer-Verlag New York, Inc.

Blankertz, B., Müller, K. R., Curio, G., Vaughan, T. M., Schalk, G., & Wolpaw, J. R. et al. (2004). The BCI competition 2003: Progress and perspectives in detection and discrimination of EEG single trials. *Biomedical Engineering. IEEE Transactions on*, *51*(6), 1044–1051.

Blower, G. (2007). *Boxing: Training, Skills and Techniques*. Crowood.

Blumer, A., Ehrenfeucht, A., Haussler, D., & Warmuth, M. K. (1989). Learnability and the Vapnik-Chervonenkis dimension. *Journal of the ACM*, *36*(4), 929–965. doi:10.1145/76359.76371

Bolander, R. P., Neto, O. P., & Bir, A. C. (2009). The effects of height and distance on the force production and acceleration in martial arts strikes. *Journal of Sports Science and Medicine*. Available: http://www.jssm.org/combat/3/9/v8combat3-9.pdf

Boulicaut, J. F., Klemettinen, M., & Mannila, H. (1998). Querying inductive database. In PKDD98, (LNAI), (vol. 1510, pp. 194-202). Springer-Verlag.

Box, G. E. P., Jenkins, G. M., & Reinsel, G. C. (1994). Time Series Analysis: Forecasting and Control (3rd ed.). Prentice-Hall.

Box, G. E. P., & Jenkins, G. M. (1976). *Time Series Analysis: Forecasting and Control* (2nd ed.). San Francisco: Holden-Day.

Compilation of References

Breiman, L. (1996). Bagging predictors. *Machine Learning*, *24*(2), 123–140. doi:10.1007/BF00058655

Brillinger, D. R. (1981, 2001). Time Series: Data Analysis and Theory (2nd ed.). San Francisco: Holden-Day.

Brillinger, D. R. (1975). *Time Series: Data Analysis and Theory*. New York: Holt, Rinehart & Winston Inc.

Brockwell, P. J., & Davis, R. A. (2002). *Introduction to Times Series and Forecasting*. Springer-Verlag New York, Inc. doi:10.1007/b97391

Campisi, P., Scarano, G., Babiloni, F., DeVico Fallani, F., Colonnese, S., Maiorana, E., & Forastiere, L. (2011, November). Brain waves based user recognition using the "eyes closed resting conditions" protocol. In *Information Forensics and Security (WIFS), 2011 IEEE International Workshop on* (pp. 1-6). IEEE.

Catania, B., Maddalena, M., & Mazza, M. (2004). A Framework for Data Mining Pattern Management. In *Proceedings of ECML/PKDD*. doi:10.1007/978-3-540-30116-5_11

Catania, B., Maddalena, M., & Mazza, M. (2005). A prototype system for pattern management. In *Proceedings of the 31st International Conference on Very Large Data Bases (VLDB05)*.

Chafik, S., & Cherki, D. (2013). Some Algorithms for Large Hidden Markov Models. *World Journal Control Science and Engineering*, *1*(1), 9–14.

Chan, N. H. (2002). *Time Series: Applications to Finance*. New York: Wiley.

Ciskowski, P., & Zaton, M. (2010). Neural pattern recognition with self-organizing maps for efficient processing of forex market data streams. In *Articial Intelligence and Soft Computing* (pp. 307–314). Berlin: Springer-Verlag. doi:10.1007/978-3-642-13208-7_39

Cole, D. (2014). The Chinese Room Argument. In E. N. Zalta (Eds.), *The Stanford Encyclopedia of Philosophy*. Retrieved July 30, 2015, from http://stanford.library.usyd.edu.au/entries/chinese-room

Cruz, R. M., Cavalcanti, G. D., & Ren, T. I. (2010). Handwritten digit recognition using multiple feature extraction techniques and classier ensemble.*17th International Conference on Systems, Signals and Image Processing*, (pp. 215-218). Rio de Janeiro, Brazil.

Curram, S. P., & Mingers, J. (1994). Neural networks, decision tree induction and discriminant analysis: An empirical comparison. *The Journal of the Operational Research Society*, *45*(4), 440–450. doi:10.1057/jors.1994.62

Czech Telecommunications Office. (2008). *163 DECREE on the method for determining terrestrial television broadcasting signal coverage*. Retrieved April 30, 2008, from http://download.mpo.cz/get/39700/50315/582024/priloha005.pdf

Davidson, I., & Fan, W. (2006). When efficient model averaging out-performs boosting and bagging. In Knowledge Discovery in Databases: PKDD 2006 (pp. 478-486). Springer Berlin Heidelberg. doi:doi:10.1007/11871637_46 doi:10.1007/11871637_46

Del Pozo-Banos, M., Alonso, J. B., Ticay-Rivas, J. R., & Travieso, C. M. (2014). Electroencephalogram subject identification: A review. *Expert Systems with Applications*, *41*(15), 6537–6554.

Deng, L., & Yu, D. (2011). Deep convex net: A scalable architecture for speech pattern classication. In *Proceedings of the Interspeech*, (pp. 2285-2288).

Dietterich, T. G. (2000). An experimental comparison of three methods for constructing ensembles of decision trees: Bagging, boosting, and randomization. *Machine Learning*, *40*(2), 139–157. doi:10.1023/A:1007607513941

Digital Video Broadcasting. (2009). *Digital Video Broadcasting (DVB); Specification for the use of Video and Audio Coding in Broadcasting Applications based on the MPEG-2 Transport Stream.* Retrieved 30 September 2009 from http://www.etsi.org/deliver/etsi_ts/101100_101199 /101154/01.09.01_60/ts_101154v010901p.pdf

Doidge, N. (2007). *The brain that changes itself: Stories of personal triumph from the frontiers of brain science.* New York: Penguin Books.

Dostál, P., & Sojka, Z. (2008). Elliottovy vlny (in Czech). Tribuns.r.o.

Draft Decree. (2008) *A method of determining the area covered by a broadcaster method determining the intensity of the electromagnetic field and the resulting derivative Population coverage television broadcasting signal (a method of determining coverage television broadcasting signal.* (in Czech). Retrieved April 30, 2008, from http://www.proglas.cz/res/data/019/002385.pdf

Dreamsky, T. S. (2013) *DREAMSKY TS-80 MultiCOMBO.* (in Czech) Retrieved 10 November, 2013, from http://www.dreamsky.cz/dreamsky-ts-80-combo.html

Drucker, H., Schapire, R., & Simard, P. (1993). Boosting performance in neural networks. *International Journal of Pattern Recognition and Artificial Intelligence*, *7*(4), 705–719. doi:10.1142/S0218001493000352

Emotiv | EEG System | Electroencephalography. (2015) Available from: http://www.emotiv.com/

Esfahani, E. T., & Sundararajan, V. (2012). Classification of primitive shapes using brain–computer interfaces. *Computer Aided Design*, *44*(10), 1011–1019.

Fabiani, G. E., McFarland, D. J., Wolpaw, J. R., & Pfurtscheller, G. (2004). Conversion of EEG activity into cursor movement by a brain-computer interface (BCI). *Neural Systems and Rehabilitation Engineering. IEEE Transactions on*, *12*(3), 331–338.

Fausett, L. V. (1993). *Fundamentals of Neural Networks: Architectures, Algorithms and Applications.* Prentice Hall.

Fausett, L. V. (1994). *Fundamentals of Neural Networks.* Englewood Cliffs, NJ: Prentice-Hall, Inc.

Compilation of References

Fink, G. A. (2014). *Markov Models for Pattern Recognition*. London: Springer Science & Business Media. doi:10.1007/978-1-4471-6308-4

Freund, Y. (1995). Boosting a weak learning algorithm by majority. *Information and Computation, 121*(2), 256–285. doi:10.1006/inco.1995.1136

Freund, Y., & Schapire, R. (1999). A short introduction to boosting. *J. Japan. Soc. for Artif. Intel., 14*(5), 771–780.

Freund, Y., & Schapire, R. E. (1995). A desicion-theoretic generalization of on-line learning and an application to boosting. In *Computational learning theory* (pp. 23–37). Springer Berlin Heidelberg. doi:10.1007/3-540-59119-2_166

Freund, Y., & Schapire, R. E. (1996). Experiments with a new boosting algorithm. In *Proc. International Conference on Machine Learning, ICML.*Morgan Kaufmann.

Freund, Y., & Schapire, R. E. (1997). A decision-theoretic generalization of on-line learning and an application to boosting. *Journal of Computer and System Sciences, 55*(1), 119–139. doi:10.1006/jcss.1997.1504

Frost, A. J., & Prechter, R. (2001). *Elliott Wave Principle: Key to Market Behavior*. John Wiley & Sons.

Fukushima, & Kunihiko. (1980). Neocognitron: A Self-Organizing Neural Network Model for a Mechanism of Pattern Recognition Unaffected by Shift in Position. *Biological Cybernetics, 36*(4), 193-202.

Fukushima, K. (1988). Neocognitron: A hierarchical neural network capable of visual pattern recognition. *Neural Networks, 1*(2), 119–130. doi:10.1016/0893-6080(88)90014-7

Gao, X., Xu, D., Cheng, M., & Gao, S. (2003). A BCI-based environmental controller for the motion-disabled. *Neural Systems and Rehabilitation Engineering. IEEE Transactions on, 11*(2), 137–140.

Garber, G. (2013). *Instant LEGO Mindstorm EV3*. Packt Publishing Ltd.

Gianino, C. (2010). Physics of Karate: Kinematics analysis of karate techniques by a digital movie camera. *Latin-American Journal of Physics Education,4*(1).

Gouriéroux, C., & Monfort, A. (1997). *Time Series and Dynamic Models*. Cambridge, UK: Cambridge University Press.

Grandell, J. (2012). *Time series analysis*. Retrieved December 31, 2015, from https://www.math.kth.se/matstat/gru/sf2943/ts.pdf

Guger, C., Edlinger, G., Harkam, W., Niedermayer, I., & Pfurtscheller, G. (2003). How many people are able to operate an EEG-based brain-computer interface (BCI)? *Neural Systems and Rehabilitation Engineering. IEEE Transactions on, 11*(2), 145–147.

Guger, C., Ramoser, H., & Pfurtscheller, G. (2000). Real-time EEG analysis with subject-specific spatial patterns for a brain-computer interface (BCI). *Rehabilitation Engineering. IEEE Transactions on, 8*(4), 447–456.

Guger, C., Schlögl, A., Neuper, C., Walterspacher, D., Strein, T., & Pfurtscheller, G. (2001). Rapid prototyping of an EEG-based brain-computer interface (BCI). *Neural Systems and Rehabilitation Engineering. IEEE Transactions on, 9*(1), 49–58.

Gurney, K. (1997). *An Introduction to Neural Networks*. CRC Press. doi:10.4324/9780203451519

Hamming, R. (1950). Error detecting and error correcting codes. *The Bell System Technical Journal, 29*(2), 147–160. doi:10.1002/j.1538-7305.1950.tb00463.x

Handley, M. (2010). *10: System Streams*. Retrieved 2 May 2013 from http://www0.cs.ucl.ac.uk/teaching/GZ05/10-system-streams.pdf

Hazrati, M. K., & Erfanian, A. (2010). An online EEG-based brain–computer interface for controlling hand grasp using an adaptive probabilistic neural network. *Medical Engineering & Physics, 32*(7), 730–739.

Hertz, J., Kogh, A., & Palmer, R. G. (1991). *Introduction to the Theory of Neural Computation*. Redwood City, CA: Addison – Wesley publishing Company.

Hillmer, C., Bell, R., & Tiao, C. (1983). Modeling Considerations Considerations in Seasonal Adjustment of Economic Time Series. Academic Press.

Homan, R. W., Herman, J., & Purdy, P. (1987). Cerebral location of international 10–20 system electrode placement. *Electroencephalography and Clinical Neurophysiology, 66*(4), 376–382.

Hornik, K. (1991). Approximation capabilities of multilayer feedforward networks. *Neural Networks, 4*(2), 251–257. doi:10.1016/0893-6080(91)90009-T

Hranac, R. (2007). *CISCO Systems. BER and MER Fundamentals*. Retrieved 10 May 2013 from http://www.scribd.com/doc/231656951/Ron-Hranac-Presentation-BER-MER-Fun#scribd

Hubel, D., & Wiesel, T. (1962). Receptive fields, binocular interaction, and functional architecture in the cat's visual cortex. *The Journal of Physiology, 160*(1), 106–154. doi:10.1113/jphysiol.1962.sp006837 PMID:14449617

IFN/ENIT. (2014). *IFN/ENIT-database*. Retrieved July 30, 2015, from http://www.ifnenit.com/

Kaper, M., Meinicke, P., Grossekathoefer, U., Lingner, T., & Ritter, H. (2004). BCI competition 2003-data set IIb: Support vector machines for the P300 speller paradigm. *Biomedical Engineering. IEEE Transactions on, 51*(6), 1073–1076.

Kearns, M. J., & Valiant, L. G. (1988). *Learning Boolean formulae or finite automata is as hard as factoring*. Harvard University, Center for Research in Computing Technology, Aiken Computation Laboratory.

Compilation of References

Kearns, M., & Valiant, L. (1994). Cryptographic limitations on learning Boolean formulae and finite automata. *Journal of the ACM, 41*(1), 67–95. doi:10.1145/174644.174647

Khalifa, W., Salem, A., Roushdy, M., & Revett, K. (2012, May). A survey of EEG based user authentication schemes. In *Informatics and Systems (INFOS), 2012 8th International Conference on* (pp. BIO-55). IEEE.

Klapuch, B. (2011). *Trading Orders Algorithm Development*. (Unpublished master thesis). University of Ostrava, Ostrava, Czech Republic.

Kocian, V. (1915). *Artificial Intelligence Algorithms for Classification and Pattern Recognition*. (Unpublished doctoral dissertation). University of Ostrava, Ostrava, CZ.

Kohonen, T., Oja, E., Simula, O., Visa, A., & Kangas, J. (2002). Engineering applications of the self-organizing map. *Proceedings of the IEEE, 84*(10), 1358–1384. doi:10.1109/5.537105

Kotyrba, M., Volná, E., Bražina, D., & Jarušek, R. (2012). Elliott waves recognition via neural networks. In *Proceedings 26th European Conference on Modellingand Simulation, ECMS 2012*.

Kotyrba, M., Volná, E., Janošek, M., Habiballa, H., & Bražina, D. (2013). Methodology for Elliott waves pattern recognition. In *Proceedings 27th European Conference on Modelling and Simulation, ECMS 2013*.

Kotyrba, M., Volná, E., & Jarušek, R. (2012). Artificial intelligence methods for pattern recognition with fractal structure. In *Proceedings of the 18th International Conference on Soft Computing, Mendel 2012*.

Kyuheon, K. (2010). *MPEG-2 ES/PES/TS/PSI*. Retrieved 4 October 2010 from http://cmm.khu.ac.kr/korean/files/02.mpeg2ts1_es_pes_ps_ts_psi.pdf

La Rocca, D., Campisi, P., & Scarano, G. (2012, September). EEG biometrics for individual recognition in resting state with closed eyes. In *Biometrics Special Interest Group (BIOSIG), 2012 BIOSIG-Proceedings of the International Conference of the* (pp. 1-12). IEEE.

Lai, K. K., Yu, L., & Wang, S. A. (2004). Neural network and web-based decision support system for forex forecasting and trading. In Data Mining and Knowledge Management (pp. 243-253). Berlin: Springer-Verlag.

Lal, T. N., Schröder, M., Hinterberger, T., Weston, J., Bogdan, M., Birbaumer, N., & Schölkopf, B. (2004). Support vector channel selection in BCI.*Biomedical Engineering. IEEE Transactions on, 51*(6), 1003–1010.

Lapkova, D., & Adamek, M. (2014a). Analysis of Direct Punch with a View to Velocity. In *Proceedings of the 2014 International conference on Applied Mathematics, Computational Science and Engineering*. Craiova: Europment.

Lapkova, D., Pluhacek, M., & Adamek, M. (2014b). Computer Aided Analysis of Direct Punch Force Using the Tensometric Sensor. In *Modern Trends and Techniques in Computer Science: 3rd Computer Science On-line Conference 2014* (CSOC 2014). Springer.

Lapkova, D., Pluhacek, M., Kominkova Oplatkova, Z., & Adamek, M. (2014c). Using artificial neural network for the kick techniques classification – An initial study. In *Proceedings 28th European Conference on Modelling and Simulation ECMS 2014*. Digitaldruck Pirrot GmbH.

Lapkova, D., Pluhacek, M., Kominkova Oplatkova, Z., Senkerik, R., & Adamek, M. (2014d). Application of Neural Networks for the Classification of Gender from Kick Force Profile – A Small Scale Study. In *Proceedings of the Fifth International Conference on Innovations in Bio-Inspired Computing and Applications IBICA 2014*. Springer International Publishing.

Lapkova, D., Pospisilik, M., Adamek, M., & Malanik, Z. (2012). *The utilisation of an impulse of force in self-defence*. In XX IMEKO World Congress: Metrology for Green Growth, Busan, Republic of Korea.

LDC. (2014). *Linguistic Data Consortium*. Retrieved July 30, 2015, from https://www.ldc.upenn.edu/

LeCun, Y., Cortes, C., & Burges, C. (2014). *The MNIST database*. Retrieved July 30, 2015, from http://yann.lecun.com/exdb/mnist/

Lecun, Y., Bottou, L., Bengio, Y., & Haner, P. (1998). Gradient-based learning applied to document recognition. *Proceedings of the IEEE, 86*(11), 2278–2324. doi:10.1109/5.726791

Leigh, W., Modani, N., & Hightower, R. (2004). A Computational Implementation of Stock Charting: Abrupt Volume Increase As Signal for Movement in New York Stock Exchange Composite Index. *Decision Support Systems, 37*(4), 515–530. doi:10.1016/S0167-9236(03)00084-8

Li, M., & Lu, B. L. (2009, September). Emotion classification based on gamma-band EEG. In *Engineering in Medicine and Biology Society, 2009. EMBC 2009. Annual International Conference of the IEEE* (pp. 1223-1226). IEEE.

Liu, P. (2000). A kinematic analysis of round kick in Taekwondo. *ISBS-Conference Proceedings Archive, 1*(1).

Lotte, F., Congedo, M., Lécuyer, A., & Lamarche, F. (2007). A review of classification algorithms for EEG-based brain–computer interfaces. *Journal of Neural Engineering*, 4.

Makhoul, J. (1980, February). A fast cosine transform in one and two dimensions. *IEEE Transactions on Acoustics, Speech, and Signal Processing, 28*(1), 27–34. doi:10.1109/TASSP.1980.1163351

Mannila, H. (1997). Inductive databases and condensed representation for data mining. In *Proceedings of the International Logic Programming Symposium*.

Muniz, A. M., Liu, H., Lyons, K. E., Pahwa, R., Liu, W., Nobre, F. F., & Nadal, J. (2010). Comparison among probabilistic neural network, support vector machine and logistic regression for evaluating the effect of subthalamic stimulation in Parkinson disease on ground reaction force during gait. *Journal of Biomechanics, 43*(4), 720–726. doi:10.1016/j.jbiomech.2009.10.018 PMID:19914622

Novák, V. (2015). Linguistic Characterization of Time Series. *Fuzzy Sets and Systems*.

Compilation of References

Novák, V., Pavliska, V., Štěpnička, M., & Štěpničková, L. (2014). *Time Series Trend Extraction and Its Linguistic Evaluation Using F-Transform and Fuzzy Natural Logic. In Recent Developments and New Directions in Soft Computing (Studies in Fuzziness and Soft Computing 317)*. Switzerland: Springer.

Oostenveld, R., & Praamstra, P. (2001). The five percent electrode system for high-resolution EEG and ERP measurements. *Clinical Neurophysiology, 112*(4), 713–719.

Oracle 11g. (n.d.). Retrieved April 10, 2015, from https://docs.oracle.com/en/

Palaniappan, R. (2005, December). Identifying individuality using mental task based brain computer interface. In *Intelligent Sensing and Information Processing, 2005. ICISIP 2005. Third International Conference on* (pp. 238-242). IEEE.

Palaniappan, R. (2004). Method of identifying individuals using VEP signals and neural network. *IEE Proceedings. Science Measurement and Technology, 151*(1), 16–20.

Palaniappan, R. (2008). Two-stage biometric authentication method using thought activity brain waves. *International Journal of Neural Systems, 18*(01), 59–66.

Palaniappan, R., & Mandic, D. P. (2007). EEG based biometric framework for automatic identity verification. *The Journal of VLSI Signal Processing Systems for Signal, Image, and Video Technology, 49*(2), 243–250.

Palaniappan, R., & Raveendran, P. (2002). Individual identification technique using visual evoked potential signals. *Electronics Letters, 38*(25), 1634–1635.

Palaniappan, R., & Revett, K. (2014). PIN generation using EEG: A stability study. *International Journal of Biometrics, 6*(2), 95–105.

Paranjape, R. B., Mahovsky, J., Benedicenti, L., & Koles, Z. (2001). The electroencephalogram as a biometric. In *Electrical and Computer Engineering, 2001. Canadian Conference on* (Vol. 2, pp. 1363-1366). IEEE.

Patuwo, E., Hu, M. Y., & Hung, M. S. (1993). Two-Group Classification Using Neural Networks. *Decision Sciences, 24*(4), 825–845. doi:10.1111/j.1540-5915.1993.tb00491.x

Pfurtscheller, G., Neuper, C., Guger, C., Harkam, W. A. H. W., Ramoser, H., Schlogl, A., & Pregenzer, M. A. P. M. (2000). Current trends in Graz brain-computer interface (BCI) research. *IEEE Transactions on Rehabilitation Engineering, 8*(2), 216–219.

Pieter, F., & Pieter, W. (1995). Speed and force in selected taekwondo techniques. *Biology of Sport, 12*, 257–266.

Poser, S. (2003). *Applying Elliott Wave Theory Profitably*. John Wiley & Sons.

Price, K. (1999). An Introduction to Differential Evolution. In *New Ideas in Optimization* (pp. 79–108). London: McGraw-Hill.

Procházka, J. (2009). *Interactive map of transmitters.* Retrieved 1 November 2009, from http://www.mapavysilacu.cz/mapcoverage.html

Quinlan, J. R. (1996). Bagging, boosting, and C4. 5. In AAAI/IAAI, (vol. 1, pp. 725-730).

Rabiner, L. R. (1989). A tutorial on hidden Markov models and selected applications in speech recognition.*Proceedings of the IEEE, 77*(2), 257-286. doi:10.1109/5.18626

Rak, R., Matyáš, V., Říha, Z., Porada, V., Bitto, O., Daughman, J., & Šimková, H. (2008). *Biometrie a identita člověka-ve forenzních a komerčních aplikacích.* Grada Publishing, as.

Ranawana, R., & Palade, V. (2006). Multi-Classifier Systems: Review and a Roadmap for Developers. *Int. J. Hybrid Intell. Syst., 3*(1), 35–61. doi:10.3233/HIS-2006-3104

Reiner, G. (2010). *Time Series. Hilary Term.* Retrieved December 31, 2015, from http://www.stats.ox.ac.uk/~reinert

Revett, K. (2012). Cognitive biometrics: A novel approach to person authentication. *International Journal of Cognitive Biometrics, 1*(1), 1–9.

Řezáč, P. (2010). *Are you watching digitally? Part 3. Antennas for the remote reception DVB-T.* (in Czech) Retrieved 4 April 2010, from http://www.itest.cz/old/videofoto/digitalni-vysilani-3.htm

Richard, M. D., & Lippmann, R. P. (1991). Neural network classifiers estimate Bayesian a posteriori probabilities. *Neural Computation, 3*(4), 461–483. doi:10.1162/neco.1991.3.4.461

Rizzi, S., Bettino, E., Catania, B., Gollfarelli, M., Halkidi, M., Terrovitis, M., . . . Vrachnos, E. (2003). Towards a logical model for patterns. In *Proceedings of 22nd International Conference on Conceptual Modeling (ER03)* (LNCS), (*Vol. 2813*, pp. 77-90). Springer.

Sammon, J. W. (1969). A nonlinear mapping for data structure analysis. *IEEE Transactions on Computers, 18*(5), 401–409. doi:10.1109/T-C.1969.222678

Schalk, G., McFarland, D. J., Hinterberger, T., Birbaumer, N., & Wolpaw, J. R. (2004). BCI2000: A general-purpose brain-computer interface (BCI) system. *Biomedical Engineering. IEEE Transactions on, 51*(6), 1034–1043.

Schapire, R. E. (1990). The strength of weak learnability. *Machine Learning, 5*(2), 197–227. doi:10.1007/BF00116037

Shumway, R. H., & Stoffer, D. S. (2015). *Times Series Analysis and Its Applications.* Springer-Verlag New York Inc.

Singhal, G. K., & RamKumar, P. (2007, September). Person identification using evoked potentials and peak matching. In *Biometrics Symposium* (pp. 1-6). IEEE. doi:10.1109/BCC.2007.4430555

Singh, Y. N., Singh, S. K., & Ray, A. K. (2012). Bioelectrical signals as emerging biometrics: Issues and challenges. *ISRN Signal Processing,* 2012.

Compilation of References

Subramanian, V., Hung, M. S., & Hu, M. Y. (1993). An experimental evaluation of neural networks for classification. *Computers & Operations Research*, *20*(7), 769–782. doi:10.1016/0305-0548(93)90063-O

Sunrise Telecom. (2010). *Measuring and Qualifying the Dosis Upstream Path*. Retrieved 5 May 2010, from http://www.gcscte.org/presentations/2010/Tom%2064QAM%20SCTE1.pdf

Telnarova, Z., & Schenk, J. (in press). The Logical Model for Pattern Representation. *International Conference on Numerical Analysis and Applied Mathematics (ICNAAM.)*

Terrovitis, M., & Vassiliadis, P. (2003). *Architecture for Pattern_Base Management Systems*. Retrieved May 13, 2015, from http://citeseerx.ist.psu.edu

Terrovitis, M., Vassiliadis, P., Skiadopoulos, S., Bertino, E., Catania, B., Maddalena, A., & Rizzi, S. (2004). Modeling and Language Support for the Management of Pattern-Base. In *Proceedings of the 16th International Conference on Scientific and Statistical Database Management (SSDBM04)*. IEEE Computer Society. doi:10.1109/SSDM.2004.1311218

Trier, O. D., Jain, A. K., & Taxt, T. (1996). Feature Extraction methods for Character recognition – A Survey. *Pattern Recognition*, *29*(4), 641–662. doi:10.1016/0031-3203(95)00118-2

Turing, A. M. (1950). Computing Machinery and Intelligence. *Mind*, *59*(236), 433–460. doi:10.1093/mind/LIX.236.433

Valiant, L. G. (1984). A theory of the learnable. *Communications of the ACM*, *27*(11), 1134–1142. doi:10.1145/1968.1972

Vlajič, N. (2010). *Analog Transmission Analog Transmission of Digital Data: of Digital Data: ASK, FSK, PSK, QAM*. Retrieved 22 April 2010, from http://www.eecs.yorku.ca/course_archive/2010-11/F/3213/CSE3213_07_ShiftKeying_F2010.pdf

Volná, E., Kotyrba, M., & Jarušek, R. (2013). Prediction by means of Elliott waves recognition. In Nostradamus: Modern Methods of Prediction, Modeling and Analysis of Nonlinear Systems, AISC 192. Springer-Verlag Berlin Heidelberg. doi:10.1007/978-3-642-33227-2_25

Volna, E., Kotyrba, M., & Jarusek, R. (2013). Multiclassifier based on Elliott wave's recognition. *Computers & Mathematics with Applications (Oxford, England)*, *66*(2), 213–225. doi:10.1016/j.camwa.2013.01.012

Volná, E., Kotyrba, M., & Kominkova Oplatkova, Z. (2013). Elliott waves classification via soft-computing. In *Proceedings of the 19th International Conference on Soft Computing, Mendel 2013*.

Wasserman, P. D. (1980). *Neural Computing: Theory and Practice*. Coriolis Group.

Wen-Hsiung Chen, , Smith, C., & Fralick, S. (1977, September). A Fast Computational Algorithm for the Discrete Cosine Transform. *IEEE Transactions on Communications*, *25*(9), 1004–1009. doi:10.1109/TCOM.1977.1093941

Wolff, Ch. (2006). *Radar Basic. Horizontal patterns.* Retrieved 3 June 2006, from http://www.radartutorial.eu/06.antennas/Half-wave%20Antenna.en.html

Wolff, Ch. (2006). *Radar Basic. Yagi Antenna.* Retrieved 10 June 2007 from http://www.radartutorial.eu/06.antennas/Yagi%20Antenna.en.html

Wolpaw, J. R., McFarland, D. J., Vaughan, T. M., & Schalk, G. (2003). The Wadsworth Center brain-computer interface (BCI) research and development program. *Neural Systems and Rehabilitation Engineering. IEEE Transactions on, 11*(2), 1–4.

XTB X-Trade Brokers Dom Maklerski Spolka Akcyjna, organizační složka. (2008). *Manual XTB-Trader.* Retrieved September, 09, 2010, from http://www.xtb.cz/obchodni_systemy/xtb_trader/navod_k_obsluze/XTB-TraderManual.pdf

Yang, S., & Deravi, F. (2012, September). On the effectiveness of EEG signals as a source of biometric information. In *Emerging Security Technologies (EST), 2012 Third International Conference on* (pp. 49-52). IEEE. doi:10.1109/EST.2012.8

Yeom, S. K., Suk, H. I., & Lee, S. W. (2013a, February). EEG-based person authentication using face stimuli. In *Brain-Computer Interface (BCI), 2013 International Winter Workshop on* (pp. 58-61). IEEE. doi:10.1109/IWW-BCI.2013.6506630

Yeom, S. K., Suk, H. I., & Lee, S. W. (2013b). Person authentication from neural activity of face-specific visual self-representation. *Pattern Recognition, 46*(4), 1159–1169. doi:10.1016/j.patcog.2012.10.023

Zadeh, L. A. (1994). Soft Computing and Fuzzy Logic. *IEEE Software, 11*(6), 48–56. doi:10.1109/52.329401

Zelinka, I., Davendra, D., Jasek, R., Senkerik, R., & Oplatkova, Z. (2011). *Analytical programming-a novel approach for evolutionary synthesis of symbolic structures.* INTECH Open Access Publisher. doi:10.5772/16166

Zellner, A. (Ed.). (1983). *Applied Time Series Analysis of Economics Data.* Bureau of the Census.

About the Contributors

Eva Volna is an associate professor at the Department of Computer Science at University of Ostrava, Czech Republic. Her interests include artificial intelligence, artificial neural networks, evolutionary algorithms, and cognitive science. She is an author of more than 50 papers in technical journals and proceedings of conferences.

Martin Kotyrba is an assistant professor at the Department of Computer Science at the University of Ostrava, Czech Republic. His interests include artificial intelligence, formal logic, soft computing methods and fractals. He is an author of more than 30 papers in conference proceedings.

Michal Janosek is an assistant professor at the Department of Informatics and Computers at the University of Ostrava, Czech Republic. His interests include artificial intelligence, multi-agent systems, modeling and simulations. He is an author of more than 20 papers in proceedings of conferences.

* * *

Milan Adamek is an associate professor at Tomas Bata University in Zlin. His research interests include sensors, measuremnt and camera systems. He is an author of around 120 papers in journals, book chapters and conference proceedings.

Denisa Hrušecká is working as a senior lecturer at Tomas Bata University in Zlín, Faculty of Management and Economics, Department of Industrial Engineering and Information Systems. Her specialisation is industrial engineering, production planning and scheduling and business information systems supporting production processes. She has studied the relationship between advanced software tools for production planning and scheduling and the aspects of process management in her dissertation. Her current research activities are focused on topics of lean management, production planning and possibilities of expert systems in production management area.

Robert Jarušek is a Ph.D. student at the Department of Computer Science at University of Ostrava, Czech Republic. His interests include artificial intelligence, neural networks, and soft computing. He is an author of more than 15 papers in proceedings of conferences.

Roman Jasek is working as an Associate Professor, head of Department of Informatics and Artificial Intelligence in Faculty Applied Informatics in Tomas Bata University in Zlin. He graduated from computer science in Palacky University in Olomouc, his Ph.D. received in Charles University in Prague. His research interests are: Artificial Intelligence, Computer Science and Data Security.

Bronislav Klapuch is a Ph.D. student the Department of Computer Science at University of Ostrava, Czech Republic. He is long life working in the IT business as a Developer, Tester, Business Analyst and Project Manager mostly on the banking information systems.

Vaclav Kocian was a Ph.D. student at the Department of Computer Science at University of Ostrava, Czech Republic. His interests include artificial intelligence, neural networks, and soft computing. He is an author of more than 20 papers in journals and proceedings of conferences.

Said Krayem lectures at UTB artificial intelligence, several PhD's doctor and students and cooperates with the Academy of Sciences in Prague. He wrote more than 20 books on computer science and more than 10 articles.

Dora Lapkova is an asistent at Tomas Bata University in Zlin. Her research interests include professional defence, self defence, physical protection, security management. She is an author of around 20 papers in journals, book chapters and conference proceedings.

Ivo Lazar was born in the Czech Republic, and went to the Tomas Bata University in Zlin, where he at present studying in the faculty Aplication Informatic to obtain his Ph.D degree in 2018. He is the author of several articles about artificial intelligence and is a lecturer Cisco academy.

Zuzana Kominkova Oplatkova is an associate professor at Tomas Bata University in Zlin. Her research interests include artificial intelligence, soft computing, evolutionary techniques, symbolic regression, neural networks. She is an author of around 100 papers in journals, book chapters and conference proceedings.

Michal Pluhacek was born in the Czech Republic, and went to the Tomas Bata University in Zlin, where he studied Information Technologies and obtained his MSc. degree in 2011 and Ph.D. degree in 2016. He now works as a researcher at the same university. His professional interests are various topics in artificial intelligence with focus on evolutionary algorithms.

Roman Senkerik was born in the Czech Republic, and went to the Tomas Bata University in Zlin, Faculty of applied informatics, where he studied Technical Cybernetics and obtained his MSc degree in 2004, Ph.D. degree in 2008 (Technical Cybernetics) and Assoc. prof. degree in 2013 (VSB – Technical University of Ostrava – degree in Informatics). He is now a researcher and lecturer at the same university (lectures from Applied Informatics, Cryptology, Artificial Intelligence, Mathematical Informatics). His research interests are: Theory of chaos, Optimal control of chaos, Softcomputing methods and their interdisciplinary applications, Optimization, Neural Networks and Evolutionary Computation. He was IPC member or session chair of many important international conferences and symposiums. He is Recognized Reviewer for many Elsevier journals as well as many other leading journals in computer science/computational intelligence.

Jaromir Svejda was born in the Czech Republic, and went to the Tomas Bata University in Zlin, where he studied Information Technologies and obtained his MSc degree in 2011. He is now a Ph.D. student at the same university.

Zdenka Telnarova is an assistant professor at the Department of Computer Science at the University of Ostrava, Czech Republic. Her interests include data modelling and ontological semantics, modelling of natural deduction and RDF data models in Oracle. She is an author of more than 20 papers in conference proceedings.

Martin Žáček is an assistant professor at the Department of Computer Science at University of Ostrava, Czech Republic. His interests include formal logic, knowledge representation and artificial intelligence. He is an author of more than 30 papers in proceedings of conferences.

Roman Zak was born in the Czech Republic, and went to the Tomas Bata University in Zlin, where he studied Information Technologies and obtained his MSc degree in 2011. He is now a Ph.D. student at the same university.

Index

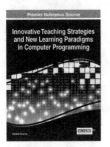

Printed in the United States
By Bookmasters